Come on back ya hear,
Eh!

Jim + Sandy

DIXIE & THE DOMINION

DIXIE & THE DOMINION

Canada,
the Confederacy,
and the
War for the Union

ADAM MAYERS

THE DUNDURN GROUP
TORONTO

Copy-Editor: Andrea Pruss
Design: Jennifer Scott
Printer: Transcontinental

National Library of Canada Cataloguing in Publication Data

Mayers, Adam
    Dixie and the Dominion: Canada, the Confederacy, and the War for the Union/Adam Mayers.

Includes bibliographical references and index.
ISBN 1-55002-468-X

1. Canada — History — 1841-1867. 2. United States — History — Civil War, 1861-1865. 3. Canada — Foreign relations — United States. 4. United States — Foreign relations — Canada. I. Title.

E470.95.M39 2003   971.04'2   C2003-903528-X

1   2   3   4   5   07   06   05   04   03

Canada

The Canada Council | Le Conseil des Arts
for the Arts | du Canada
since 1957 | depuis 1957

ONTARIO ARTS COUNCIL
CONSEIL DES ARTS DE L'ONTARIO

We acknowledge the support of the **Canada Council for the Arts** and the **Ontario Arts Council** for our publishing program. We also acknowledge the financial support of the **Government of Canada** through the **Book Publishing Industry Development Program** and **The Association for the Export of Canadian Books**, and the **Government of Ontario** through the **Ontario Book Publishers Tax Credit** program, and the **Ontario Media Development Corporation's Ontario Book Initiative**.

                                        J. Kirk Howard, President

Printed and bound in Canada.⊕
Printed on recycled paper.

www.dundurn.com

Dundurn Press
8 Market Street
Suite 200
Toronto, Ontario, Canada
M5E 1M6

Dundurn Press
2250 Military Road
Tonawanda NY
U.S.A. 14150

To Bruce Blackadar,
for his insights and encouragement,
and to my parents and grandparents,
whose stories made me realize that the
shared memories of history are important.

"They coveted Florida and seized it; they coveted Louisiana and purchased it ... they picked a quarrel with Mexico, which ended by their getting California.... The acquisition of Canada was the first ambition of [America].... Is it likely to be stopped now, when she counts her guns afloat by thousands and her troops by the hundreds of thousands?"

D'arcy McGee, Canadian cabinet minister
February 1865

TABLE OF CONTENTS

PROLOGUE:
No Silence From Canada

A flawless September day in Ottawa, Canada's capital. The sky is a deep cobalt blue, and a slight warming breeze stirs the air. The flags at half-mast move in a slow, graceful salute. On Parliament Hill, a red carpet extends towards a dais. Prime Minister Jean Chrétien, Governor General Adrienne Clarkson, and U.S. Ambassador to Canada Paul Cellucci walk slowly together. It is midday on a national day of mourning. Clarkson and Cellucci take their seats. Prime Minister Chrétien takes the podium:

> Mr. Ambassador, you have assembled before you, here on Parliament Hill and across Canada, a people united in outrage, in grief, in compassion, and in resolve. A people of every faith and nationality to be found on Earth. A people who, as a result of the atrocity committed against the United States on September 11, feel not only like neighbours, but like family.
>
> It is our feelings, our prayers and our actions that count. By their outpouring of concern, sympathy and help, the feelings and actions of Canadians have been clear. The message they send to the American people is clear: "Do not despair. You are not alone. We are with you. The world is with you."
>
> Martin Luther King, in describing times of trial and tribulation, once said that: "In the end, it is

not the words of your enemies that you remember, it is the silence of your friends."

Mr. Ambassador, there will be no silence from Canada. Our friendship has no limit. Generation after generation, we have travelled many difficult miles together. Side by side, we have lived through many dark times, always firm in our shared resolve to vanquish any threat to freedom and justice. And together, with our allies, we will defy and defeat the threat that terrorism poses to all civilized nations.

Mr. Ambassador, we will be with the United States every step of the way. As friends. As neighbours. As family.

Canadians and Americans have always shared time and place. The accident of geography has forced them to share history as well. But the same events have had different impacts, evoked different memories, created different consequences, and shaped national destinies in different ways. Sometimes, as Prime Minister Chrétien noted, the miles travelled have been difficult. Among the most difficult for both countries was the American Civil War, the last great military struggle on the continent. Over the course of the war's four years (1861–1865), while America fought, Canada watched and worried. In the last year of the war, as the tide turned against the South, Southern leaders sent spies and saboteurs to Canada. These men used the long, undefended border between the colonies and the Northern states to raid and loot along the frontier: mid-Victorian terrorists, if you like. One team firebombed New York. Another sacked and burned the town of St. Albans, Vermont. Their weapon was Greek Fire, a nineteenth-century napalm made from sulphur, naptha, and quicklime, which thankfully caused few, if any, deaths. The raiders' purpose was the same as that of the people who committed the acts of September 11, 2001 — to inspire fear and exact retribution for wrongs real or imagined. Another Confederate plot involved bioterror of the time — mailing trunks of clothes infected with yellow fever to northern hospitals. It failed because yellow fever could not be transmitted this way. Where today's assassins are strangers from afar, these terrorists were Americans, disaffected former citizens of the Union. They found Canada a convenient base of operations to further their aims.

As the Canadian colonists tried to contend with the events beyond their border and those within, they nurtured their own dream of independence. There was a quickening sense that destiny beckoned; the time had come for British Canadians to seize their future, to make a nation of themselves if only to unite against the chaos to the south. In 1867, within two years of the end of the Civil War, the Confederation of British North American provinces would be complete.

Since the end of the war, with one exception in 1866, Canadians and Americans have enjoyed one of the greatest friendships in the world, a legacy of peaceful coexistence. It is a relationship that is unrivalled among nations. As Prime Minister Chrétien said, our friendship has no limit. Yet, it has not always been so. The year 1864 was such a time.

NORTH AMERICA IN MAY 1864

British Colonies and territories

United States

Confederate States

ALASKA (Russian)

THE NORTH-WESTERN TERRITORY

NEWFOUNDLAND

BRITISH COLUMBIA

RUPERT S LAND (Hudson s Bay Company)

PROVINCE OF CANADA (Canada East)

(Canada West)

P.E.I.

N.B.

NOVA SCOTIA

U.S. TERRITORIES

UNITED STATES

CONFEDERATE STATES

MEXICO

Map by Brian Hughes

THE CONFEDERATE COMMISSIONERS IN CANADA

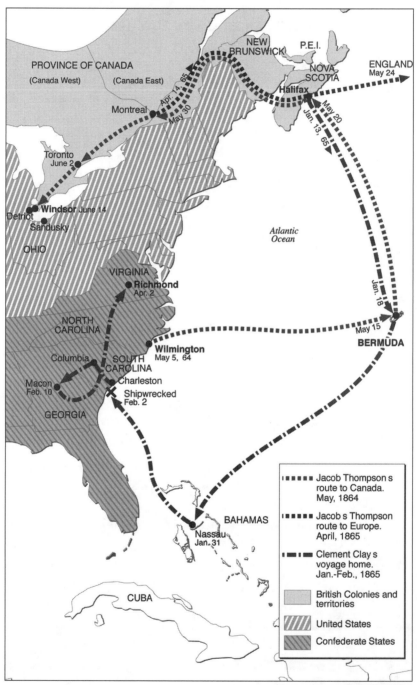

PROVINCE OF CANADA
(Canada West)   (Canada East)

NEW
BRUNSWICK   P.E.I.

NOVA
SCOTIA

ENGLAND
May 24

Halifax

Montreal
May 30

Apr. 14, 65

May 20
Jan. 13, 65

Toronto
June 2

Detriot
Windsor June 14
Sandusky

OHIO

Atlantic
Ocean

VIRGINIA
Richmond
Apr. 2

Jan. 18

NORTH
CAROLINA

May 15

BERMUDA

Columbia

Wilmington
May 5, 64

SOUTH
CAROLINA

Macon
Feb. 10

Charleston
Shipwrecked
Feb. 2

GEORGIA

BAHAMAS

Nassau
Jan. 31

CUBA

▮▮▮▮▮ Jacob Thompson s
route to Canada.
May, 1864

▮▮▮▮▮ Jacob s Thompson
route to Europe.
April, 1865

▮▬▮▬▮ Clement Clay s
voyage home.
Jan.-Feb., 1865

British Colonies and
territories

United States

Confederate States

Map by Brian Hughes

CHAPTER 1:
The Celebrated Stranger

"May peace and prosperity be forever the blessing of Canada, for she has been the asylum of many of my friends, as she is now an asylum for myself ... May God bless you all."
Jefferson Davis

The slap of the *Champion*'s paddle wheels was heard long before she was seen, though the steamer eventually slid out of the Lake Ontario fog at about 10:45 a.m. on May 30,1867. As she drew alongside Milloy's Wharf in Toronto's harbour, thousands of people — Southern exiles, the curious, and prominent local citizens alike — waited in anxious agitation.

The papers that day were full of the news that Queen Victoria had given royal assent to the British North America Act. It meant that on July 1 the clutch of five colonies that made up Britain's possessions on the continent would be forged into a new nation called the Dominion of Canada. But the papers had been full of Confederation news for months. A far more spectacular, but unpublished, piece of news had brought a crowd of a thousand or more to the waterfront — a Confederate of a different sort. As the *Champion* drew alongside the wharf, the crowd watched for a glimpse of the celebrated stranger on board.

The rumour had spread through Toronto that Jefferson Davis, President of the late Confederate States of America, would be among the passengers. The papers had closely followed Davis's

Milloy's Wharf at the foot of Toronto's Yonge Street, where Jefferson Davis disembarked from the *Champion* in May 1867.

release from prison a few days earlier and his journey by train through Washington to New York and from there Montreal, where his family had lived for the past two years. Now Davis was coming to Toronto on a mission he would later tell General Robert E. Lee probably saved his life.

As the *Champion* hove to, her great paddle wheels fell silent and Davis appeared on deck. He walked slowly, with the help of a cane. His jacket and trousers were black and his coat collar was turned up against the chill. On one side stood the massive, athletic figure of James Mason, a one-time U.S. senator from Virginia and the late Confederacy's ambassador to Great Britain. On the other stood Major Charles Helm, former Confederate consul in Havana.

For some, the sight of Davis's frail and emaciated frame was a shock. Lieutenant-Colonel George T. Denison, a Canadian officer and Southern sympathizer, stared in disbelief at the change prison and

Jefferson Davis told General Robert E. Lee that his trip to Canada in 1867 immediately after he was released from prison saved his life.

James Mason, Confederate ambassador to England, lived in exile in Niagara-on-the-Lake, Ontario, after the Civil War.

defeat had wrought on Davis. "I was so astonished that I said to a friend near me: 'They have killed him,'" Denison wrote in his memoirs.[1]

Denison scrambled to the top of a pile of coal and began to cheer. The crowd took up his cry as Davis moved carefully down the wharf. Davis seemed stunned by the reception and paused to shake outstretched hands. The papers reported next day that clutching his hat and bowing repeatedly, Davis said again and again, "Thank you, thank you, you are very kind to me."[2]

The press of people was so thick that police were forced to clear a way to a waiting carriage. From the wharf, it was a short ride to Helm's home, where the party rested. About two hours later they boarded the *Rothesay Castle* and resumed their voyage to the small town of Niagara-on-the-Lake. As the party walked up the hill from the wharf, Davis turned and for a moment stared at Fort Niagara, New York, across the Niagara River, where an oversized Stars and Stripes fluttered in the evening breeze.

"Look there Mason," he said, "there is the grid iron we have been fried on."

After dinner, the local band came to the brick cottage where Mason lived. The band struck up "Dixie" and Davis came out onto the verandah. There was brief applause and then silence.

"I thank you for the honor you have shown me," he said. "May peace and prosperity be forever the blessing of Canada, for she has been the asylum of many of my friends, as she is now an asylum for myself ... May God bless you all."[3]

It was a rousing start to an extraordinary five-month Canadian visit, a journey that allowed Davis to restore physical and mental equilibrium after four years of civil war and two more of prison. When Davis arrived in Canada his nerves were so frayed, ordinary sounds tormented him. The voices of people "sounded like trumpets in his ears," his wife, Varina, later wrote in her memoirs.

In the United States, the railway coach Davis travelled in had been pelted with rotten fruit and crowds had jeered as he passed. In Canada, he was hailed as a tragic, even noble, fallen hero. Yet, on Davis's orders in the spring of 1864, a team of guerrillas had used Canada as a base to launch raids against the Union. If these plans had succeeded, Canada would have been drawn into the war, a reluctant player in a larger Confederate game to gain peace at any price. Instead, the passage of three years had left Davis tormented by his failures and mourning his lost cause. These Canadians, these British Americans who greeted him with such affection, on the other hand, were making a peaceful and proud transition from colony to country.

Davis might well have wondered, that day, how different might things have been had the mission of Jacob Thompson, the man he'd sent to Canada in the last year of the war, succeeded.

CHAPTER 2
Spring Summons

"I am on my way to Canada. It is a very difficult and delicate duty for which I am not suited by my talents, tastes or habits. I cannot enjoy secret service."
Clement Clay, April 1864

The *Thistle* was long, low, and very fast. She cast off from the Wilmington, North Carolina, wharf in the early afternoon of May 5 and steamed slowly out of sight. Her hull and deck were painted gray and she lay low in the water, heavy with baled cotton, barrels of turpentine, tobacco, rice, and sugar. These were the staples that the Confederate States traded for guns and manufactured goods in the marketplaces of Europe. Within a short time, the 201-foot blockade-runner seemed to disappear from sight, giving the illusion of invisibility.

In the late afternoon, the *Thistle* hove to eighteen miles down river in the shadow of Fort Fisher. The captain rowed ashore to confer with the Fort's commandant, Colonel William Lamb. They agreed the *Thistle* would wait a day for a better chance of eluding the blockading Union cruisers lying offshore.

All that night and throughout the next day the *Thistle* waited patiently, until some thirty hours after leaving Wilmington, in the evening of May 6, she steamed into the confused waters where the mouth of the Cape Fear River meets the North Atlantic Ocean. She followed in the wake of the C.S.S. *Raleigh*, an ironclad Confederate naval ram, as the *Raleigh* snaked her way across the shallow Wilmington bar into the open sea. The *Raleigh* would act as a decoy, teasing, then eventually engaging, six of the blockading ships of the Union Navy to draw them away from the *Thistle*. Where the *Raleigh* headed south, the *Thistle* went north, running parallel to the shore for some time before turning eastward towards Bermuda. The island lay about 675 miles away, or about 72 hours of sailing time.

The *Thistle*'s passengers were sent below for safety and the captain offered his cabin to the two preferred guests on board. One was Jacob Thompson, a burly, bearded Mississippi planter. The other was Clement C. Clay, a smaller, wispier man who was a lawyer from Alabama. The men were offered the captain's compliments and, if needed, brandy from his personal store.

"The night was quite dark and very favourable for escape," Clay later wrote in his diary. "We had not long crossed the bar when I saw the flash of a gun and after several minutes heard the report. I saw and heard the same six or seven times more, but whether proceeding from our guns or the enemies I could not tell."[4]

Clay believed the fire was aimed at the blockade-runner *Young Republic*, which had headed out a day earlier on a southerly course for Nassau. As it turned out, the guns were turned on the *Raleigh*, which for the rest of the night engaged two Union cruisers and then four more in the early hours of May 7. It was a spirited and courageous display by the Confederate ram, all the more remarkable for how little damage was done to any of the ships involved.[5]

The occasional muzzle flashes from the battle lit up the sky as the *Thistle* threaded her way through the blockading vessels. She came so close to her enemies that it seemed to Captain William Cleary, who was accompanying Thompson and Clay, as if he could reach out and touch the side of the ships as they passed.

"We twisted our perilous way through the blockaders [and] could easily distinguish their towering hulks although they could not see us," Cleary later recalled. "It seemed at times, as if a stone could have been pitched from our vessel into one of those dangerous neighbours."[6]

As dawn's light broke, the *Raleigh* retreated toward the inlet and the protective umbrella of Fort Fisher's guns. At about the same time, aboard the *Thistle*, Thompson, Clay, and Cleary woke from a light sleep. The *Thistle* had been spotted and a cruiser was giving chase.

In the rigging, a lookout kept his binoculars on the smoke in the distance. Although on paper the *Thistle* could do fourteen knots, that assumed ideal conditions, including an empty hold and calm seas. The lookout shouted to the captain that the cruiser was coming closer. If conditions held, the pursuing ship would be near enough to fire in a few hours. Reluctantly, the captain urged Thompson, Clay, and Cleary to prepare for their capture. "This was pleasant intelligence for gentlemen going out on diplomatic business," Cleary wrote. "I thought I might as well have remained and been shot the regular way on land."

The trio divided the twenty-five dollars in gold coins that they carried. Personal baggage was sorted and small valises packed with personal effects. "I did not feel alarmed, yet not quite as easy as I desired," Clay wrote. "Preparations were made for throwing over the cotton to save it from the Yankees. All our papers, tending to show our missions, were put in the bag with the government dispatches to be burned."[7]

Thompson and Clay assumed that upon capture they would soon be recognized. Both had been well-known in public life before the war. Between 1856 and 1860, Thompson had been Interior Secretary in the cabinet of President James Buchanan, the last administration before the outbreak of war. Clay had served his second term as a U.S. senator from Alabama during the same years. It would quickly be deduced that they were not common passengers, but agents in the service of their government.

Their orders had come directly from Confederate President Jefferson Davis a month earlier. On April 7, Davis sent a telegram to Thompson, summoning him to Richmond, Virginia, the Confederate capital. "If your engagements will permit you to accept service abroad for six months, please come here immediately," Davis said.[8]

Within a few days Thompson arrived in a city that was still absorbing the shock of General Robert E. Lee's defeat at Gettysburg nine months earlier. Richmond's overflowing hospitals still held some of the twenty thousand men wounded during the three days of battle. Since then, the news seemed to have gone from bad to worse. Vicksburg and Port Hudson, the Confederate garrisons on the Mississippi, had fallen the same day that Lee began his retreat from Maryland. A gloom had settled over the Confederate States, and nowhere was it more visible than in Richmond.

John B. Jones, a clerk in the Confederate War Department, recorded in his diary that month: "We are a shabby-looking people now, gaunt and many in rags."

In the spring of 1864, the outlook for the Confederacy was bleak. After three years of struggle the final grapple was at hand, and the South's remarkable resiliency and extraordinary capacity to wage war would soon face a final test. Of the eleven states that had seceded with such high hopes in April 1861, only the six in the heartland remained intact, and they were threatened at almost every point. Union General William Tecumseh Sherman was about to begin his march through Georgia. In Virginia, General Ulysses S. Grant was pressing towards Richmond. Texas, Louisiana, and Arkansas had been cut off by the fall of the Mississippi Valley forts. In the north, Kentucky and Tennessee were largely in Union hands. The South's ability to carry the war into the North had ended with Lee's withdrawal after Gettysburg.

Abraham Lincoln's war policy had also become clear by early 1864. The North had more men, more factories, and more guns, and Lincoln would bring all these resources to bear in a total war. He would grind the Confederate spirit and break their will to fight. Union armies were to use all means to deny the Confederacy resources to wage war by razing their cities, destroying their factories and railroads, burning their crops, and laying waste to their farms.

The South had given up believing that Britain and France would give it diplomatic recognition. This status would have enabled it to break the tightening Union blockade because more ships would use its ports, making it harder for the Union to enforce the blockade. More ships meant more vital goods coming in and more cotton out. Official recognition would also have the intangible effect of shoring up Southern spirits as much as it would be a blow to Northern morale.

Early in the war, the Confederacy had misplayed its diplomatic cards, hoping to bully Great Britain into support by withholding cotton exports. But King Cotton diplomacy hadn't worked. Britain, at the height of its Imperial power, had no intention of being held hostage to warring parties in its former colony. Instead Britain chose neutrality, supporting neither North nor South and trading with both. Of necessity it found new sources of cotton in Egypt and India, and the South resumed exports.

Any hope for a diplomatic victory seemed to rest on the presidential elections in the North. In November, Abraham Lincoln had to stand for re-election. As in the South, weariness had settled over the North. Many Northerners saw Lincoln's great weakness as his conduct of the war. The critics' voices had grown louder, saying the price of victory was too high and perhaps even unachievable.

Just weeks after the Union victories at Gettysburg and Vicksburg, Lincoln sought to press his advantage by calling for the draft of five hundred thousand more men. When New York papers published the news, it triggered three days of rioting in the city that saw government buildings, black-owned businesses, and churches ransacked and burned. Almost one thousand people were killed or injured. It took thousands of troops to quell the unrest. If the South could help that resentment spread, who knew what might be achieved?

Stories had reached Richmond for almost a year, telling of how large parts of the so-called Northwest — today's American Midwest of Illinois, Indiana, Ohio, and Michigan — were desperate for peace at any price. The war was killing their men and destroying their commerce. Traditional trade and transportation routes along the Mississippi for corn, cattle, and lumber were closed. It was causing ruin everywhere along the upper reaches of the river. Fathers and brothers were being drafted to fight and die for a cause with which they had little connection. They neither owned slaves nor found common cause in trying to free them.

It was also said that secret societies had sprung up in the Midwest and armies numbering in the thousands were ready to rise up in rebellion. Davis hoped to encourage such seditious acts and couldn't think of a better place to do it than from bases in British Canada. The Canadian colony's long, virtually undefended border with the Northern states was ideal for infiltration. Southern agents could move freely and many Canadians had pro-Southern sympathies.

Davis had first turned to Alexander H. Stuart, a former U.S Secretary of the Treasury, who was invited to Richmond to discuss a matter "too delicate for correspondence."[9]

Davis flattered Stuart, telling him he would have a "sort of diplomatic family ... the mission of which was to foster and give aid to the peace sentiment then active among the border states," Stuart later recalled. His mission would be well financed and he was to have free hand in spending the money. Stuart believed success hinged on a "remarkable delusion" about the extent of the Northern peace movement and how the Confederacy might capitalize on it. He declined on the grounds of pressing "family obligations."

Within a week Davis had settled on Thompson. The men had known each other for almost half a century. Both lived in Mississippi, and their paths had crossed many times in the course of long political careers. Thompson had been a tireless worker for the Democratic Party. In 1856, when Thompson lost the Mississippi senate race to Davis, the party rewarded his loyalty with the cabinet post in Buchanan's administration.

Thompson was a bookish, keenly intelligent man who spoke French and Italian fluently and was obsessed with education. He was one of the founding fathers of the University of Mississippi in Oxford. He also started Oxford's first female academy. He was instrumental in founding the University of the South in Sewanee, Tennessee, after the Civil War, giving freely of his money and time. Before the war, when his extended family ran into financial trouble, Thompson paid for nieces and nephews to attend colleges in Boston and Baltimore. He was always reading, always learning, and deeply religious, a puritan with all its nineteenth-century connotations.

But if friends and family saw him as generous and supportive, others described him as humourless or as someone who could be vindictive and cruel. He also had an awkward personality that made him seem taciturn and sour at times. Captain Thomas Hines, Thompson's military commander in Canada, would describe him as a man of sterling integrity, undoubted ability, and great political experience. But he "was unluckily inclined to believe much that was told him, trust too many men, doubt too little and suspect less." Hines's friend Captain John Castleman noted more gently that while Thompson was always a gentleman, "he was no diplomat" and was unable to realize that "many men were not as honorable as he."[10]

Thompson, fifty-four, had other assets. He was well connected in the North from his days in Washington and had the stature of a pre-war national politician. From a Canadian base he could quietly seek out old friends and those who would embrace anything that furthered the Confederate goal of peace. Thompson had some military experience, having served as Inspector General with General John Pemberton in the Western Theatre, seeing action at the Battle of Shiloh and Vicksburg in 1862–63. Now he was at loose ends in Mississippi, tending to his business affairs in Oxford and dabbling in the politics of the state legislature. He could be convincing and he was certainly resourceful and shrewd. Although there would be many criticisms of Thompson's behavior, one consistent measure of the man was loyalty. He stood by his cause, his family, and his friends long after it might have been prudent or practical. He also held a fundamental belief in the power of positive thinking and, like all optimists, thought anything possible as long as one had conviction.

Thompson was elected to Congress in 1839, a position that he held for a remarkable six consecutive terms. He wasn't known for his public speaking, but he often seemed to best his opponent with sound argument. He worked hard for the Democratic Party and in 1852 declined the prestigious post of U.S. Consul to Cuba. The following year he lost the Mississippi senatorial race to Jefferson Davis, but his devotion to the party was rewarded in 1856 by being appointed Secretary of the Interior in the newly elected Buchanan administration.

Thompson was a hardline secessionist by 1860 and threatened to resign his cabinet post if Buchanan sent a troop ship, the *Star of the West*, to relieve the besieged federal garrison at Fort Sumter in Charleston's harbour. When Buchanan did this, Thompson resigned on January 9, 1861, and returned home. He took no part in the formation of the Confederate government, but when General P.G.T. Beauregard was sent to command the Confederacy's Army of the West, Thompson offered his services as an aide.

He fought in the Battle of Shiloh in Tennessee in the spring of 1862 and had a horse shot out from under him, although he was unhurt. In mid-1862, when General John Pemberton took over as Commander in the West, he joined Pemberton's staff as Inspector General. He fought with Pemberton at the siege of Vicksburg, and when Vicksburg fell he returned to Oxford, where he took a seat in the state legislature. That was where President Davis found him in early 1864.

At a meeting that lasted much of the night, Davis and Thompson discussed the plan for the Canadian mission. Thompson was to use all necessary means to mobilize the thousands of men who belonged to the secret societies in the Midwest, give shape and direction to their energies, and help bring an end to the war. He was to round up any stray Confederates in Canada who had escaped from Northern prisons and use them as his guerrilla force. He was entrusted with a large secret fund for which he was not required to account, other than in his reports to Richmond.[11]

Thompson was informed that Clay would accompany him. Davis served two ends with Clay's appointment. He rewarded Clay's loyalty while tempering Thompson's impetuous ways. Thompson was opinionated and confident in a way that self-made men often are. He was an entrepreneur and a businessman, owning land and slaves in and around his hometown. He had prospered because of his drive and hard work, and he wasn't afraid to tell people abut his success.

Clay, on the other hand, came from a clan where politics in all its subtle forms was a way of life. Clay was smoother, more refined, and less impetuous. He was ever the politician, looking for the main chance that would carry his tide higher. He had supported Davis before the war and defended him since from attacks within the Confederate Congress.

Clay had hoped for a foreign post or even a place in the Confederate cabinet following his defeat for a seat in the Confederate senate in 1863. Neither had happened. He had already turned down a minor appointment and so, when Davis offered him the Canadian mission, he accepted it, though with deep misgivings.

"I am on my way to Canada, for the purpose of serving the country as best I can," Clay confided to Texas Senator Louis Wigfall days before leaving. "It is a very difficult and delicate duty, for which I am not suited by my talents, tastes or habits. I cannot enjoy secret service. I have accepted it with extreme reluctance."[12]

For Davis it was a small moment of triumph in an otherwise bleak landscape. He had moved towards this end for months, incrementally, but with persistence. He had persuaded the Confederate Congress to pass a Secret Service Act and to free up $1 million for clandestine operations, much of it earmarked for Canada. It meant the commissioners had plenty of money. The investigation into the assassination of Abraham Lincoln concluded the sum was $650,000, a fortune at the time. Another estimate suggests it was $910,000, mainly from the proceeds of the cargo of cotton and turpentine aboard the *Thistle*, which had carried them to Bermuda. Thompson and Clay would be an odd couple from the start, separated by experience and temperament as much as by the rigours of their mission.[13]

Davis wrote the same set of orders for Clay and Thompson. They were vague and suggestive, giving the pair wide latitude in the execution of their tasks. "Confiding special trust in your zeal, discretion, and patriotism, I hereby direct you to proceed at once to Canada, there to carry out such instructions as you have received from me verbally, in such a manner as shall seem most likely to conduce to the furtherance of the interests of the Confederate States of America. Jefferson Davis."[14]

Ten days later, they boarded the *Thistle* for the
adventure of a lifetime,
though on the morning of
May 7, both commission-
ers feared their mission
would be a rather short
misadventure. But after
a five-hour chase, the
Thistle's captain let out a
cry. She was pulling away
from her pursuer. He sup-
posed their engines had
failed. "We all agreed afterward we were very cool
and calm — that is, each
man, said he was," Cleary
recalled. "Fortunately, we
never learned how we
would have stood it."

The steamer hoisted

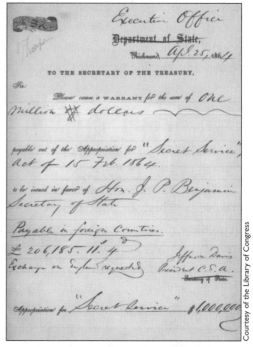

The Confederate Secret Service Act of
April 25, 1864, set aside $1 million for
clandestine operations. Much of it went to
the Canadian mission.

the Confederate ensign and made for St. George's, Bermuda, arriving just before sunrise on Tuesday, May 10.

The experience shattered any illusions Clay might have had
about the dangers of the mission. In truth, the odds had been very
much against the *Thistle*, and but for the *Raleigh*'s efforts, both
Thompson and Clay would likely have been dead or in prison
within hours after heading out to sea.

The *Young Republic*, which Clay believed to be the target of
Union cannons, had been captured after a six-hour chase, not long
after the *Thistle* ran the gauntlet. She had dumped 319 bales of
cotton, cut away her anchors and anchor chain, cast her lifeboats
adrift, and thrown personal effects overboard in a vain effort to
elude her captor.

Likewise, early on May 7, the *Raleigh* fell back towards the
Wilmington sandbar just before dawn. In front of her lay certain

destruction. Behind her, the ebbing tide made it impossible to recross the Wilmington bar. Her draft was too deep, and coated with all that iron, she weighed too much. Her commander, Lieutenant Pembroke Jones, chose the lesser of two evils and set a course for the sandbar, beaching the ship in a vain attempt to defeat the laws of physics. She was close enough to shore to fall under the protection of the fort's guns. Salvagers later stripped the ironclad of her guns and armor, and a military court later cleared her commander of misconduct.

Later that morning, the campaigns that would end the war within a year began. General Ulysses S. Grant crossed the Rapidan River into Virginia with his eye on Richmond. In Tennessee, General William Tecumseh Sherman, under orders from Grant, crossed into northern Georgia. Sherman's immediate target was Atlanta. From there, Sherman's army would march through the state's heartland and by Christmas set the city of Savannah on fire.

On May 15, with none of these facts known to Thompson, Clay, or Cleary, they boarded the British mailship *Alpha* for Halifax, Nova Scotia.[15]

CHAPTER 3
Arrival

"I inform Your Excellency that [I wish] to avoid most scrupulously any infringement of public law, particularly the laws for the preservation of Her Majesty's Neutrality."
James Holcombe to Governor General Monck

Less than a week later, the Commissioners arrived in Halifax, Nova Scotia, after an uneventful journey. In 1864, the British colony was at the zenith of its mid-century prosperity, savouring a commercial glory not seen before or since. The colony was one of five that made up British North America, and its population of 350,000 was spread out along 4,500 miles of rocky coastline, a fact that smugglers had long since learned to use to their advantage. Halifax was the largest city and had played a major role in sea communications between Britain and the United States for most of the century. Ships from England bound for New York and Boston regularly called at Halifax. Those heading east to Portsmouth or Liverpool stopped for fuel and provisions. The massive stone fortress at the top of Citadel Hill was the place from which England had ruled its half of the North American continent for almost a century. In summer, Halifax was home to the North American and West Indian squadrons.

The outbreak of war had created feelings of sympathy in Nova Scotia and the rest of the British Canadian colonies for the North. For Nova Scotia, Boston was regarded as the business centre of the universe. The Reciprocity Treaty, which allowed for a tariff-free flow of many goods between Nova Scotia and the United States, had produced close economic links between the colony and New England. The anti-slavery movement had influenced Nova Scotia, and even though many Nova Scotians had fled the American Revolution eighty-five years earlier, they still had family and friends across the border. As the *Halifax Chronicle* noted soon after war was declared: "There are no more Union men in Massachusetts than Nova Scotia."[16]

In 1861, Nova Scotians saw the dispute as a fight between the forces that favoured slavery and those committed to abolishing it. But when the first year of the war passed and Abraham Lincoln had done nothing to free slaves, there was a sense of bewilderment and a subtle shift in public opinion. If the fight wasn't about slavery, then what was it about? If the South wanted to go its own way because of a different culture surely this was no different than the desire of the original Thirteen Colonies who had declared independence from Britain in 1776. Seen in that light, the disintegration of the Union was merely a continuation of events begun some eighty-odd years earlier. In fact, throughout the war, Canadian[17] newspapers referred to the conflict as the "American Revolution."

By mid-1864, when Thompson and Clay arrived, attitudes were more divided. The war was a huge economic opportunity, whichever side was right. The South offered free trade without taxes on goods coming in and out of its ports, while trade with the North involved haggling over tariffs and a neverending dispute over control of the rich Georges Bank fishing grounds, which straddled the coast of Nova Scotia and northern Maine. The fair and free trade promised by the Reciprocity Treaty wasn't always easy to administer. The South, on the other hand, paid a huge premium to anyone wishing to run goods through the blockade, no questions asked. Business was so brisk in 1864 that two new banks, the Merchants Bank and the People's Bank, opened their doors in Halifax.[18]

Southerners were also the winners in the propaganda war. Southerners in Halifax were more likely to be sophisticated and educated, leaving good impressions on their hosts. Most, like Clay, Thompson, and James Holcombe, the third Canadian commissioner, were agents of their government. They spoke with a united voice, leaving no doubt that the South was strong and resolute, its cause just. Southerners were also good customers, priming the economic pump with the goods they bought to ship home.

Thompson and Clay's first stop was a room above a confectionery store in Barrington Street, in the business district, where Holcombe rented a room. The Virginia law professor had been in British North America for three months, sent there by Jefferson Davis to defend Southern interests in the *Chesapeake* case. Davis hoped Holcombe would be successful in laying a legal claim to the merchant steamer, which a group of Confederate sympathizers had captured off Cape Cod in December 1863. The ship had been recaptured by a Union naval vessel and taken to Halifax, where it had since been tied up in a lengthy legal battle.

Holcombe brought the pair up to date on the progress of his campaign to help escaped Confederate soldiers return to the South. This was the second reason he was in Canada. It was Holcombe who had organized Halifax shipper Benjamin Weir to run goods and soldiers back to the South. Holcombe had set up a network of agents in Montreal, Toronto, and Windsor, opposite Detroit, to funnel the men to Halifax. Not surprisingly, he had found that very few escaped prisoners were eager to return to Confederate armies. However for those "brave and enterprising men" wishing to do so, there was a network.[19]

Holcombe had informed Canadian Governor General Viscount Stanley Monck of his presence in British North America and the purpose of his mission. In a letter to Monck on May 9, which Monck later forwarded to Colonial Secretary Edward Cardwell, Holcombe said he did not plan any hostile acts from Canadian soil. In contrast to the way the mission would develop, Holcombe went out of his way to tell Monck he would not violate any local or Imperial laws.

"I have been sent to the British provinces for the purpose, among other duties of placing funds in the hands of these unfortunate men to return to their country," Holcombe wrote. "As this may lead to some misrepresentation by our enemies, I have been charged to inform Your Excellency of the fact, and to communicate instructions which I have received, to avoid most scrupulously any infringement of municipal or public law and in this connection, particularly the laws for the preservation of Her Majesty's Neutrality."[20]

On May 20, just two days after he arrived, Thompson had learned enough and was off with Cleary, travelling by boat across the Bay of Fundy to St. John, New Brunswick, and from there by carriage up the St. John River Valley to Rivière du Loup and then by train to Montreal. The broad plan they had discussed with President Davis was to disrupt the North by fostering the growing peace sentiment in the Midwest. Captain Tom Hines, formerly an officer in Kentucky General John Hunt Morgan's command, was now in Canada West organizing these escaped Confederate prisoners into a clandestine fighting force. Thompson was anxious to begin.

It was an eight-day trip that highlighted the difficulty of communications in the Canadas. The fastest route to Toronto by rail took only two days, but was denied them. It crossed the U.S. border to Portland, Maine, and from there to Montreal and Toronto. Clay, overcome by "a sudden and quite severe disposition," stayed in Halifax for nine more days, making contact with Southern sympathizers in Holcombe's circle. Among the social rounds was a visit to Thomas Connolly, the Catholic Archbishop of Halifax. Clay and Thompson had met Connolly in Bermuda and the trio had travelled together to Halifax on the *Alpha*. The friendship of the three typified the confused Canadian sensibilities.

Connolly was a powerful Catholic cleric, known for his energy and his causes. He fought for the poor and the underprivileged and poured his energies into the business of building schools, orphanages, convents, and safe houses for sailors. Yet, he welcomed the Southerners and their cause with open arms. Clay wrote that Connolly "dispenses the most liberal hospitality to every respectable Confederate who visits Halifax." Connolly gave Clay an open letter of introduction, which urged every Canadian Catholic Bishop to give him as much help as needed to help fight for the "cause that commands the respect and sympathy of the world."[21]

Clay was also introduced to one of Holcombe's strays, a young man who had fought hard, been captured, escaped from a Northern prison, and made his way to Canada. He was a Kentucky cavalry officer named Bennett Young who had fought with Morgan during his raid into Ohio in the summer of 1863. Young, twenty-two, was captured just north of Cincinnati with the rest of Morgan's command, but escaped a few months later from a federal prison in Chicago. He made his way to Toronto and enrolled at the University of Toronto, taking courses that would have led to his ordination as a minister. After a year he dropped out and made his way to Halifax, where Clay found him.

Young had what Clay later described as feasible plans for raiding and looting towns along the U.S. frontier. These plans would, of course, violate Canadian and British laws, despite Holcombe's promise of "scrupulously" avoiding such infringement. Young had letters of introduction from people whom Clay knew by reputation as friends of the South. They vouched for Young's integrity, "his faith as a Christian and his loyalty as a soldier of the South." Clay dispatched him to Richmond for a formal commission and then ordered him to return to duty in Canada.[22]

On May 30, a week and a half after Thompson's departure, Clay left Halifax, making his way overland to Montreal via Quebec City in a perambulating trip that took eleven days but was "most invigorating and refreshing," as he wrote to his wife.

CHAPTER 4
Northwestern Conspiracy

"The belief was expressed that by a bold, concerted movement, the three great Northwestern states could be seized and held. This in 60 days would end the war."

> Jacob Thompson to Confederate Secretary of State
> Judah Benjamin

By the time Clay arrived in Montreal on June 10, Thompson had settled in at the Queen's Hotel in Toronto, his headquarters during his Canadian mission. Thompson chose the Queen's for many reasons, high among them that it suited his taste for fine living. Its foods, wines, and service were renowned, and the main floor telegraph office offered instant communication with allies and emissaries. The hotel carried the latest American newspapers, whose classified ads were another of Thompson's forms of communication with Richmond. The hotel was well situated on the waterfront, opposite the main railway station, so that Thompson's many spies, couriers, and informants could easily make contact with him.[23]

Action was how Thompson had built a personal fortune, and action was how he had climbed the ladder within the Democratic Party. Unlike Clay, who had been born to power and privilege, Thompson's achievements had been carved out of the Mississippi wilderness after twenty-five years of hard work. He had left North Carolina in 1831, at the age of twenty-one, for Mississippi, then on the frontier. He eventually settled in Oxford, where the Choctaw

Confederate prisoners outside an unknown Union prison, possibly Chicago's Camp Morton, in 1864.

Indian lands were being opened to settlement. Soon he had a busy law practice and arranged to marry Kate Jones, daughter of the richest landowner in northern Mississippi, although she was only sixteen. He packed her off to Paris to complete her education. He gradually accumulated the wealth that by 1864 included two plantations encompassing five thousand acres and land in six other Mississippi counties and in Texas, most of which was undeveloped. He also owned a sawmill, a hotel in Oxford, and three cotton gins.

Jacob Thompson was a wealthy planter with decades of national political experience, but he had no experience as a spy.

40

He wanted to move quickly toward the goals he had discussed with Davis in Richmond. Foremost was Davis's instruction to find out whether the conditions were ripe for a rebellion in the Midwest, led by so-called Copperhead groups. Thompson was intrigued by these possibilities. These disaffected Democrats were opposed to war and to the government of Republican president Abraham Lincoln. The Copperheads wanted to make peace with the Confederate states because many simply believed the conquest of the South was either illegal or impossible — or both. They saw the cost in Northern lives and economic ruin, and felt the war was simply not worth the effort.

According to reports that had trickled back to the South with increasing frequency after the Battle of Gettysburg in July 1863, the Copperheads had well-organized armies numbering in the hundreds of thousands. The reports said the Copperheads were not only ready to bring an end to the war, but were prepared to go one step further — to overthrow Lincoln's government and form a new Northwestern Confederacy including Illinois, Indiana, Ohio, and Missouri. All they needed was a helping hand and the former United States would be broken into three pieces, assuring the Confederacy's survival.

The chief proponent of this story was Clement Vallandigham, an Ohio congressman who, through a series of events, had become a rallying point for the views of the various Copperheads groups. In early 1863, Vallandigham had been imprisoned for sedition after urging Northerners to overthrow the federal government and make peace with the South. Lincoln commuted his sentence and instead banished Vallandigham to the Confederacy. While there, Vallandigham spread his myth of mighty Copperhead armies. After spending some months touring the southern states and wearing out his welcome there, Vallandigham ran the blockade to Halifax.

As Vallandigham travelled west, some Canadians praised him for his support of peace and his courage in standing up to Lincoln's policy of war. In Quebec, British financier Edward Watkins presided over a private dinner at the exclusive Stadacona Club. Similar status was accorded him in Montreal, and so impressed were the Canadians that the Grand Trunk Railway provided him with a private car for a trip to Niagara Falls.[24] Yet the Governor General and leading Canadian politicians held their noses as Vallandigham moved through the provinces. He embarrassed them with his hysterical and inflammatory rhetoric, but under British law, as a political exile, he was entitled to stay.

The second week of June 1864 found Vallandigham in Windsor, across the St. Clair River from Detroit. Thompson fully expected to meet the man who would help him in his task of overthrowing the U.S. government. Thompson had sent Hines ahead, and on June 11, the three met to discuss how Thompson might help Vallandigham stir opposition to the war to a state of open rebellion.

Thompson was dazzled. Vallandigham was tall with a powerful presence and an imposing voice. His legal training and his practice in Congress making speeches made his arguments fluid and convincing. He devoured books on law, religion, and philosophy and devoted an hour a day to the Bible. These traits appealed to Thompson, because of his love of books and his personal religious beliefs. Hines, on the other hand, would describe Vallandigham as a fool and fanatic, a vain, hopeless dreamer "who believed all that was told to him."[25]

Vallandigham told Thompson that a feeling of fatigue and rising anger had been building in the North following the staggering casualties at Gettysburg and Lincoln's call just a few weeks after that battle for a draft of 500,000 more men. The New York draft riots showed just how angry Northerners were, and with just a little push, Vallandigham said, an uprising in the Midwest would create a second Confederacy and end the war.

The various military wings of the Sons of Liberty would be put on alert, arms and ammunition secured. There would be simultaneous uprisings throughout the Ohio Valley with prisons and arsenals seized.

As soon as the prisoners were released they were to be armed and equipped and then join the battle to separate the Northwest from the union. Hines would be the liaison between the various groups, and Thompson would coordinate the plan.[26]

Thompson was initiated into the group's secret rites so he would have a better understanding of the order. In a letter to Benjamin some months later, Thompson said he saw the Sons of Liberty as the Confederacy's salvation.

"Its organization was essentially military. It had commanders of divisions, brigades, of regiments, of companies," Thompson wrote. "The belief was boldly expressed that by a bold, vigorous and concerted movement, the three great Northwestern states of Illinois, Indiana and Ohio could be seized and held. This being done, the states of Kentucky and Missouri could easily be lifted from their prostrate position and this in 60 days would end the war."[27]

Thompson was equating Copperhead disloyalty to the Union and unhappiness with the war with support for the Confederate cause. If he was right, rebellion and personal glory, vindication of the cause, and peace for the South were at hand. If he was wrong, what lay ahead was military and financial disaster.

Back in Toronto, Hines sent a ciphered message to Secretary of War James Seddon in Richmond. He reported that he had met Thompson and formulated a plan.

Hines would lead two regiments that were being formed in Chicago. They would move on nearby Camp Douglas to free Confederate prisoners once the uprising was in full swing. Simultaneously, Democrats in all counties in Illinois and Ohio would rise and rally to arms. Some three thousand of these men would help free the seven thousand prisoners at Rock Island, Illinois, another federal prison camp. "State governments ... will be seized and their executives disposed of. By this means we hope to have, within 10 days after the movement has begun, a force of 50,000 men."

Thompson was optimistic about the prospects for success. "I have a great many things to communicate which I feel unwilling to commit to paper," he wrote to Clay in Montreal.[28]

CHAPTER 5

The Irish Lord

"[Canadian] sympathies are with the southern states not because they are anti-abolitionists. They sympathize with the South from a strong dislike of the aggression and insolence they have felt upon their own borders."

Anthony Trollope, on Canadian antipathy
for the North

As Thompson took the first steps towards his goals, Governor General Monck faced his own tests. The U.S. Consul in Halifax had duly noted the Commissioners' arrival, and of course, Holcombe had communicated with Monck just days before Clay and Thompson arrived. Thompson had likewise informed Monck of his presence in Canada before he left Montreal for Toronto. Confederate emissaries were nothing new. As long as these Confederates didn't break any Canadian laws, as Holcombe had promised, they were welcome to stay. But in a larger sense, Thompson and Clay represented the menace and destabilizing threat of the great American war.

As Queen Victoria's highest representative in North America, it was Monck's job to defend British interests, a job he took seriously.

By the spring of 1864, Monck, Canadian government officials, and the American government were willing partners in efforts to keep Confederate plots from maturing on Canadian soil. Public sympathies may have been mixed, but the official response was not. Often the incidents involved nothing more than rumours. Such was the case in the fall of 1863, when Canadian Premier Sandfield Macdonald — whose brother-in-law Eugene Waggaman was a colonel in the Confederate Army[29] — intervened with Monck to expose a vague plan to buy a boat, arm it, and set it loose on Lake Erie. The activities of boat-buying Confederates in Montreal came to the attention of the U.S. Consul, Joshua Giddings, who informed Seward as well as Monck.

Giddings was also told that boats were to be used in concert with a large Confederate force to free prisoners held at Johnson's Island in Sandusky, Ohio. Monck found no evidence of a raiding party, but worked with Sandfield Macdonald to alert authorities in Detroit, Cleveland, and Sandusky. Macdonald even travelled to Buffalo to talk to Mayor William Fargo and General John Dix. In the end the raid did not material-

Canadian Governor General Viscount Stanley Monck was a cool, level-headed administrator who adroitly managed relations between Canada and the U.S. during the Civil War years.

ize, but as events in the fall of 1864 would show, the Confederates still found Johnson's Island an attractive target.

By the time the Confederate Commissioners arrived, the Canadian authorities had plenty of experience dealing with the various agents of both governments passing through the colonies. Within months of the outbreak of war, Canada became the meeting place for displaced Southerners, skedaddlers from both armies, exiles, agents, and spies. Southern couriers and officials on their way to Europe often came overland to Windsor or Niagara Falls and from there to Toronto, Montreal, and Halifax. From Halifax, fast blockade-runners took them home via Bermuda or Nassau to Wilmington, North Carolina or Charleston, South Carolina.

The long, largely open frontier made crossings easy. In winter, you could walk across the St. Clair River to Detroit. In summer, you could sail a boat across Lake Erie or Lake Ontario from the Canadian side and disappear without a trace. As John Surratt, the courier whose mother was executed for her part in the Lincoln assassination, described some years later, passing oneself off as "a Canuck" was an easy and effective cover.

From 1862 onward, the U.S. state department populated all large Canadian cities with consuls who reported on the comings and goings of Confederate officials and agents. The Canadian government tolerated this misuse of diplomatic privilege because it suited them. As the Confederates became more of a menace, a virtuous diplomatic circle helped convince American authorities of Canadian sincerity in stopping raiders from basing themselves on Canadian soil. When the communications weren't urgent, the consuls would write to Seward in Washington. Seward would inform the British Ambassador to Washington, Lord Richard Lyons, and Lyons would pass the message on to Monck. Monck would relay whatever action was needed to Canadian authorities.

The neutrality policy forbade Monck and Lyons from favouring either side, so often the official response to small irritants was to turn a blind eye. Another tactic was the judicious use of the press to make the rumours public. That way there was no official need for action, but the warning was sent nonetheless.

Monck was, at forty-five, a large, comfortably built man, bearded, square-shouldered, and with no intrinsic interest in colonial affairs. He had taken the job because he was bored with his sedentary life in Ireland as lord of his inherited manors, on estates in the counties of Wicklow and Wexford. He was "very tired of doing nothing at home," and saw no better public appointments on the horizon.

Monck had served in the British House of Commons for seven years and had been a Lord of the Treasury in the liberal government of Henry Temple, Viscount Palmerston, between 1855 and 1858.

After that he was a landed gentlemen out of office, something that Palmerston corrected when he became prime minister again in 1860. At best, though, Monck appeared to be destined for junior positions. He had impressed those who had worked under him as "a man of good sense and judgment and of fair abilities and application." Palmerston hoped to offer him the comparatively insignificant office of Irish Lord of the Treasury. When that couldn't be arranged, he got Canada.[30]

Monck was frank and amiable, good at business affairs, and enjoyed sports, horses, dogs, and all things connected with country

John A. Macdonald, Canada's first prime minster, had an anti-American bias and viewed the republican system of government as open to corruption.

life. He had a British aristocrat's healthy contempt for the common man, colonial politicians, and Americans, though not necessarily in that order. In early 1862, when Canadian Members of Parliament failed to pass a bill calling for higher taxes to raise a militia, Monck was dumbfounded. Here a great war was raging a few hundred miles from their border, and the Canadians weren't in the least interested in raising and equipping a modest citizen's army for their defence. He lamented in a letter to his superiors that Canada's political leaders were a "wretched lot." Not one of them was "capable of rising above the level of a parish politician" and they were "led away by all the small jealousies and suspicions to which minds of that class are prone."

Monck had some legal training but no other formal qualifications for the job. However, he had less tangible assets: tact, energy, and patience, all in short supply in Canadian politics. He was an efficient administrator who proved prudent, levelheaded, and occasionally wise. He remained Governor General until 1868, a year after Canadian Confederation, and concluded that in his seven years of stewardship his most "anxious and responsible" duties were conducting foreign relations with the United States.

From Britain's point of view, the dramatic growth and development of the United States during the first half of the century was cause for alarm. The *Times of London* sent a full-time correspondent to the United States in 1854, and those reports, along with first-hand accounts like Alexis de Toqueville's *Democracy in America* and Anthony Trollope's *North America*, showed how America was maturing socially, politically, and economically.

In Britain and Canada, the events of the American War of Independence and the invasions during the War of 1812 were still recalled. Canada was peopled with Empire Loyalists who had fled the American Revolution. While Americans might have viewed them as traitors, their descendants formed Canada's political elite. Their views influenced wider thought in British North America. Naturally, they had no sympathy for America or its politics, viewing republican government as inherently unstable, an unseemly popularity contest where one voted for an individual at a winner-takes-all convention. Canadians preferred the British parliamentary system of government, where parties elected leaders, leaders laid out platforms, and whichever party garnered the most votes became the government. John A. Macdonald, who would become Canada's first prime minister, typified the mid-Victorian horror of the American system that he referred to as "immoral" and "horrid." Macdonald attended a party convention in the 1856 and was shocked at the lobbying on the floor, which meant that "talent and worth counted for little and low trickery very much."[31]

As the slavery debate consumed the American political stage, Canadians and Britons once again saw it as a failure of the American system. How could a Constitution that promised liberty, justice, and the pursuit of happiness for all men also make room for slavery? The Bishop of Montreal, George Jehosaphat Mountain, spoke for many Canadians when he noted that slavery was an unsurpassed political contradiction. In the United States, millions of men were in bondage, in a state of "studied and carefully contrived degradation," yet America "vaunts itself to the world, as the only free country on earth."[32]

In Britain and Canada, America was portrayed as a country rife with disharmony, where politicians were incompetent and corrupt and the issue of slavery consumed political life and was never far from the surface. George Brown, publisher of Toronto's *Globe* newspaper and a leading liberal politician, had lived for a time in New York. As early as 1850 in a series of editorials in the *Globe* he returned to the subject of slavery, reminding Canadians that they should keep in mind that American conquest of Texas had meant slavery for an area that the Mexicans had kept free of the institution. Americans were eager to denounce the tyranny of monarchies in Russia or Austria, but their "national hypocrisy" forced them to shy away from the evil in their midst. In fact, by allowing the onward march of slavery they had regressed since the War of Independence seventy-five years earlier.

Britain had outlawed the slave trade in 1807 and had managed to secure international acceptance of the ban, along with the right to board suspected slavers on the high seas. The United States refused to sign the agreement. Memories of their colonial status and British interference with shipping during the War of 1812, along with an unwillingness to antagonize Southern interests, made sure of that. As a result, a thriving slave trade continued.

Economically, the interests of Britain and United States were also diverging. Freer trade meant that British manufactured goods could be traded for American raw materials without high tariffs. But paradoxically, British investment was also creating the American industrial might that was challenging Great Britain's supremacy. American trade was beginning to penetrate markets in Europe, Africa, and Latin America. Textile mills in New England were absorbing more and more cotton that had been traditionally exported to mills in Lancashire. No less disturbing was the American challenge to the British merchant marine. In the decade after 1847 the United States was the world's biggest shipbuilding nation. American ships won the best cargoes and most of the passenger business across the Atlantic.[33]

In 1842, the Webster-Ashburton Treaty had ceded a large part of what is now Maine's Canadian border to the Union. And in the West, the Oregon Settlement ceded most of the Pacific Northwest to the United States by drawing the border at the 49th parallel. To British and Canadian nationalists these moves smacked of capitulation. So it was with unfriendly eyes that Britain viewed the United States in 1861 when the war broke out. It boiled down to disapproval, distrust, and apprehension.

It was then natural in Britain and Canada that the Confederate cause excited a widespread sense of sympathy. Didn't Southerners have the same right to leave the Union as their ancestors had had to withdraw from the British Empire? Wasn't the conflict just a continuation of that process and a glaring reminder of the mistake the Americans had made? Britain also sensed a strategic advantage for its interests in a divided Union. Canada might emerge as a dominant power if the Union should shatter for good. Disunion would leave the United States less aggressive and less irritable than it had been. The division of one large bullying state into two meant that each would be more occupied with its immediate neighbour than anything else.

Colonel Garnet Wolseley, who was sent to Canada as part of a general reinforcement of its defences, was quick to see that. In 1862, Wolseley spent a month visiting the Confederacy to observe the war first-hand. Wolseley, who later became commander-in-chief of the British Army, argued that Britain should grant the Confederate States diplomatic status. He concluded in a letter to his superiors that his main reason for saying this was because the division of the Republic into two weak countries would immediately strengthen the position of Britain's Canadian colonies. Wolseley liked the Southern people, but had no love of their cause. He confided to a friend that most of his good wishes for the South stemmed from "my dislike of the people of the United States and my delight at seeing their swagger and bunkum rudely kicked out of them."[34]

Anthony Trollope, who visited Canada during his North America tour, also recorded the Canadian sympathy for the South. He found it curious because Canadians didn't own slaves, cared little about cotton, and actually had more in common with Yankee New England. He said:

> Their sympathies are with the southern states not because they are anti-abolitionists, not because they admire the hearty pluck of those who are endeavoring to work out for themselves a new revolution. They sympathize with the South from a strong dislike to the aggression, the braggadocio and the insolence they have felt upon their own borders.[35]

It did not clarify matters for Canadians when, at the outbreak of war, President Abraham Lincoln said publicly and carefully that he did not regard himself primarily as the emancipator of slaves, but as the protector of Union. Lincoln's first inaugural address, captured in the *Globe*, said in part:

> My paramount objective in this struggle is to save the Union and is not either to save or destroy slavery. If I could save the Union without freeing any slave I would do it; and if I could save it by freeing all the slaves, I would do it; and if I could do it by freeing some of the slaves and leaving others alone, I would do that.

In the end Great Britain chose a course of neutrality because it realized that to do otherwise gambled with the security of its Canadian possessions. Neutrality offered a diplomatic protection for Canada and assured the Northern states that Canada would have no part to play in support for the South. So Britain refused to give the Confederacy diplomatic recognition, but British ships ran the Northern blockade to buy Southern cotton. The Confederate government also found sympathetic financial markets in Britain to raise money to pay for the war. British shipyards built raiders for the Confederate Navy. But in an effort to keep Canada clear of the dispute, the colony passed laws forbidding the sale of arms, ammunition, or coal to either side, while the allowing the sale of foodstuffs, medicines, and other manufactured goods.

By 1864, the fear of Northern invasion lingered, and as events would show, it was not unfounded. The Union Army had grown from the group of hastily recruited civilians of 1861 into the largest standing army in the world. As General Sir Charles Hastings Doyle observed in a letter to his Canadian commander Sir Fenwick Williams: "They are formidable. If they persevere they must ultimately succeed."

And what if the North won and turned its eye to Canada in anger? Or if the South won independence and the North turned to Canada as compensation? Hastings Doyle, who was commander of British Troops Atlantic, which included Bermuda, put this to Williams, relating a conversation he'd had with American military commander Ulysses S. Grant and General George Meade during a visit to the siege of Richmond.

"I sympathize with neither side, for they both hate us cordially," Hastings Doyle wrote. "I used to chaffe them a good deal about when they planned to pay you and me a visit. The reply I invariably received was: 'Oh, we do not have anything to say to you until we have taken Mexico.' There is but one feeling. Mexico will be theirs when the war with the South is over."[36]

In January 1862, the Canadian government established a Commission to consider the question of defence. A new post was created, the Minister of Militia Affairs, with John A. Macdonald its first minister. Its recommendation was framed as the Militia Bill. The bill called for a volunteer force of 100,000 men, half active and half in reserve. The problem was it would have cost nearly $1 million a year. The bill was attacked by Brown's *Globe* as economically unfeasible, noting that that it would be the fourth rise in taxes in four years. When John A. put it to a vote, his government fell, persuading Monck to utter his unkind words about Canadian politicians.

The defeat was jeered at in the Northern press as proof that Canada would never fight. In London, the *Times* attacked the pampered colonials who lacked the fortitude to defend themselves. The British government was appalled. What sort of people were these Canadians that they were so unprepared to pay for their own defence? In the end, all the Canadians would pay for was an active force of 10,000 men and another 10,000 in reserve at an annual cost of $250,000. It was the best that could be done.

Monck wasn't pleased with the idea of a volunteer force, but ever the practical administrator, he accepted that a volunteer army was the only resource at hand. "If we can get nothing better we must put up with it and try to do the best we can with the instruments with which we are supplied," he wrote.[37]

That's pretty much where it stood in mid-1864. In early 1864 Colonial Secretary Cardwell insisted that British forces be stationed at key points in the St. Lawrence River Valley, rather than strung out in small units from Quebec to Windsor without the support from a militia in the event of any American action. It meant that in the event of an invasion most of what is now Ontario would be abandoned.

The Canadians defeated the first Militia Bill because in 1862 they were not convinced that the war posed a threat to them. If it did, they believed any conflict would be between the United States and Britain, in which case they would have little, if any, say. In this they were largely correct. So if Britain wanted a large force in Canada to protect British interests, Britain should pay. Yet from that moment on the pressure increased on Great Britain to withdraw from military responsibilities in North America.

All of these things added up to opportunity and a favourable climate for Jacob Thompson when he first arrived. Canada's vast border was an invitation to his intrigues and an easy way to infiltrate the North, meet with the secret societies, and move ahead with his plans for the overthrow of Abraham Lincoln's government.

CHAPTER 6
Failed Rebellion

"A large amount of money has been expended and it now seems for very little profit. But in reviewing the past, I do not see how it could have been avoided."

> Jacob Thompson, on the
> Northwestern Conspiracy

In Toronto, Thompson found himself surrounded by many veterans of Morgan's Cavalry. They were young, battle-hardened, and committed to the Southern cause, trained in the arts of guerrilla war and keen to strike back at their enemy. Hines, who was Thompson's main military aide, recruited Captain John Castleman and Lieutenant George Eastin. Upon his return from Richmond, Lieutenant Bennett H. Young would join the team.

There were others, like Dr. Luke Blackburn, who would later become governor of Kentucky and who had been surgeon general in the Confederate command of General Sterling Price in Missouri. Blackburn would hang on the fringes of the mission, and his most notable act would come late in the game. In the fall of 1864, Blackburn would send trunks of clothes contaminated with yellow fever to Union hospitals in hopes of infecting and killing as many wounded Union soldiers as possible. It was a diabolical plan that failed only because the fever could not be transmitted that way. The courier, Godfrey Hyams, got as far as taking the trunks to Boston but abandoned them there, unable to carry out the plan.[38]

Thompson used Hyams, an Arkansan who had escaped to Toronto with his wife, as a go-between. He later turned traitor, spilling everything he knew about their plans to the U.S. Consul in Toronto, David Thurston.[39] Hyams ended up testifying against the Confederates in Canada at the trial of the Lincoln conspirators.

Young, whom Clay had met in Halifax, was commissioned by Secretary of War Seddon as a lieutenant and was sent back to Canada in secret service. On the fourth of July, Young was back in Toronto, reporting to Thompson.

Another member of the Confederate guerilla force was Colonel George St. Leger Grenfel. He would die in chains in a Union prison camp on the Dry Tortugas off the Florida coast. In 1864, Grenfel still cut an impressive figure, standing six feet tall, with blue eyes and a shock of shoulder-length white hair, set off by a deep tan and leathery face burned dry by the desert sands of North Africa.

"He displayed a love of fighting, which amazed the wildest and boldest of the Kentucky and Tennessee cavalrymen," Hines wrote. "On one occasion leading a charge and riding down upon a strongly garrisoned railway depot, he received 11 bullets in his horse and person. Yet he seemed to think only that 'It wasn't a very good day for the bullets.'"[40]

The mission's secretary, William Cleary, had been sent to New York to buy guns for the uprising and had used ex-mayor Fernando Wood as his contact. The meeting place for the subversives was a violin shop off Washington Square. There, Cleary bought rifles, pistols, ammunition, and components to make Greek Fire. They were smuggled into Canada, where the Confederates packed them in boxes stencilled "prayer books" and sent them back across the border into Ohio and Indiana. The boxes were buried in haystacks, graveyards, and barnyards.

But the Sons of Liberty had been infiltrated, and their movements were known to federal authorities.[41] The most important double agent was a man called Felix Stidger, a mild-mannered, nondescript-looking clerk whose later testimony helped shatter the Copperheads in the Northwest. While Hines paid tribute to Stidger, lamenting, "He ruined us all," author Robin Winks described Stidger's accounts as "highly unreliable." In regular dispatches to his superior, Colonel Henry B. Carrington, military commander of Indianapolis, Stidger tracked the Copperheads' movements and plans.

The thirty-one-year-old Stidger was a native of Kentucky. An ardent supporter of the Union, he had joined the adjutant general's office when the war broke out, and later joined the provost marshal's office in Tennessee. It was there that he came to Carrington's attention. In late 1863, Carrington had become alarmed at the extent of the Copperhead movement. He gathered a staff of six men, including Stidger, and told them to infiltrate the secret societies. Soon Stidger was indoctrinated into its many rites and was introduced to Dr. William Bowles, a prominent Democrat. Bowles had served in the U.S. Army as a colonel during the Mexican War and was a rabid foe of Lincoln's war policy. Gradually Stidger worked his way into the inner council. By the summer of 1864 he was the secretary of a large Copperhead group in Indiana, and all the orders for guns, plans for their distribution, and details of the uprising were coming through him. He was so afraid for his life that he begged Carrington not to "speak of me to anyone, nor tell anyone what work I am doing, for if you do I shall be betrayed and murdered in my sleep."

Carrington moved when a note arrived from Stidger that Judge Joshua Bullitt, Grand Commander of the Knights of the Golden Circle in Kentucky, was returning to Louisville following a meeting in Windsor with Thompson. Bullitt would have letters, bank drafts, and other incriminating documents in his possession. Bullitt was arrested, and among the papers found on him was a $10,000 cheque drawn on the Bank of Ontario, signed by Jacob Thompson.

Clay and Thompson worried that another round of arrests was imminent. In a letter to Thompson on August 3, Clay wrote: "The arrest of Judge Bullet is ominous and may be followed by others, which will prevent our success. The secret of the order, its officers, its signs are all out."[42]

There was another discouragement in store. Joseph McDonald, the democratic candidate for governor of Indiana, had gotten wind of the conspiracy and, fearing that it would ruin his chance for election, called a meeting of the Copperhead leaders on August 5 and told them to call it off or he would expose it.

The mood was one of deepening gloom. In the end the Copperheads agreed to August 29, but as conspirator Lieutenant John Headley noted in his memoirs, it was with great reluctance. "We leave for Chicago to do our best, but with heavy hearts and drooping hopes for the cause," they said.

To make matters worse, Governor Oliver P. Morton of Indiana had received an anonymous note reporting the shipment of arms and ammunition shipped from New York via Canada. It said the weapons could be identified in crates as prayer books and would be found at the printing company in Indianapolis of H.H. Dodd, one of the remaining Copperhead leaders. It was raided on the night of August 20, and the crates were found to contain 400 army revolvers and 35,000 rounds of ammunition. News of the raid was widely reported throughout the North.

On August 24, Thompson gave Hines and Castleman $25,000 to defray the costs of the Chicago expedition. He also made Castleman second-in-command, giving him authority for an expedition against American prisons and "such other services as you and Capt. Hines have been verbally instructed about." Hines and Castleman were left to select their men, choosing those who "are suited to so perilous an undertaking." They split their force in half, with each taking thirty-five men. At the last minute, in typically naive and foolish fashion, Thompson sent another twenty men, impressed by their "high connections." Hines was worried by the appearance of some, the loose tongues of others, and the sobriety of yet more. Nonetheless each received $100, a pistol and ammunition, and a round-trip train ticket from Chicago to Toronto. During the days before the convention they filtered into Chicago in groups of two and four. The conspirators were given a little hope with the news that the federal garrison in Chicago was being reinforced for the convention. If this irritant could become a spark for riots, it could give the Copperheads a reason to fight. As Castleman later noted, "We knew that any arrest would supply our best hope for success and that it mattered little who would be arrested. An inflammatory crowd might thus be led beyond retreat."

On August 28, Hines and Castleman met with the Copperhead leaders. They expected energetic and passionate men, but the Copperheads seemed frightened and anxious, not empire builders at all. When Hines asked if everything was set, he was told that while the groups had been ordered to converge on Chicago they had no instructions, no organization, and no command structure. They were nothing more a mob. Hines was in a rage. But there was nothing he could do.

That night three thousand troops moved into the city as federal authorities responded to pleas from the commandant at Camp Douglas for reinforcements. By morning Hines knew the rebellion had failed. He met with the Copperhead leaders one last time, asking for their help in launching assaults on the prisons at Rock Island and Camp Douglas. Hines pleaded as he unveiled his plan. He would divide his men into squads, cut the telegraph wires in and out of the city, move in and capture a federal arsenal, and, so armed, attack the prisons. By dawn the Northwest would be in flames. The commanders said they could not do it.

Hines called his men together and told them to scatter. They were free to return home to Kentucky or they could come with him and Castleman through Indiana and Ohio. Twenty-five took tickets home. Twenty-two went with Hines and Castleman. Twenty-three returned to Canada with Bennett Young.

Thompson was livid when he learned of the rebellion's failure. He had believed in its success, he had spent so much money and devoted so much planning to that end. He described those that returned, including Young, as "deserters" and ordered Young to return to the Confederate States. Writing to Clay on September 2, Young said he was surprised by the reaction. "Col. Thompson orders me home. I refuse. The Secretary of War reserves that right and nowhere is it delegated to Col. Thompson."[43]

The plan failed for many reasons. For a small group to succeed in overthrowing a government the attack had to be decisive and unexpected. It also had to be secret, an essential advantage that the conspirators didn't have. The federal authorities knew most of the movements of the Copperhead groups, because the groups were honeycombed with informers like Stidger. The Copperheads had no real plan to govern, nor any mechanism to take over once the rebellion took place. They weren't really an army, but rather men who played at being soldiers. Nor did they have any desire to support the Confederate cause, as much as they disliked Lincoln and the war. Many had family serving in the Union Army fighting the Confederates. When it came time to betray those people as well as their country, they couldn't do it. As Hines put it some years later, "They had no personal sympathy for the Confederates at all. They desired that the War should cease ... While they wanted the armies withdrawn from the South, few wished for the success of the Confederacy. We very soon discovered that this was the temper of these people."[44]

Thompson refused to believe any of this. Months later, in a December letter to Benjamin, he maintained that:

> The feeling among the masses is as strong as ever. They are true, brave, and I believe, willing and ready, but they have no leaders. The large bounties paid for treachery, added to the large military force stationed in those states, make organization and preparation almost an impossibility. A large amount of money has been expended and it now seems to have been for little profit. But in reviewing the past, I do not see how it could have been avoided.[45]

Holcombe believed a rebellion was just wishful thinking. "The Northwest is not now ... and may never be ripe for rebellion," Holcombe wrote to Benjamin. However, Holcombe felt that as long as federal authorities believed in the possibility, it worked to the advantage of the Confederacy, because it would force the government to keep heavy concentrations of troops throughout the Northwest, creating "an important diversion in our favor."[46]

Meanwhile, at the Democrat Convention, the mood had changed. The Convention elected Major General George McClellan, Lincoln's indecisive former general, as their candidate for president in November. Clement Vallandigham's delegates forced the convention to accept a platform of peace with the South.

A few days after the Convention convened, the stalemate around Atlanta ended. General William Tecumseh Sherman advanced through the smoke into a ruined city. "Atlanta is ours and fairly won," wired Sherman to the War Department. Vallandigham and his peace democrats saw their platform crack. The way to the Southern heartland lay open. The end was in sight.

On August 22, as the final plans for Chicago were being laid, a federal force under General Albert "Whiskey" Smith entered Jacob Thompson's hometown of Oxford, Mississippi. For the better part of the month Oxford had changed hands in vicious fighting. On the seventh of August it was evacuated. On the ninth, it was recaptured by General Nathan Bedford Forrest. Forrest held it until forced to withdraw on August 22 after two days of street fighting. That morning a large force of black and white troops occupied the town.

In a one-day orgy of looting, thirty-four stores and businesses were burned. Five homes, including Thompson's, were put to the torch. Smith supervised the carnage, refusing to allow anyone to remove anything of value from their homes. Thompson's wife, Kate, salvaged one thing she valued above all else, a photograph of their only son, Macon, before he was badly disfigured in an accident. As she clutched the photo on the lawn, a union soldier grabbed it and threw it into the blaze. In the official report to the Confederate War Department some days later, the commandant at Oxford wrote: "General Smith's conduct and that of his staff was brutal in the extreme, they having been made mad with whiskey. The soldiers were licensed for any crime — robbery, rape, theft and burning."[47]

Thompson regrouped. With the fall of Atlanta it became clear that what the South needed more than ever was relief on the battlefield and men to fill her thinning ranks. In Northern prisons, Thompson might find the means to serve both aims. If he could free the thousands of men there he could build an army and a threat to Northern security that would cause troops to be diverted for their protection.

He sent Captain Charles Cole to Sandusky, Ohio, and set into motion a plan that had been rumored for the better part of a year: assaults on the Johnson Island prison. For one brief moment, a Confederate naval pennant would fly on the Great Lakes.

CHAPTER 7
Peace Plans

"In my long life, I have known no counterpart to this man. He was a constant menace to the interests for which the commission-ers were responsible. He controlled Mr. Clay and while he was there Mr. Holcombe."

Captain Tom Hines on George Sanders

As Thompson and Hines put their Northwest Conspiracy in action, Clement Clay had made his way to the city of St. Catharines, on the shores of Lake Ontario some fifteen miles from the Falls and sixty miles from Toronto. There he would remain for the rest of his Canadian stay, partaking of the curative spa waters and renting a room in a house owned by a refugee from Georgia, Robert Cox.

It is clear from the letters Clay sent home to his wife that he was lonely and lost. Once he had separated himself from Thompson, the two communicated mostly by mail. He was as worried about his wife, Virginia, as he was about his mission, writing to her weekly and sending back many of the items denied Confederate women because of the war. She often wrote back with shopping lists, including such things as silk dresses and even Hudson Bay furs. Bennett Young carried one such missive back to Clay upon his return from Richmond, where he had received new orders from Secretary of War Seddon. In a return letter to Ginnie, dated July 28, Clay wrote that he had found the requested combs,

Courtesy of the Niagara Falls Heritage Foundation

The Clifton House Hotel in Niagara Falls was the setting for peace talks between the Confederate Commissioners in Canada and U.S. President Abraham's Lincoln's chief of staff, John Hay.

fans, and braid, which he enclosed by parcel post, noting that ivory tuck combs "are all the rage here" and cost eight dollars each. Clay also sent a top and some marbles to his son Matt, giving detailed instructions on how to use it and proudly adding the results of a personal test drive, where he found the top "spins 15 times if properly handled."[48]

In St. Catharines, Clay was able to pursue his own plans at a leisurely pace. They included making overtures to important men in the North in order to try to negotiate peace.[49] It was grandiose, naive, and ill-conceived, overestimating the power of the peace sentiment in the North. It would likely not have come about at all, but for the meddling of George Nicholas Sanders.

While in Montreal, Clay learned that Sanders was living in Niagara Falls. Clay wrote to Confederate Secretary of State Judah Benjamin that Sanders was staying at the Clifton House and "representing himself as sent by our government to encourage peace.

He actually talked of calling a peace meeting of citizens of the US and CS to devise joint action to that end. I hope he will not do so silly a thing, but wish he were in Europe, Asia or Africa."[50]

Clay may have wished Sanders away, but he was soon captivated by Sanders' charisma, charm, and passion. Captain Castleman, who observed his effect on the Confederate mission, thought him devious and dangerous.

"In my long life I have known no counterpart to this man," Castleman wrote in his memoir *Active Service*. "Commissioner Clay soon yielded entirely to his influence, most men were swayed by his plausible theories and he was a constant menace to the interests for which the commissioners were responsible. He controlled Mr. Clay and while he was there Mr. Holcombe."[51]

Official biographies describe Sanders as a promoter, revolutionary, and Confederate agent. He was born in Lexington, Kentucky, the son of a horse breeder, and was fifty-two at the time of his Canadian adventures. He spent most of his life on the political fringes as a fixer, lobbyist, go-between, and financial promoter. In the early 1840s he was urging Washington to annex Texas from Mexico. Later that decade he worked for a time as an agent of the Hudson's Bay Company, adjusting its claims to the Oregon territory that had been ceded to the United States. He was accused of cheating the Bay Company of a vast sum of money, yet was perpetually broke.

In the 1850s, Sanders was in Europe, promoting the cause of American republicanism. His reward in 1853 was to become U.S. Consul in Liverpool, which is where he met many of the exiled revolutionaries who became his friends. He recklessly promised any and all comers American aid and arms, using his diplomatic protection to send their communications with each other throughout Europe. He wrote to the *Times* advocating the assassination of France's Napoleon III and urged in the so-called Ostend Manifesto that the United States should annex Cuba. These erratic and embarrassing actions caused his recall to the U.S. — supportive letters from Garibaldi and Victor Hugo notwithstanding. At the outbreak of war, Sanders returned to Europe in an unofficial capacity, drumming up support for the Confederacy and helping it finance the war. In August 1862, the U.S. Consul in Quebec spotted Sanders preparing to board the liner *Luna*. He was bound for Europe carrying dispatches from Jefferson Davis. Sanders had met with then Canadian premier Sandfield Macdonald, who later relayed his comings and goings to the U.S. consul. In early 1864, he was back in Canada for the duration of the Confederate operations. He later claimed in a letter to Jefferson Davis that Davis had approved his attempt at peace plans with the North, since Davis had agreed to let Sanders go to Canada to try to forge an alliance with northern Democrats eager to end the war.[52]

What it meant was there were at least three parallel operations being run in Canada. Thompson focussed on an uprising in the Northwest. Holcombe and Clay wanted to return escaped prisoners to the South and mount an anti-war campaign by influencing men in the North. Sanders had grandiose plans for making peace with the North, which quickly involved Clay. Sanders also had a fast and loose view of Canadian law and would persuade Clay to authorize the St. Albans raid. Who was in charge?

Sanders' strategy was to draw Lincoln into secret peace talks and then embarrass him by exposing the talks. If this came to pass, it might affect the outcome of the presidential election in November. Sanders was soon meeting a steady stream of northern Democrats at the Clifton House. Word spread, and by early July the eccentric, pro-peace publisher of the *New York Tribune*, Horace Greeley, was involved. Although skeptical about the rumours, Greeley turned to a Sanders confidante, William Cornell Jewett, known as "Colorado" Jewett.

The exact nature of Jewett's relationship with the people of Colorado was a matter of some speculation. He claimed he had helped develop the state's vast mineral wealth. His critics maintained he promoted worthless stocks, had fleeced investors, and was generally someone more suited to jail than to public life. Although born and raised in Portland, Maine, the outbreak of war found him in favour of peace and the Confederate cause. He had at several points been in touch with Greeley, whose pro-peace sentiments were well known in the North. Clay thought Jewett a fool. In a letter to Secretary of State Judah Benjamin, he characterized Jewett as "a man of fervent and fruitful imagination and very credulous of what he believes to be true."[53]

In response to Greeley's inquiry, Jewett said Sanders had authorized him to say that there were two ambassadors of the Confederacy in Canada "with full and complete powers for peace." It was lie, since neither commissioner had any such power. Jewett urged Greeley to come to Niagara to meet Sanders, or if Lincoln would offer a safe conduct pass, they would go to Washington.[54]

The message was received at a time when Union morale was at its lowest ebb. Federal losses around Atlanta and in the wilderness near Richmond were staggering, and here it seemed was a way to stop it. Greeley dutifully forwarded the note to Lincoln along with an urgent letter of his own. He wrote, "Our bleeding, bankrupt, almost dying country longs for peace, shudders at the prospect of fresh conscription, of future wholesale devastation and new rivers of blood." Greeley urged the president to offer safe conduct passes to prove he was eager to end the war.

Lincoln was aware of the need to show his desire for peace and drew up a statement he probably knew the Confederates would reject. He wrote to Greeley that if he could find anybody having a proposition from Confederate president Davis embracing "the restoration of the Union and abandonment of slavery, whatever else it may embrace, say to him that he may come to me ... and he shall have safe conduct."[55]

Greeley didn't pass on Lincoln's complete terms to the Confederates. He invited Clay and Holcombe to Washington, which they agreed to as long as they were to have complete protection. Greeley, of course, couldn't offer that, given the terms of Lincoln's letter. In the meantime, Lincoln impatiently waited the arrival of the commissioners. In another letter, he asked Greeley what was the delay and also forwarded on his safe conduct pass.

The commissioners told Greeley they were not ambassadors but merely employed in the confidential service of their government. They were confident, however, that should the discussions be made known to Richmond, they would achieve that desired status.

The commissioners were jubilant with the turn of events. It seemed that a serious attempt at peace was within their grasp. They rushed off a letter to James Mason in London with copies of the notes exchanged with Greeley and announcing a "great change" in Lincoln's attitude toward the South. They were convinced there could be peace as well as an independent southern Confederacy. Since Greeley had not informed them about the full contents of Lincoln's letter they had no reason to believe otherwise. Their disappointment was complete when Lincoln's aide John Hay arrived at the Falls on July 20 with Greeley and delivered a note from Lincoln that repeated the same message Lincoln had given to Greeley.

While Hay waited impatiently the commissioners drafted a long letter to Greeley. Jewett thoughtfully provided a copy to Associated Press. It talked of deception, Lincoln's lack of good faith, false promises, and false dealings. In fact, Lincoln had been entirely consistent and forthright. It was Jewett and Greeley who had twisted the message and created the false impressions. The wide publication of the letters probably did more than any peace talks could have. It galvanized opinion in favour of the Confederates and pointed a suspicious finger at Lincoln.

Canadians were puzzled by the turn of events. The *Toronto Leader*, a conservative pro-Southern paper, blamed Lincoln for the failure of the talks. Its first dispatches, carried on July 22 under the headline "Strange Stories From Niagara Falls," accused him of bad faith, which in the end made sure the talks "degenerated into a kind of nonsense which forms the best commentary on the whole affair." The next day the paper sniffed that Lincoln had failed to seize a "favorable opportunity for peace." On July 22, the liberal *Hamilton Times* also blamed Lincoln's intransigence for the failure, but felt he was justified in doing so. Yet the *Times* fairly observed,

"Blood enough has not yet been shed to reduce either party to that state of exhaustion that will render peace an absolute necessity.

The *Toronto Globe*, which first reported the talks as an odd rumour, noted on July 23, "Strange as the story is, there is evidently something to it." The *Globe*'s analysis was that Lincoln deserved unqualified praise, and it called the Southerners "man-stealers," dismissing Holcombe and Clay as simply exiled Confederates looking for a little notoriety. It is a particularly revealing statement, for it indicates that as yet, the Canadians were still unaware of the grand Confederate plans underway in their province, even though the evidence was all around them. The *Globe* further stated, ever pushing its anti-slavery crusade: "Those who have looked upon the dreadful civil war now raging in the seceded States as a means of removing the curse of slavery from this continent, will rejoice to find Mr. Lincoln making the abandonment of slavery equal with the restoration of the whole union an indispensable part of any proposition."

The events at Niagara offered more hope to the Confederates that should the Copperheads succeed in their uprising, the Confederacy could at last break free of the Union and forge its own destiny.

Thompson gained more optimism in those middle weeks of August from a visit to Toronto by Judge Jeremiah Black, who had served in President Buchanan's cabinet with Thompson in the last administration before the war. Within Lincoln's cabinet there was discontent with the course of the war, and War Secretary Edwin Stanton, fearing Lincoln's defeat, disclosed his views to Black. He suggested Black visit Thompson to learn more about Southern morale, their determination to fight, and feelings about peace. The men met at the Queen's Hotel on August 20, where Black said his mission was to learn whether negotiations could be opened with the Confederate government "without the final ultimatum of separation," if the southern states could be made secure in their rights.[56]

Thompson said the Confederate States would not surrender their rights to regulate their own affairs, including their slave laws. Their demand for independence was merely a means of protecting their institutions, but if they could have the proper guarantees that the same goal could be achieved under a reunion government, they might be persuaded to end their struggle. In a lengthy report to Stanton, Black predicted that a suspension of hostilities coinciding with negotiations could settle the business. He asked Stanton to advise Lincoln to call a truce for four to six months and begin immediate talks with the Confederates. He suggested that, as a show of good faith, Holcombe should have a safe pass through the United States to Richmond to get the official Southern view.

Black's report met with a cold reception. Stanton had already been embarrassed by the publicity surrounding Black's visit to Toronto and wished to cut his losses. He told Black that Thompson's ideas about peace proved that he "will accept no peace but upon the absolute independence of the Confederate government, the dissolution of the Union and the establishment of two or more governments within the territorial limits of the United States."[57]

All of this was unknown to the commissioners. They were so encouraged by Black's visit they arranged for Holcombe to sail to England to confer with Confederate ambassadors James Mason and John Slidell to persuade them once again to induce the major powers to intervene and press for peace.

Holcombe left for Europe via the Confederacy at the end of August. At Halifax, he boarded the blockade-runner *Condor* for Wilmington. It was caught in a storm off the mouth of the Cape Fear River and ran aground on the Wilmington bar, the same sand-bar that had broken the back of the *Raleigh*. Holcombe managed to gain the shore. Seriously ill, he retired to his home near Lynchburg, Virginia, and his letters did not reach England until the end of the year, by which time they were irrelevant.

CHAPTER 8
Canadian Coalition

"The day which I have long expected has arrived.... Let us unite to consider and settle this ... in a manner worthy of us as a people."

George Brown, Leader of the Opposition
June 1864

If those weeks in July and August held hope for the Confederates, they were also full of promise for Canadians digesting the news of the Canadian Coalition. This dramatic event held out hope of smashing a quarter-century-old political deadlock and finally unlocking a way for the colonies to unite and create one country out of five provinces. The coalition had come about quite extraordinarily because two men, who dominated the political stage and loathed each other, had managed to come together for a common purpose. George Brown, the fiery, reform-minded *Globe* publisher who led the Reform Party, or liberal movement, in Canada West, and Brown's enemy, John Alexander Macdonald, leader of the Conservative Party, had formed the most unlikely alliance seen before or since in Canadian history.

On June 14, the day that Thompson returned from meeting Vallandigham in Windsor, Macdonald's coalition government collapsed after forty-five days in office. A vote in the House on a minor government motion had been defeated, forcing Macdonald to submit his resignation to Governor General Monck. But Monck urged Macdonald to try to find the combination of allies that would allow the government to continue.

A week later, as Clay settled in at St. Catharines and plotted a peace strategy with Sanders and Holcombe, the historic moment unfolded in the Canadian legislature at Quebec. At a little past 4:00 p.m. on June 22, John A. uncoiled his thin, gangly, six-

Courtesy of the Ontario Archives

George Brown set aside bitter feelings towards John A. Macdonald to join forces with his political foe to achieve Confederation.

foot frame and stood up. In a subdued and matter-of-fact tone, he explained to the 130 members that a week-long series of secret negotiations had taken place with George Brown, leader of the opposition.

Brown had approached Macdonald and argued that both parties had tried to govern the country without success, and repeated elections had only arrayed the majorities against themselves in even stronger opposition. Another election offered little hope of changing anything, but the two sides had never been better placed than now to work together. If Macdonald was prepared to promise to do this, he, Brown, would help in any way possible. After some discussion, the pair agreed that a coalition government would also have as its central aim negotiations for a confederation of all the British North American provinces, including the Maritimes and the Northwestern Territory.[58] The basis of government would be a parliamentary system where the number of seats in the legislature would be based on representation by population.

As Macdonald sat down, the normally voluble assembly sat in silence. Brown and Macdonald had been bitter enemies for a decade. They had not spoken a civil word in ten years. And yet here they were partners in a new and unknown venture. All eyes were on Brown.

Macdonald and Brown stared at each other for a brief minute, and then Brown rose slowly. As the *Globe* reported the next day, he was "evidently laboring under the deepest emotion, which for a time choked his utterance."[59]

Gesturing toward Macdonald, he said:

> For 10 years I have stood opposed to the gentleman opposite in as hostile a manner as it is possible to conceive of public men arrayed against each other ... But I think the House will admit that if a crisis has ever arisen in the political affairs of any country, such a crisis has arrived in the history of Canada.

Since 1851, when Brown was first elected, he had seen men of "substance and high hopes" try again and again to make sense of the Canadaian political gridlock. One by one, they had been stripped of their aspirations and given up. The problem was, as always, "We have two races, two languages, two systems of religious belief, two sets of laws, two systems of everything, so that it has been almost impossible that men in both sections could come together in the same government."

But at last there was a chance to change that. What was at stake was nationhood, larger meadows and wider fields of play. And if it meant setting aside old friendships and enmities, party allegiances and cherished goals, he would do it.

"That day which I have long expected has arrived," Brown said. "Let us try to rise superior to the pitifulness of party politics," he urged. "Let us unite to consider and settle this question as a great national issue, in a manner worthy of us as a people."

Brown begged his French Canadian adversaries to believe him when he said he sought no advantage from them, only equality. "We have no desire but a just settlement of our difficulties."

He praised the French Canadian members of John A. Macdonald's cabinet:

> It is a great thing, a bold and manly thing for Sir Etienne Taché and the member from Montreal East Mr. Etienne Cartier to take up this question. They deserve the highest praise for this bold and patriotic stand and for the way they have placed at hazard their political position.

The House could be proud that the formation of such a coalition involved men from Ontario and Quebec, French and English, Reform and Conservative. It was a peaceful way to solve a national problem, a solution that had eluded politicians in the United States, now engaged in a great war.

"Look at the present situation of the great nation along side of us," Brown said.

To cheers and applause, Brown sat down. The Speaker adjourned the House and a crush of humanity descended on Brown, pumping his hand, clapping his back, crowding, cheering, and congratulating him. The Canadian Coalition was born.

The papers next day declared their surprise at the turn of events and their support for its goals. "The Crisis Terminated!" said Brown's *Globe*. Letters of praise and more kind words from newspapers throughout the province. Even the paper owned by Cartier, *La Minerve*, a traditional enemy, described his actions as "truly great and admirable."[60]

Brown revelled in the praise. "It is great fun," he wrote to his wife Anne next day. "The unanimity of sentiment is without example in this wooden country."[61]

This unanimity that Brown spoke of was a collective hope for a resolution to a problem that had plagued Canada for twenty-five years. The source of the problem lay in the fair and even-handed way in which an earlier Governor General, Lord John Durham, had tried to soothe the agitation in the colony in the wake of the Rebellion of 1837.

Britain, not wishing to see a repeat of the American Revolution, sent Durham, known as "Radical Jack," to the colonies in May 1838. The previous year, what were then Upper and Lower Canada (Ontario and Quebec) had rebelled against the Crown, chafing against economic and political inequities in much the same way as Americans had sixty years earlier.

In Lower Canada, the revolt centered on French Canadian nationalism. The economic booms and busts of the 1830s, agricultural failures, and overpopulation created tensions between the majority French-speaking population in Lower Canada and the minority English speakers who held the levers of political and economic power. When Britain refused to remodel the provincial legislature, it boiled over into agitation and armed revolt in the fall of 1837. The rebels, led by French Canadian patriot Joseph Papineau, were ill-equipped and quickly defeated, but the mood spread to Upper Canada.

There colonists were also dissatisfied with a network of political and economic control known as the Family Compact, in which a group of descendants of Empire Loyalists who had fled the American Revolution exerted tight political and economic control through a web of favouritism and patronage. On December 5, 1837, William Lyon Mackenzie, a radical armed with a draft constitution and eight hundred supporters with pitchforks, rifles, and staves, marched toward the legislature in downtown Toronto. They were quickly dispersed and order was restored, but the point had been made. Durham was dispatched. After five months of research, he made two main recommendations in what became known as Lord Durham's Report. In Upper Canada, he criticized a system where power was monopolized by a "a petty, corrupt, insolent Tory clique."[62]

His answer was "responsible government," where the government would be elected by the people and would have a great deal of control over domestic affairs. The Governor General's role would be limited to foreign affairs. The Governor General would also be the colonies' link with the mother country. Durham believed this system would tie the colonies more closely to Britain, allow for economic growth by breaking up the corrupt Family Compact, and keep Canadians out of the American orbit.

In Lower Canada, he found different problems. "I expected to find a contest between a government and a people," he wrote in his report. "I found two nations warring in the bosom of a single state: I found a struggle, not of principles, but of races; and I perceived that it would be idle to attempt any amelioration of laws or institutions, until we could first succeed in terminating the deadly animosity that now separates the inhabitants of Canada."

Durham hoped that a gradual assimilation of French Canadians would solve that problem. Immigration from Britain was swelling the English-speaking population in the province, and over time, he assumed French culture would be absorbed by the dominant English one and cease to be an issue. So, Durham recommended tying Upper and Lower Canada into a new political configuration with one legislature. The two former colonies would be known as the Canadas. Each half would have thirty-seven seats in a new legislature.

What Durham could not have foreseen was that this perfect balance of power was a recipe for disaster. Instead of breaking down animosities, it fuelled them. Instead of absorbing French Canadians into English culture, it sharpened the divisions. It quickly became apparent to French Canada that while the English voted along party lines, they could vote on issues that affected French language and culture. French legislators supported the parties that best represented their views and so held the balance of power, protecting their institutions, their language, and their religion from any and all assaults.

By 1864, the problem was a constant irritant. Canada West's population was four hundred thousand greater than Canada East, but taxes and advantages flowed into eastern Canada, paid for by those in the west. George Brown, through the pages of the *Globe*, pounded away at unfairness. Brown's solution was "representation by population." The seats in the legislature would be divided up based on the numbers of people in each part of the colony. This would give Canada West more seats and the upper hand. Naturally, French Canada wasn't interested.

John A. Macdonald's conservatives had a strong power base in Quebec and had been adept at trading off English and French interests in such a way that, if not in power, he was never very far out of it. It had also meant that until now he had deferred to the French Canadian objection to the plan.

The initial public reaction was one of shock at such scandalous compromises by both Brown and Macdonald. The choice of the federal government was also suspect, given the evidence of three years of civil war in the United States. After all, the weakness of the American federal system, with the limited powers of the government in Washington, had been the real cause of the war. Why would Canadians want to repeat that experiment?

In Montreal, *Le Pays* called the French-Canadian ministers in the coalition traitors. In Quebec, the *Courier du Canada* more temperately suggested that Brown's Reformers were in a distinct minority in the cabinet, so nothing dangerous could happen to French Canadian interests. *La Minerve*, which was quick to praise Brown at first, said flatly, "Ce n'est pas possible." The *Montreal Gazette*, a conservative English paper, noted suspiciously, "One cannot touch pitch and not be defiled; one cannot have intercourse with Mr. George Brown and not make some lamentable sacrifice of principle."

In English Canada, they had their own worries, but the Reformers found it easiest to recover. Brown was their patriot, who had sacrificed all: he was the hero of the hour. The hope was that a centralized government would minimize French control over their affairs. The *St. Catharines Constitutional* fairly typically reported that although one couldn't help but be astonished and confused by the turn of events, it sincerely hoped that "a new and happier political era is about to dawn upon the country." Brown's *Globe*, naturally, was all for it.[63]

Within a week of the Coalition's announcement, Parliament was recessed. While the Confederate commissioners in Niagara

77

played their game of peace, the government planned its drive for a general British North American Union. A mission would be sent to the Maritimes to coincide with a conference those colonies were organizing to talk about a confederation of their own. The Canadian cabinet saw this as a great opportunity to lay the wider scheme before them.

It would mark the beginning of a new era in Canadian politics, of inter-provincial conferences and high state missions, of ceremony, diplomacy, and the business of drafting a national constitution.

CHAPTER 9
The Lake Erie Raid

"I told him to go to hell and he shot at me, the ball passing between my legs."

Philo Parsons *pilot describing his capture*

In early July, Charles Cole presented himself to Holcombe. Word had spread that Holcombe would provide the means for passage back to the South, and Cole, acting on that belief, sought Holcombe out. Holcombe was convinced that Cole could help the mission and persuaded Cole to stay. As he wrote to Clay on July 10 that same day, "Some Memphis people know him. He is not smart, but I suspect a bold and desperate fellow and I have detained him, thinking he might be useful."

In an interview with Thompson four days later, Cole said he had served with the rank of captain in General Nathan Bedford Forrest's command, been captured, escaped, and subsequently held a commission as a lieutenant in the Confederate Navy. Thompson, unable to confirm Cole's claim, nonetheless believed him to be the right man for a mission that was to run parallel to the uprising in Chicago. He put Cole on the payroll and sent him around the lakes to familiarize himself with the ports, their defences, and in particular the gunboat USS *Michigan*, sitting in the harbour of Sandusky, Ohio, on Lake Erie, guarding the Confederate prison at Johnson's Island.[64]

Cole took with him a prostitute called Annie Brown,[65] whom he passed off as his wife, and a boy, John Robinson, whom he used

Courtesy of the U.S. Naval Historical Research Centre

The USS *Michigan* was the only American gunboat on the Great Lakes. She was anchored in Sandusky, Ohio, a few hundred yards away from Johnson's Island prison.

as a courier between himself and Thompson. Thompson provided $4,000 for this adventure, and Cole was soon in residence at the West House in Sandusky, where, posing as a Philadelphia business-man, he spent the money as quickly as Thompson could provide it.

In Sandusky, Cole had made the acquaintance of Captain Carter, who commanded the *Michigan*. Cole described Carter as an unpol-ished man who was disgruntled because he had not been given a more responsible post. Cole, despite thinking the captain could not be bought, nonetheless sent cases of whiskey to Carter and his offi-cers as a token of his friendship. Cole asked Thompson's permission to organize a force to board the *Michigan* and take her by surprise and asked to be placed in secret service to do so. Thompson happily issued the orders, ordering Cole to strictly obey the neutrality of the British provinces in any plan he was to devise. Thompson assigned another exiled rebel, John Yates Beall, to help in the plan.

That was the beginning of the plan that came to be called the Lake Erie Raid. Its purpose was the release of about 2,500 Confederate prisoners held on the chunk of rock in the middle of

Sandusky's harbour, just a few hundred yards from where the *Michigan* was anchored.

As prisons went, Johnson's Island was probably fairly humane. By September 1864, it was home to 2,500 Confederate officers, many of them veterans of Morgan's Kentucky command. They lived in wooden barracks that were cramped, but reasonably warm in winter and well built. The rations were enough to keep a man alive, though hungry, and the camp's mortality rate was probably the best proof of its record. Less than 2 percent of the 12,000 men who passed through its gates died there, some 10 percentage points better than the average among all Northern prisons during the war.

The prison boasted a library of between five hundred and eight hundred books, and prisoners could write as many letters as they liked, though none longer than a page.

But Johnson's Island was still a prison.

In the barracks the bunks were in tiers of three, with two men per bunk. In the middle of the room was a wood-burning stove. From early 1864 onwards, daily rations were a small loaf of bread and piece of meat, no coffee, no sugar, and no longer any packages from home. As the severe conditions in Southern prisons became known in the North, there was a public backlash against allowing Southerners any more than was necessary to keep them alive, so they were also denied the chance to supplement their diets with food purchased from Sandusky stores. By the last winter of the war they were hungry enough to look at all options. Repulsive things were greedily devoured — rats, rotten meat, bones, and bread from the slops.[66]

It offered little chance for escape, and anybody thinking of it only had to look across the harbour at the *Michigan*, a 582-tonne vessel with 15 guns. That was why it was all the more remarkable when the prison and the *Michigan* became the target of the only Confederate naval action of the Canadian campaign.

Cole's reconnoitre had led him to believe that the *Michagan*'s officers and crew could not be bought. So Cole and Beall came up with a plan — to drug the officers and crew, seize the boat, and let it loose on northern cities along the lakes. It was the perfect plan, for the *Michigan*'s rampage would be unimpeded. As John

Castleman recalled in his memoirs, "There was no military achievement which promised results so important, because at that time and for the then immediate future the destructive agencies of an unopposed gunboat was inestimable."[67]

This intelligence was passed back to Thompson via courier John Thompson and through Bennett Young, who was carefully doing his own survey of the border states with an eye to towns that the Confederates could raid and burn. Cole was given another $25,000 in American currency.

Beall came from Virginia, where his family were successful farmers. He was an earnest, committed, and some said fanatical young man whose beliefs were anchored by strong religious convictions. The combination made him a particularly dangerous undercover agent, fearless and bold. Castleman described Beall as "a very competent and aggressive officer who did what others said they might do," and Headley's view was that Beall was a modest and unassuming man, one who did not talk unless he had something to say, resourceful, self-possessed, and an interesting companion.

Beall joined the Confederate infantry early in the war. In a skirmish near Harper's Ferry in October 1861, a musket ball shattered three ribs. After a long convalescence, he made his way to Iowa, where his brother lived. The discovery that Beall was a Confederate forced him to flee to Canada in November 1862, where he lived for a short time in Dundas, near Hamilton. In early 1863, he was on the move again, back in Richmond. There he proposed the idea of taking the *Michigan*. It was the second time the project reached the desk of Confederate Navy Secretary Stephen Mallory. Mallory considered it carefully, but abandoned it again because he did not think it could be achieved without breaching the neutrality of the British Canadian colonies.[68]

But Mallory assured Beall that should the plan be put into action he would be part of it.[69] By May 1864 he was back in Richmond. He was soon sent north again, and by August was in Toronto reporting to Jacob Thompson.

John Yeats Beall was fanatically committed to the Confederate cause.

In Toronto, Beall was delighted to find one of his former comrades, an adventuring Scot by the name of Bennett Burley. Like Beall, he was a religious man who drank nothing stronger than soda water and did not smoke or chew tobacco. By the time he turned up in Richmond at the age of twenty-two, he had already served in Italy on the side of Garibaldi and at another time against them in the Papal Guards. He brought a torpedo to the Confederacy that he said his father had designed. It was attached to the side of a ship and then ignited by a fuse. He managed to secure a naval commission.

Burley was captured in May 1864 during a raid along the Maryland coast. He was taken to Fort Delaware, forty miles below Philadelphia, and imprisoned. He soon escaped by climbing down through a drain and swimming underwater for twenty-five yards until he came out into the Delaware River. Burley made his way to Toronto and found Jacob Thompson.

In Sandusky, Cole passed himself off as an executive with the Mount Hope Oil Company. He was about thirty-eight years old, short, with bright gray eyes and a mustache. By one account, he was under constant surveillance well before the moment when he first pressed his attentions on Captain Carter. The source of this confession was Charles Wilson Murray, a gunner aboard the *Michigan* who later became a detective of some renown in Canada. According to Murray, Captain Carter was suspicious of Cole from the start and, worried about persistent rumours of a Confederate attack on Johnson's Island, detailed Murray to find out what he could.

Murray's first stop was Detroit, and hearing that Clement Vallandigham was across the river in Windsor, he turned there for his first lead. Among Vallandigham's visitors was Cole, who on Thompson's instructions was doing his Great Lakes tour. Murray overheard enough at the hotel bar to conclude that something was up. So Murray followed Cole back to Sandusky. Murray reported all this to Carter and rented a room at the West House, Sandusky's grandest hotel, with a view of the harbour and Johnson's Island. There, in the bar over a few drinks, he struck up an acquaintance with Cole and soon had a job.

Cole, meanwhile, was enjoying Thompson's money. He bought a yacht and a fast team of horses and made the acquaintance of officers aboard the *Michigan*, winning their friendship with cigars and liquor. Through them he was able to tour the prison and alerted the men in the camp that liberty was at hand.

Captain Archibald McKennon, of the 16th Arkansas Infantry, a Johnson's Island prisoner, later recalled of the plans for the raid:

> We were organized into companies and regiments and had armed ourselves with clubs, which were made of stove wood and other materials at hand with which to fight. We were in constant expectation of orders, which never came, to make the fight. It would have been a pitiable affair, for the undertaking was wholly impractical.[70]

The plan called for Cole to arrange for a party ashore for some officers and entertainment aboard the *Michigan* for those on duty, who were to be drugged by a potion in their wine. Beall and his men were to steal a boat, make for Sandusky, and, at a signal from a confederate aboard the *Michigan*, bring their vessel alongside, board the *Michigan*, turn its guns on Johnson's Island, and free the prisoners. From there, the *Michigan* was to be loosed on Detroit and Buffalo. But exactly how 2,500 sick, injured, and malnourished officers were to be organized into a fighting, foraging army was never explained.

On the evening of September 18, Bennett Burley boarded the *Philo Parsons* in Detroit, a small coastal steamer plying between that city and Sandusky. He asked the clerk whether it would be possible to stop briefly at Windsor on the Canadian side to pick up three of his friends, one of whom was lame and disabled. The clerk agreed on condition that Burley board the boat in Detroit. He did the next morning, and at Windsor the three men came on board. One of the men was Beall. The captain later remarked at how quickly the lame man's limp disappeared. A little further down river at Amherstburg, also on the Canadian side, another sixteen men were taken on, carrying with them an old trunk, which appeared very heavy. They seemed to have no connection to Burley, and Atwood took them for American draft dodgers returning home.

At Middle Bass Island, one of a handful of small islands near the American side, the captain went ashore and was replaced by his first mate and the clerk, who was a part owner in the boat. At 4:00 p.m. the boat reached Kelly's Island, little more than eleven miles from Sandusky. There, two or three other men boarded. They had spent the last few days posing as sewing machine salesmen, something that the locals found curious. The boat pulled away, and not long after, Beall walked up to Ashley and told him he was a Confederate officer and the boat was being commandeered. As Ashley related in a deposition the following day:

> I was standing in front of my office when four of the party came to see me and drawing revolvers said if I offered any resistance I was a dead man. At the same time the trunk flew open and in less time than it takes to write it, the whole gang were armed to the teeth with revolvers and hand axes. They stationed two men to watch me and rushing into the remainder of the cabins threatened to shoot anyone who offered resistance.[71]

Michael Campbell, the pilot, saw one of the raiders chasing the engineer with a cocked revolver and ordering him into the hold.

"He turned on me and made the same order," Campbell said. "I told him to go to hell and he shot at me, the ball passing between my legs." On the upper deck he saw five other armed men driving the passengers down into the hold. There the prisoners remained, with the exception of the pilot, engineer, and fireman. The ship had been running without a pilot for about thirty minutes and was soon headed towards Sandusky. After cruising in that direction for almost an hour, the raiders discovered they didn't have enough wood to make the trip. So they returned to Middle Bass Island to resupply. After taking a few shots at the wood lot owner, they began loading in haste. The wood lot owner's son, meanwhile, raced to Captain Atwood's house. He told Atwood that his father was being killed by robbers who were taking his wood. The perplexed captain ran to the wharf and demanded in a loud voice, "What the hell is going on." With pistols aimed at his head, he was soon back aboard in the hold under guard. With the loading of wood underway again, another problem arrived.

It was another small steamer, the *Island Queen*, which plied between Sandusky and the islands, arriving with several dozen unarmed federal soldiers who, as it turned out, were absent without leave from their units. Beall's men jumped on board and ordered the ship to surrender. The *Queen*'s captain instead rang the go-ahead bell, and as the engineer tried to start the boat he was shot through the cheek by one raider, followed by others who set upon the crew with hatchets. The crew and most of the passengers were then transferred to the crowded hold of the *Philo*, with the women and children being gallantly set ashore.

Now with more than fifty prisoners, the Confederates decided to put them all ashore, forcing them to swear not to tell of this little adventure for twenty-four hours, nor to take up arms against the Confederacy. The *Island Queen* was lashed to the *Philo Parsons* and, about five miles off the island, scuttled and sunk on a reef. From there the *Philo* made haste for Sandusky, and it was 9:00 p.m. before she arrived. She waited for the signal flare from the *Michigan*, but it never came. They could see through night glasses that the ship had changed position so that it faced the prison, the decks were cleared for action, and smoke was rising from the funnel. Something was wrong. First the messenger from Cole had failed to reach Kelly's Island with final details of the plan, and now this. Disheartened, seventeen members of the crew decided they would go no farther. They approached Beall and told him so. He was furious, but no amount of shouting, persuasion, or threats could move them. So he ordered them to write down their mutinous intentions, which was done on the back of a bill of lading, and had each one sign it as proof of their insubordination and vindication of himself. They did so, at the same time recording their admiration for their commander, along with the equal conviction that the plan could not succeed.[72]

Beall reluctantly turned the *Philo* around and headed her back towards the Detroit River. The people of the islands, who were convinced a Confederate invasion was imminent, were outside burying their valuables only to be astonished by the sight of the *Philo* steaming by at full speed in the dark, looking rather like a "scared pickerel." For a time on that return journey, an indignant Beall forced the mate to hoist the Confederate ensign, the first and last time one flew on the Great Lakes. In the early morning, a small boat laden with plunder was put ashore about three miles above Amherstburg, and a little later the remaining prisoners were beached at Fighting Island. The *Philo* continued on to Windsor, where she was stripped of everything, down to her piano, mirrors, chairs, trunks, and linens. The injection pipe was severed, the boat was left to sink, and the raiders disappeared. Two were arrested for a few hours and then released, and customs officials managed to round up some of the *Philo*'s possessions on the grounds that they had been landed without duty being paid. Both the *Philo* and the *Queen* were salvaged and were running again in about a week. However, for the rest of the season they understandably carried few passengers.

In Sandusky, Cole had arranged for an afternoon and evening of refreshment and women at an inn outside of the town. He expected the officers to come ashore in the early afternoon, leaving a skeleton crew on board. When they didn't, he asked Murray to go find them. Before they could do so, Ensign James Hunter, dispatched by Carter, came to the hotel, where he found Cole's bags packed and bills paid in preparation for a quick departure. After a few drinks he told Cole that the captain had refused him permission to attend the party and he asked Cole to come back to the ship and help persuade the captain to change his mind. They walked down to the wharf; reaching the *Michigan*'s barge, Hunter roughly pushed Cole aboard, shouting for the crew to give way.

Cole protested and insisted on being put ashore, but Hunter told him he was a prisoner, something that Cole at first refused to believe. Instead, he offered to buy whiskey for all the men on board, but by their reaction he knew the game was over. Cole was hustled into Carter's cabin, where he offered to explain everything in private. Carter instead ordered Hunter to search Cole while Carter covered him with Cole's pistol. Among the papers they found was a commission as a major in a Tennessee regiment. There was also $600 in cash and a handful of certified cheques drawn on the Bank of Montreal for $5,000 each, according to Murray. Cole offered the money to his captors if they would let him go. Instead they arrested him.

Carter prepared his ship for action. All night a keen watch was held for the *Philo*, but nothing was seen, which seems inexplicable since the boat was at least twice in view of the *Michigan*. At daylight, the *Michigan* got underway in search of the pirates; at Kelly's Island, the people were so frightened by the previous day's events that they refused to come to the wharf to help the ship tie up, until the ship's pilot, a three-hundred-pound hulk of a man who was well known, showed his face. Finding no sign of the boat at the mouth of the Detroit River, they decided to go back to their station in Sandusky.

Beall spent the next few weeks in northern Ontario at a hunting camp while the excitement died down. Burley went to Guelph, about sixty miles from Toronto, where he experimented making munitions until he was arrested for his part in the drama at the behest of the American authorities. Annie Brown was arrested and later testified against Cole and was released.

The *Globe* called the raid "Piracy on Lake Erie" and the work
done of desperados "who went to their disgraceful work from
Canadian soil." The *Globe* deduced that the attack was the work
of Southern refugees in Canada and added that "our people
regardless of their sympathies in the American war will pronounce
the affair a shameless outrage upon our hospitality." Even the
Leader said the action was an abuse of Canadian neutrality.[73]

The northern port cities quickly demanded that the Canadians
be chastised for harbouring the criminals, some even going so far
as to suggest that troops be dispatched to the Canadian side to
round them up. John A. Macdonald, whose portfolios included
Solicitor General, felt obliged to ask the Governor General to send
regulars to Windsor to persuade the Americans not to retaliate.

The news reached Monck on September 21 at Quebec, as the
vice-regal party, including the visiting British ambassador to
Washington, Lord Lyons, headed off for a day's outing at the falls at
Lorette. For Lady Frances Elizabeth Monck, the Governor General's
sister-in-law, the news caused quite a stir. "News of ships being
burnt on Lake Erie; telegrams coming and going."[74]

Monck wrote a hasty telegram to his military commander, Sir
Fenwick Williams, asking him to keep the Canadian Rifles in
Windsor, though they were due to be withdrawn. Williams did so,
and a few days later Monck thanked him, saying it was a sound policy "in view of the recent outrage." Monck expressed relief that the
Americans couldn't blame Canadians in any way for the Johnson's
Island plot, "but in the present excitable condition of the public mind
in the States, it is wise to take every precaution against anything that
may give them a handle against us."[75]

Monck also wrote to the Colonial Secretary, telling him that
Anglo-American tensions might increase to the breaking point if
Southern refugees continued to use the Canadian side as a ren-
dezvous point as they had in the case of the *Philo Parsons*. He
repeated his desire of earlier in the year for a small naval force to
patrol the lakes. It had been turned down as too expensive by the
Imperial government. It was rejected this time because the Colonial
Office feared the Americans would retaliate, leading to an escalation

of naval power on the lakes. Monck also indicated that Canada's neutrality laws were neither strong enough nor explicit enough to stop these Southern incursions, and while it was too late in the season to take any measures before the closing of navigation, he urged Cardwell to give him more legal authority to combat the Southern menace. Monck wanted the power to seize vessels and munitions on the lakes, including the incendiary materials used by the rebels to fire American cities. He also wanted legal authority to expel anyone suspected of violating neutrality laws, or to keep them in jail on charges of "levying war from Her Majesty's Dominions against a friendly power."

American Secretary of State William Seward called on the British Chargé d'Affairs in Washington, Hume Burnley, notifying him that in view of what had happened the United States intended to breach the terms of the Rush-Bagot Treaty, which limited each power to one armed cruiser on the lakes. Burnley was in charge in the absence of Lyons. General John Dix, the military commander in the Northeast, did a quick survey of the lakes and recommended that five tugboats be armed and placed at harbour entrances. At Detroit and Buffalo an additional regiment of men was sent to patrol the border, and by early autumn the frontier was an armed camp.

For Jacob Thompson, the failure at Johnson's Island was another bitter defeat. He had moved to Windsor on September 17, anticipating that within days he would have a force of thousands at his command and, with the *Michigan*, control of the Great Lakes. In a letter to Secretary of State Judah Benjamin some months later, Thompson said the plan was well conceived and held out the promise of success, but was betrayed by "some treachery."

For the Confederates, their second failure in Canada would call for yet another revision of strategy, one that would turn away from peaceful attempts at ending the war to one aimed at dragging Canada into it.

CHAPTER 10
Confederates in Charlottetown

"It is for us to ... arrive ... at such a plan as will avoid the mistakes of our neighbours. If we can attain that, we shall not be New Brunswickers, nor Nova Scotians, nor Canadians, but British North Americans."

John A. Macdonald
August 1864

As Thompson pondered his failures at Chicago and Sandusky, the Canadians were making strides towards their goal of a confederation of British interests in North America. The initial shock that Brown and Macdonald were allies gave way to a broader acceptance of the plan as the pair stumped the country-side in support of the scheme.

Still, it was hard to imagine more unlikely partners. Brown, at forty-five, was an awkward and passionate man, a newspaper publisher with firm views, great ambitions, and too much energy. He was intense, focussed, and unwavering in his views, qualities that made him well suited to newspaper publishing, but less so to the subtleties of politics. He was anti-slavery and anti-South, having helped establish an abolitionist society in Toronto. When John Brown came to Chatham, Ontario, in 1858 to drum up support for his slave rebellion, Brown was there. He was pro-Lincoln and believed the Northern cause was just, but felt it was in Canada's best interests to stay out of the way until the war was over.

Macdonald, four years older, had also been born in Scotland. He was a lawyer and voracious reader, a man with a dry sense of humour who enjoyed debating and public speaking as much as the social aspects of politics — the parties, the talk, the food and drink, things that Brown did not enjoy. Macdonald had an enormous feel for statecraft and was an unrivalled leader of men. Macdonald was flexible, better able to compromise, and with a talent for using the system to his advantage. He was less principled perhaps, but more practical, and had visions of nationhood as large as Brown's. For Brown, it was the whole loaf or nothing. Macdonald

Courtesy of the Ontario Archives

The brilliant Alexander Galt first proposed Confederation in 1858. He was the plan's financial genius.

would take half now, while continuing to persuade his opponent to give up the rest. When it came the United States, Macdonald had what American author Robin Winks has described as "a bundle of anti-American prejudices." It is true that he disliked the American system of government. He saw the electoral process as a popularity contest between candidates and the separation of the executive and legislative branches as inefficient and lacking the checks and balances found in the parliamentary system. He disliked Lincoln's suspension of civil rights, including habeus corpus, which allowed for arrest and detention without trial. He believed the war was a result of the defects in the way the Americans had devised their Constitution and wanted to ensure that it did not happen in Canada.[76] When it came to slavery, Macdonald certainly didn't approve of it, but unlike Brown he had no passionate urge to actively rid the world of it.

In late August, as Thompson awaited word of a Northwest Rebellion, Brown and Macdonald, together with a large delegation, visited Charlottetown, Prince Edward Island, to persuade the Islanders and their fellows in Nova Scotia and New Brunswick to join the grand plan. The Maritimers saw an easygoing, disarming, and friendly John A., a man whose legendary capacity for alcohol was very much in evidence. A well-oiled John A. was at his best, telling wonderfully bawdy stories, doing cruelly effective mimes of friends and foes, and stirring any gathering to a fever pitch. Macdonald, the expert in political possibility, had seen that the notion of a broad confederation, an idea he had long thought impractical, might actually work. And once committed to it, his shrewd improvisations had a way of making things happen.

George Brown was regarded as famous, if not notorious. His passionate convictions on a wide variety of issues, his unlimited capacity for moral indignation and biting invective, and his gift for indiscreet words had stamped a powerful personality on the minds of all British North Americans. He had none of Macdonald's polish. Brown was a rough-and-tumble, no-nonsense sort of man, an evangelist of Upper Canadian rights, and a fearless defender of English Canada. For French Canadians, Brown was the embodiment of bigotry and fanaticism; for Conservatives, he was their most dreaded opponent. In Parliament and in his paper he attacked the Conservatives for their reliance on French Canadian votes and subservience to French Canadian pressure.

The Brown-Macdonald feud went back to 1848, when as a gesture of respect to the growing popularity of Brown and his paper, the Reform government rewarded him with the relatively insignificant post of secretary to a commission investigating the province's prisons. Brown found a corrupt system that offended his sensibilities as a crusading journalist.

At one prison, the commission founds numerous instances of casual cruelties, indifference, and neglect. One prisoner received 168 lashes in 28 days. A ten-year-old boy received six lashes for laughing, and an eight-year-old earned solitary confinement for shouting in his cell. "We can only regard this as a case of barbarity disgraceful to humanity," Brown wrote in his report.[77]

The warden was charged with neglect of duty, and the warden's son, a Conservative member of parliament, turned to Macdonald for help. Macdonald concluded that the evidence against the warden was circumstantial, that it had been distorted, and that the man had never been given a fair chance to respond. Having formed this opinion, Macdonald clung to it stubbornly. He asked that the matter be referred to a special committee of inquiry. This was done, but nothing in it cleared the warden's name. Brown was outraged that Macdonald could overlook the basic wrongs and injustices. He saw cheap politics in Macdonald's support, a symptom of the man's wider moral corruption. In the face of such obvious crimes, what did it matter if the procedures were slightly irregular? The men had been bitter enemies from that day on, and only the mutual desire for a better future for Canada persuaded them to join forces and now make this momentous trip to visit their cousins in the three Atlantic coast colonies.

In the Maritimes, Confederation was not a burning issue. It had been a favourite after-dinner subject but was never pressing enough to actually get on with. It might offer benefits, but so did a Maritime union of the three provinces that were once Nova Scotia. As well, the economic prosperity of the Civil War had blunted the edge for a broad union. Yet, as the Maritimers would be quick to admit, the Chesapeake affair and the actions of the warring Americans could all too easily end up involving Canada.

Brown and Macdonald arrived in Charlottetown, the capital of Prince Edward Island, on September 1. A few days earlier, Confederate General John Bell Hood, who would later live in exile in Niagara-on-the-Lake, had abandoned Atlanta. In a single week of frontal assaults on federal positions where he was outnumbered four to one, the hot-tempered and impatient Hood broke the army that his predecessor, General Joe Johnston, had so carefully preserved. Hood's retreat northward into Tennessee with the remnants of that force left the city open and defenceless. Union General William Tecumseh Sherman burned it and then everything else in his way as he began his march to the sea, which would end at Savannah by Christmas. It was the beginning of the end of the Confederacy.

The peace platform at the Democratic Convention in Chicago, which had looked so promising in early August, was now crumbling. Northern morale, which had reached low tide after a summer of military failure, surged with Atlanta's fall. For Thompson, the failures in Chicago and on Lake Erie would mean a change of tactics, all of which would place renewed pressure on Canadian authorities. But for now the thing on the minds of the Canadians was how to bring the Maritimers on side.

The meetings were private and informal, which the Canadians hoped would avoid grandstanding for public consumption. Their task was to prove that Confederation was desirable and even necessary. It was difficult because a basic feature of the scheme was its immediacy. The Maritimers weren't convinced that immediate action was the answer. They would probably agree that the vast, empty wilderness of British North America should one day be a nation, but that monumental undertaking would take place at some point in the future. In the meantime, life in the provinces with control over domestic affairs was a fairly satisfactory state of existence with which few — the Canadians excepted — were dissatisfied.

George-Étienne Cartier, Macdonald's Quebec lieutenant, led off with the general arguments in favour of Confederation. Cartier, short with a rugged countenance, had an unforced heartiness that made him a natural ambassador. He enjoyed company, talk, songs, parties, and dances with unabashed gusto. His voice was high-pitched, his manner intense and almost explosive, and his English came tumbling out without regard for grammar, idiom, or pronunciation. The effect was a candour that was disarming and impressive. Cartier and Macdonald had long been allies. Like Macdonald, Cartier maintained a strong attachment to the monarchy, despite his role as chief defender of French-Canadian interests. Like Macdonald, he thought poorly of republican government and felt that if French Canada had to choose between the evils of the English and the Americans they would choose the English. He believed in the constant possibility of an

American invasion, and saw the Confederacy as a way to distract the Northern States from such a move. If the South was victorious it removed the possibility entirely.[78]

Macdonald followed Cartier with a discussion of the precedents and practices for such a union and the faults to be avoided, in particular those that had become self-evident in the United States. Macdonald's debating style was much more casual and conversational, but the range of his knowledge and the scope and organization of his ideas were impressive from the start. His tall, spare frame and jaunty, genial ways were soon winning him friends. They worked well together: Macdonald advocated the strongly centralized federation, while Cartier, a representative of a cultural minority whose first duty was to defend those things, stood out in the eyes of the Maritimers as proof that local loyalties would survive under the plan. They were effective and powerful speeches, and as the *Saint John Telegraph* reported, "great it is said is the effect ... and the arguments almost irresistible."[79]

The Canadian Minister of Finance, Alexander Galt, laid out the fiscal framework for Confederation. By one account Galt, a large, moody man, was a magician who with a great theme to inspire him could give a spectacularly brilliant performance. New Brunswick's Governor General, Arthur Gordon, who spoke to Galt at some length during the meeting, thought Galt by far the ablest of the Canadians. He had a strong creative instinct, a vigorous expansionist urge, an infectious and enthusiastic capacity for designing large projects, and an amazingly fertile mind. This was one of the great moments of his career. He was financing nothing less than a transcontinental nation; and he could talk not only in generalities and rhetorical flourishes, but also with a wealth of convincing detail. The federal government would assume all the debts and in turn provide revenue to the provinces, apportioned on the basis of population. He set it all out in its parts and then as an integrated whole. His delivery and impact were no less great than the other ministers' a day earlier.

Brown laid out the framework of the proposed federation, the sharing of powers between the federal and provincial governments, and how the judiciary would work. He proposed that the legislature would have sixty seats, twenty each from Canada East and West and twenty more from the Maritimes. On the trickier division of powers, the Canadians had decided that the tragedy of the American experiment had to be avoided at all costs. They believed that the Confederate States had been encouraged in their rebellion by the fatal clause in the American Constitution that provided that all powers not specifically assigned to the central government were reserved by the states. This error could be avoided by doing the opposite — investing the federal government with all powers not vested with the provinces.

After a week the answer could scarcely have been in doubt. "They were unanimous," crowed Brown to his wife, "in regarding Federation of all the provinces to be highly desirable — if the terms of union could be made satisfactory — and they were prepared to waive their own more limited question until the details of our scheme could be more fully considered and matured."

The Canadians moved on to Halifax, where Brown and Macdonald made two of the rare public speeches of the trip. It was the first dinner where the delegates could voice the spirit of their deliberations. Brown's was recalled years later by Prince Edward Island Premier John Hamilton Gray as one of great power. His presentation was masterly. He set out the assets and potential of a united British North America. What he had at first believed only to be a solution for the two Canadas, he now recognized was greater than that. The great assets brought to a wider union by the Maritimes included shipping, shipbuilding, mines, markets, and people. To achieve this union completely the Inter-Colonial Railway was not too great a price to pay. He dealt with the objections of the Maritime press to the process.

True, Canada had debts, but its resources were so great that population growth and exploiting the wealth would easily overcome it. The new federal state would not endanger any of the strong tries the Maritimes had with the mother country, and in fact they would be strengthened. United colonies made the Empire stronger. Nor was Confederation simply a way for Canada to overcome its own internal problems. The Canadians hadn't come to the Maritimes to seek relief from these problems, but to embrace something greater. "Our sole object in coming here is to say to you: 'We invite you to join with us frankly and earnestly — whether it would, or would not, be for the advantage of all the British North American colonies to be embraced under one political system.'"

Macdonald's speech was a bookend, a persuasive address filled at turns with humour and earnest entreaty. "Everyone admits that Union must take place some time. I say now is the time," Macdonald said. "For twenty long years I have been dragging myself through the dreary waste of Colonial politics. I thought that there was no end, nothing worthy of ambition, but now I see something which is well worthy of what I have suffered."

He worked his theme of the need for a strong federation. He turned to the Constitution of the United States. He praised its wisdom, he admitted its defects, "and it is for us to take advantage [of] and see if we cannot arrive by careful study at such a plan as will avoid the mistakes of our neighbours." But this could only be done through a strong federal union that would have all the rights of sovereignty except those specifically reserved for the provinces. "If we can attain that, we shall not be New Brunswickers, nor Nova Scotians, nor Canadians, but British North Americans."

Macdonald told his audience they could make a great nation, capable of defending itself, and he reminded them of "the gallant defence that is being made by the Southern Republic — at this moment they have not much more than four millions of men — not much exceeding our own numbers — yet what a brave fight they have made."[80]

For two more days, there were speeches and parties in Fredericton and St. John. From there a special train carried the Canadians back to the *Queen Victoria* in Charlottetown for the trip to Quebec. The weather had turned, and on September 19, three weeks after they left and the day of the raid on the *Michigan*, they arrived back in Quebec.

As Brown noted, "Our expedition has been all and more than we could have hoped."

The failure of the peace talks and the fiascos in Chicago and Sandusky strained relations between Clay and Thompson even more. Clay predicted that Thompson would try to pin the debacle at Chicago on him. Clay feared Thompson believed the talks at Niagara Falls raised the possibility that the Confederacy could solve its problems by the ballot box, precluding the need for a revolution. "He may throw on us the blame for his own shortcomings," Clay said in a letter to Holcombe. "Look out for such a coup d'etat."[81]

He was right. Some days later, Thompson wrote to Benjamin that the effect of the talks was to lead people to believe that under some conditions the South would agree to return to the Union and "this belief diminished the war spirit in the West. They began to hope they could accomplish at the ballot box what they had determined to do by revolution."[82]

As always, there was a third point of view. Holcombe, in his report of the peace talks, backpedalled with the skill of a lawyer and an academic, putting as much distance between the commissioners and Sanders as possible. He told Benjamin that although Greeley supposed "we held a quasi diplomatic position, we had never written a line or uttered a word to justify such an inference." Sanders had led Greeley to believe this and then insinuated himself into the negotiations as an equal partner. Although there was "serious objections to his association," the commissioners thought that Sanders' "peculiar talents might render him useful." In other words, Sanders conned his way in to the inner circle and once there wouldn't leave.

Clay wrote to Benjamin that the Chicago uprising had failed because the group most likely to be useful, the Sons of Liberty, was largely crushed and its organization in ruins. "As to revolution in the Northwest, I am growing skeptical," Clay wrote. "These people need a leader and I fear they will not find one."

Clay settled back into his bachelor's life in St. Catharines, where Holcombe and Sanders were his constant companions. He was a sick and lonely man who refused to believe accounts in Northern papers about Union victories — all Northerners were liars. He wrote to his wife, Ginnie, weekly, complaining that he never heard from her, and he took every opportunity to send parcels with things denied her by the war. One package he sent through the blockade with George Sanders' son, Lewis, included tops and marbles for his son Matt, which he noted with satisfaction cost only fifty cents.[83]

Holcombe, meanwhile, was on his way back to the South. On September 20, he boarded the blockade-runner *Condor*, "a staunch, three-funneled vessel, superbly adapted to her trade and as swift as a swallow."

The ship's more famous passenger was Rose O'Neal Greenhow. "The Wild Rose," as she was known in Washington, was an extraordinary Confederate spy whose ring of female socialites in the capital provided invaluable intelligence to the Confederates throughout the war. Greenhow was returning to the South from London, where she had arranged to publish a best-selling account of her activities and imprisonment by federal authorities.

On September 30, the last day of the voyage, the *Condor* was caught in a storm. It was built to take such weather, and in the late afternoon it made a run through the gauntlet of blockading ships off the mouth of the Cape Fear River. She was spotted, and two ships took up the chase. At 3:00 a.m. on October 1, as the *Condor* knifed her way through the seas where river mouth and ocean met, she ran aground on New Inlet Bar, two hundred yards from the safety of Confederate guns at Fort Fisher. As the ship wallowed on the sandbar, listing to starboard, the heavy seas pounded the hull and threatened to break it up. Greenhow demanded that the ship's captain, Admiral Hobart Hampden, the eighth Earl of Buckinghamshire, put her ashore in a boat. Hampden at first refused, pointing out that such a trip would be suicidal. But Greenhow had been in a federal prison once and she was determined not to do so again. Finally, exhausted by her harangue, Hampden ordered a boat lowered.

Holcombe decided to go with her. He stored his mail, including letters from Thompson, under the stern seat, four sailors took the oars, and the boat was set free. Within moments mountainous breakers lifted the tiny boat high in the air, only to let it go with a sickening drop into the deep troughs. Eyewitnesses reported that the lifeboat struggled close to shore, and a few dozen yards off the beach, a giant wave lifted the craft and it overturned. All six people were tossed out and dragged down by an undertow in the surf.

Holcombe fought his way to the surface and clung to the keel of the overturned lifeboat. The wind and waves almost tore away his grip, but he managed to hang on and finally, in a last dash, struck for shore. He made it, and there he lay "like a dead man" until the crewmen found him.[84]

Holcombe and the crew scoured the beach for Greenhow. Her body was found some hours later; her jewellery and the cash in her purse were gone. The Wild Rose was buried the next day in Wilmington. On October 2, Holcombe left Wilmington for Richmond, and he met briefly with Confederate officials. He did not send an official report of his actions and an accounting of moneys spent in Canada to Secretary of State Benjamin until November 16. Holcombe apologized for the lack of financial detail, saying that a notebook containing those entries was lost when the *Condor* went down. Holcombe said he sent home between fifty-five and sixty escaped Confederate soldiers from the Canadas, a meagre return for seven months in the provinces and the expenditure of thousands of dollars.[85]

Holcombe's departure meant the loss of an ally for Clay, so he was no doubt pleased to see the return to Canada of Bennett Young, whom he had met in Halifax in May. Young had gone on to Richmond, been commissioned as a lieutenant in the Confederate Army by Secretary of War James Seddon on June 16, and, curiously, been ordered back to Canada to report to Clay, rather than Thompson. His specific instructions were to collect Confederate soldiers who had escaped from Northern prisons, but no more than twenty of them, and "execute such enterprises as may be indicated to you." In a supplementary dispatch received in Toronto on August 20 he was ordered to reconnoitre towns along the frontier, select the ones most exposed to attack, and feel free to sack and burn them. "It is but right," wrote Seddon, "that the people of New England and Vermont especially, some of whose officers and troops have been foremost in these excesses, should have brought home to them some of the horrors of such warfare."[86]

Young had enormous respect for Clay, seeing a renowned lawyer and politician, a man of letters and religion, and possibly a mentor. This became clear later, after the St. Albans raid. Young was hurt when Clay distanced himself from the raiders.

Young was born in Kentucky, the son of a hat manufacturer turned planter. His father's wealth afforded Young the best schooling, and at the outbreak of war he was preparing to follow his older brother into the ministry. According to a story he told later while in jail in Montreal, his life's course changed early in the war when Union troops raided his hometown, raping and beating the young woman whom he hoped one day to marry. She died several weeks later, and Young, grieving and longing for revenge, joined Morgan's Cavalry. There he met Hines, Castleman, and many of the Kentucky cavaliers who ended up in Canada. He was among the 2,500 men captured in Ohio in July 1863; he escaped from Camp Douglas, near Chicago, by bribing a guard and made his way to Toronto, where that fall he enrolled in the University of Toronto, planning to resume his studies. As the war news grew bleaker, he left Toronto for Halifax and Holcombe's pipeline back to the South. It was while waiting to go home that he met Clay.

Clay had a good feeling about Young. "He showed me letters from those whom I knew by reputation to be true friends of Southern independence, vouching his integrity as a Christian and his loyalty as a soldier for the South," Clay wrote to Benjamin. Clay added that he was satisfied Young's heart still burned with the fires of the cause and that he found Young's plans for retaliating against the North feasible. So Clay sent him home with a note to the War Department. Young explained his strategy to Seddon, which may explain Seddon's supplementary instructions urging him to carry out the raids after finishing his assignment in Chicago. In those orders, Seddon specifically named Burlington and St. Albans, Vermont, as targets.[87]

Captain John Castleman had also raised the idea of sacking Northern towns soon after fleeing from Chicago at the end of August. Castleman and Hines had moved south into Indiana with the intention of burning and destroying federal depots. Thompson was distressed by their plans. He feared these adventures would be linked to him and he told Clay that Castleman's idea of raids on banks and public buildings "embarrasses me." If it was traced back to the commissioners the actions would "place us in an awkward position with the Canadian authorities." Despite his misgivings, Thompson wrote to Castleman that the plan he proposed "is very desirable. We do not believe you could do a more valuable service and we shall take pleasure in according you every aid."[88]

Thompson would no doubt have been more embarrassed by the plans for the St. Albans Raid, but he didn't find out about it until it was too late.

CHAPTER 11
The St. Albans Raid

"We are Confederate soldiers and you are my prisoner. We have come to give you a taste of Sherman's idea of war."
St. Albans raider Tom Collins to a bank teller

Wednesday, October 19, was cool and threatened rain, so the streets of St. Albans, Vermont, were nearly empty. Lieutenant Bennett H. Young turned away from the third-storey window overlooking the town square to study his reflection in the mirror. The Montreal tailor had done a fine job on his uniform, its soft gray wool accented by the wide yellow stripe that stretched down the length of his trousers.[89]

Young knelt and, hand to forehead, calmed himself with a prayer. A moment later — refreshed, strengthened, and with renewed resolve — he left the room and padded down the staircase of the American Hotel, past the bewildered gaze of the hotel clerk. The bell on the Town Hall struck three as Young stepped out onto the wooden sidewalk. With a nod to the men scattered within sight, he raised his revolver, fired once into the air, and shouted, "This city is now in the possession of the Confederate States of America!"

So began the raid that came to be known, to the Confederates at least, as the great "Vairmont Yankee Scare Party." It took place only forty miles from Montreal, making it the northernmost battle of the Civil War.

Courtesy of Frank Leslie's Illustrated Newspaper

The St. Albans raiders were treated like heroes in Montreal. Locals visited them in jail, bringing food, wine, and tobacco and ensuring they had all the local papers to read.

Before the day had ended, three banks in the town along the shores of Lake Champlain would be plundered of $208,000, worth some $20 million today. One villager would be dead and another three wounded. The town — indeed, the whole northern U.S. frontier — would be left in shock. In Washington, Congress would call for an invasion of Canada. In Quebec City, Governor General Monck would dismiss the attack as the work of "miscreants" — mere bandits, marauding under the guise of soldiers. And for Canada's Fathers of Confederation gathering at Quebec to craft a constitution, this chain of events would give a new urgency to their talks.

Preparation for the attack had begun eight days earlier, on the morning of October 11, when two well-dressed and well-spoken men had arrived at the Lafayette Hotel in Philipsburg, Quebec, a way station for travellers located less than a mile from the American border. Several more had arrived in the afternoon. And that evening after dinner, Young's plan unfolded in his hotel room in Philipsburg, as he explained how the operation would work. None of the team had reached the age of twenty-five, yet all were veterans who had escaped from Yankee prisons and made their way north. As Young talked, they studied the crumpled map laid out before them. Ringed in red ink were St. Albans and, eight miles to the northeast, the town of Sheldon.

Young had picked St. Albans for what he hoped would be the first of many raids after a careful reconnoitre of upstate New York and Vermont. It was close to the border, allowing for a quick escape as well as easy infiltration by road, rail, and water. It was also a prosperous market town, where the coming and going of strangers would not attract undue attention. The First National Bank, the St. Albans Bank, and the Franklin County Bank were all located on Main Street in the centre of the town, less than half a block apart.

The raiders should arrive separately in pairs by horse, train, and carriage to avoid suspicion. Young opened his carpetbag. Inside were forty glass vials containing a clear liquid. The concoction was known as Greek Fire. Young said he'd call another meeting when they were all in St. Albans, divide up the Greek Fire, and after they'd hit the banks they'd burn the town. It was 11:00 p.m. when Young rolled up the map and told the men to check out of the hotel in the morning, leaving in pairs. They were to meet again in St. Albans.

Young left for St. Albans the next day, where he continued a careful scouting of the town, visiting each of the three banks he planned to rob. And during the following week, the raiders drifted into St. Albans by horse, train, and carriage, all the while gathering intelligence about the banks, where the best horses could be had, as well as which routes north were the safest and fastest.

Tom Collins, one member of the twenty-two-man group, decided to spread the word — for anyone who cared to know — that the young men were members of a Montreal hunting and fishing club who had selected the town for their annual fall outing. But they were short of guns, he said, and would be most grateful to borrow some. Collins received no offers, however.[90]

The raid had been planned for Tuesday. But upon learning it was market day, and that the town would be busy, Young postponed the raid until the following afternoon, "the dullest of the week."

As he had predicted, there were very few people on the streets when Young fired his gun into the air on that Wednesday afternoon in St. Albans. Some of the townspeople, hearing the pistol shot, emerged from their homes and businesses, looked at Young, and laughed. Most believed it was a joke or a prank — understandably, since they had never actually seen a Confederate, let alone one in uniform. For them, Gettysburg and the wilderness were war stories they'd read about in the *St. Albans Messenger*. In the next forty-five minutes, they were to learn something more about the reality of things.

"We are Confederate soldiers and you are my prisoner," said Tom Collins, pointing his twin Colts at the head of the teller sorting bills behind the counter of the St. Albans Bank. "We have come to give you a taste of Sherman's idea of war."

Assistant cashier Cyrus Bishop, eyes wide with fright, jumped backwards off his stool and retreated to the inner office, where his boss, Martin Seymour, was also counting cash. Together, the two men tried to close the door, but the raiders were too fast. The hapless Bishop and Seymour were grabbed by the throat and pinned to the wall.

"Not a word," Collins hissed. "We have come to take your town."[91]

As Collins stood guard, his team scooped up the bills on the table and rifled the safe, stuffing the notes into their valises and the deep pockets of their coats. A bag containing $1,500 in coins was deemed too heavy to take. A sheet of uncut St. Albans bank notes worth $50,000 was overlooked, too, as was a similar sheet of bearer bonds. But when local merchant Samuel Breck came in with $393 to repay a loan — representing years of savings — a pistol was shoved into to his chest and the cash was taken. A young man came in to deposit cash for his employer. Similarly relieved of $210, he joined the line of prisoners.

Collins next forced everyone in the bank to swear an oath of allegiance to the Confederate States. The oath administered, Collins ordered the prisoners into the back room, closed the door, and locked it. The robbery had taken twelve minutes, a scene repeated throughout the town.

While thirteen of the raiders stripped the banks, the remaining nine, including Young, herded the astonished townspeople onto the village green. Young was aware that each passing minute put their mission at risk, yet it was vital that passersby be contained in the square. To the west, toward the train depot and lake, hundreds of men worked either at the station or neighbouring machine shops and warehouses. If mobilized, they could easily overwhelm his small force.

The man who rallied the town was nineteen-year-old Captain George Conger of the 1st Vermont Infantry, home on leave. Ignoring the flying bullets, he slipped away from the green, grabbed a horse, mounted, and set off through the town raising the alarm. Soon groups of men had joined Conger and they began sniping at the mounted rebels from behind trees and windows.

Young ordered his men to retreat and to burn buildings as they went. The men hurled their bottles of Greek Fire onto the roofs of downtown buildings and, where possible, through windows. While the raiders believed they had fired the town, the crude firebombs ultimately had little effect: at the American Hotel, the mixture was smeared all over the washroom and burned until the next day. The wood was kept wet, however, and little damage was done.

Young's group crossed the Missisquoi River at Enosburg Falls, some twenty-four miles northeast of St. Albans, reaching the Canadian border at about 9:00 p.m. Abandoning their stolen horses, they donned civilian clothes. From there, they were to proceed on foot to Montreal.

While all the raiders made it safely across the border by midnight, their troubles were not over. By the following day, thirteen of the men had been arrested by Canadian authorities or had given themselves into voluntary custody.

The next afternoon, when news of the arrests reached Young, he decided to give himself up. "I am their leader," he said to one of his companions. "Their cause is my cause. I alone had the command of the raid." Young rode south and, that evening, remained in Canada at a farmhouse five miles north of Philipsburg. The farmer agreed to give him bed and board and care for his horse for the not inconsiderable sum of five dollars. After supper, an exhausted Young stretched out in front of the living room fireplace and soon fell asleep, his guns hanging on the back of a chair in his bedroom.

He would not have done so had he known that, earlier in the day, Conger and his posse (now in Canada) had stopped by, asking the farmer to keep a lookout for any rebels who might want shelter. And now that Young was asleep, the farmer had sent one of his hands to find Conger.

Young awoke to find the room crowded with men, all pointing revolvers at his head. A grinning Conger said, "You are my prisoner."

Conger later testified it was all he could do to keep the Vermonters from hanging Young then and there. Young was tied and thrown into a wagon with a rope around his neck, as the outraged posse members "kept cocking their pistols at him, telling him, what they would like to do."

As the wagon started down the farmhouse lane, Conger jumped in, turning to shout instructions to his men. For Young, convinced that he was about to be hanged, it was too good an opportunity to miss. He lunged at Conger, catching him in the stomach with a knee. Grabbing the reins, Young cracked the whip, sending the wagon bolting down the road.

A half-mile down the road, the chase ended and Young was recaptured. He tried to leap out but was caught and beaten with rifle butts by his enraged captors. Suddenly the melee was interrupted by a crisp British voice. The men turned to find a scarlet-clad officer sitting stiffly on horseback. The British officer told them that seven rebels captured earlier were to be escorted across the border next day. He suggested that Young join them. Conger agreed, but some of the mob refused to leave without exacting personal revenge on the rebel leader. The major's eyes narrowed. "This would be a violation of our neutrality," he said, a note of hostility creeping into his voice.

"We don't give a damn for your neutrality," came the reply.

The major stared hard. "But you will respect our arms, sir," he said. "If you leave with this prisoner, I will send a company of regulars to bring him back."

The threat was enough to change the villagers' minds. They reluctantly helped escort Young to Philipsburg. At the garrison, he was handed over to the commanding Captain, while the St. Albans posse were unceremoniously "escorted" back to the road to Vermont.

Young joined seven of his comrades, where they were comfortably confined in the soldier's barracks. Over food and ale, the story was recounted to the admiring audience of red-coated officers. Later that evening, Young and his men were taken to St. Jean-sur-Richelieu, twenty miles north, where they were treated as heroes.

In the besieged rebel capital at Richmond next day, news of the raid was a welcome tonic. "A war with England would be our peace," wrote John B. Jones, a clerk in the Confederate War Department.

The raid caused pandemonium on both sides of the border, which was one of its goals. In the words of one of the residents of St. Albans, Albert Sowles, who would later write an account of the raid:

> Terror reigned throughout the frontier. It was the prevailing opinion that the raiders were but an advanced guard of an army from Canada that had temporarily overpowered the local government and were marching through our states, carrying all the horrors of war to our doors.[92]

In St. Albans, stores were closed and doors barred. By morning four companies of militia, along with two cannon, had arrived, dispatched by Governor Gregory Smith. When the news had arrived in Montpelier the previous evening, there had been panic in the state capital. The legislature was quickly adjourned and officials hastily armed and organized themselves for the defence of the town. When hours passed with no further news, hysteria reached a fever pitch and everyone assumed it was because the telegraph wires had been cut. Governor Smith sent a telegram to Monck informing him of the raid, which he at first believed had been the work of a raiding party one hundred strong, killing five people, including a child, and leaving the town in flames. Smith, who was also president of the Central Vermont Railway, recalled a train and immediately sent seventy-five invalid soldiers to St. Albans. Smith also assumed the rebels were an advance party, so he placed the border under military guard. Cadets from Norwich University at Northfield were called out and sent to the border. By morning, 1,300 men were under arms.

That evening in nearby Burlington pandemonium broke out when word spread that a Confederate force was moving on the city by steamer down Lake Champlain, intent on sacking and burning everything in its path. All able-bodied men were called on to prepare for battle with the invader.

The news reached General John Dix, Military Commander of the East, at a dinner party, whose guests included British Ambassador Lord Richard Lyons, recently returned from Quebec. Dix ordered the commanding officer at Burlington to send troops to St. Albans, find the raiders, and, if necessary, pursue them into Canada and destroy them.

A seriously worried Lord Lyons asked pointedly whether Washington had authorized the orders, to which Dix replied that it was not needed. He informed Lyons and other guests that such a course was justified by international law, presumably referring to the ambiguous concept of "hot pursuit."

The fear spread along the frontier with papers in Ogdensburg, Rochester, Buffalo, and Cleveland calling their citizens to arms to repel the invaders. In Plattsburg, New York, across Lake Champlain, the residents ripped up a section of railroad track after learning the rebels were coming by rail. As Sowles put it, "The rumours would fill the air until spring."

On the Canadian side the sympathies were split. Spiting the Yankee was always popular, but burning the town of neighbours was not. The raid seemed a mere excuse for bank robbery, but they were angry that the Americans would assume they could cross the border with impunity and impose their own summary justice at will. The *Montreal Gazette* quickly labelled the affair "the Outrage at St. Albans," saying it had been carried out by "misguided men" and, regardless of whether it turned out to be an act of war or robbery, it was uncivilized conduct likely to excite "the universal execration of mankind."

In the midst of the mayhem, Bennett Young wrote to the *Montreal Evening Telegraph* from jail. He protested his innocence as a common criminal and also raised the issue of Canadian sovereignty.[93] Young wrote that he went to Vermont "for the purpose of burning the town and surrounding villages, as a retaliation for the recent outrages in the Shenandoah Valley and elsewhere in the Confederate States." He said he hadn't broken any Canadian laws while the Vermonters had insulted Canadians by chasing him across the border, arresting him, beating him, and threatening to kill him, all without respect to the fact that they were in another country.

"Surely the people of Vermont have forgotten that you are not in the midst of a war," he wrote.

Monck at first wasn't sure what to believe. He received the telegram from Smith, but the papers on the morning of the twentieth failed to carry any news about the raid. In a letter to Colonial Secretary Cardwell, he admitted, "I was at first inclined to doubt the authenticity of the telegram."[94]

He called a hasty meeting with John A. Macdonald and George-Étienne Cartier, then in the middle of intense discussions at Quebec. He also wisely ordered Judge Joseph Coursol, the police magistrate, to dispatch a police force to the border to arrest any raiders they could find. Monck next sent a telegram to his military commander in Halifax, Sir Fenwick Williams, asking him to use the detachment at St. Johns to help Coursol. Unsure of the size of the raiding party, he knew only that should they put up a fight, the

DIXIE & THE DOMINION

handful of police would be easily overpowered. Monck told Sir Fenwick the raid was no more than a "marauding expedition, though I dare say they were using the name of the Confederates to cloak their designs."[95]

The raiders had thought themselves safe in Canada and so made no particular effort to conceal themselves. One by one the local military commander, Colonel Edward Ermatinger, rounded them up. Within three days of the raid fourteen of them were in custody. Nineteen thousand dollars was surrendered to the sheriff at St. John, Quebec,

Sir Fenwick Williams, a Crimean War hero, was Commander-in-Chief of British North American forces. He feared and respected the Union Army.

and some money dropped on the road by the raiders in their haste was brought in by farmers.

Thompson was mortified and reproached Clay in a telegram. Clay, in a dissembling panic over the possibility of his own arrest, lied and said he'd had nothing to do with it. "I am no less surprised, shocked and disturbed than you can be," he wrote. "I will explain when we meet. I have full proof that I discountenanced it. I did not know that anything would be attempted." Having denied any complicity, Clay went on to say that it was his duty to see to the defence of the raiders and he would do so, "notwithstanding it looks like mere selfish plunder."[96]

That same day, Clay sent a cheque for $6,000 to George Sanders in Montreal for the defence of the raiders. It was clear by then that the Americans would ask the court to extradite them to the United States under the terms of the Webster-Ashburton Treaty.

114

However, Clay admitted in a letter to Judah Benjamin that he authorized Young to proceed, but he gave Young strict orders to "destroy whatever was valuable, not to stop to rob; but after firing a town he could seize and carry off money or treasury notes, he might do so on condition they were delivered to the proper authorities of the Confederate State."

Clay called on the raiders in jail some days later, then publicly denounced them and wished that the lot of them, with the exception of Young, "were in a warmer climate than that in which they had been born."

The raiders were disgusted. They refused his request to turn over any money they had, or had hidden, from the raid. Young was stung by the betrayal. He wrote to Clay from jail that "I have ever done my duty to you and my country. I ask that you make me right with the War Department. That the raid has done good no one can deny and I trust that you will give a fair and just statement of all that I did." He would have turned the money over to Clay, but his men stopped him. "The boys would have yielded, but after they heard the language you used in regards to them, they all expressed a determination to be extradited rather than yield."

"I have ever loved you Mr. Clay," Young wrote, "more so as a father rather than a superior and come what will ... my heart will ever be open to you with a warm gushing spring of love. I love my country and I love you and there's nothing I won't do to serve them."[97]

Monck, meanwhile, had received an official request from U.S. Secretary of State Seward for the extradition of the raiders and had appointed Judge Coursol to hear the case in Montreal. The news had reached him in the midst of the most hopeful series of developments since he arrived in Canada. The Canadians and their Maritime cousins, energized by the success of the Charlottetown Conference, were meeting in Quebec to hammer out the framework for Confederation. Monck did not want to see it derailed. For Lady Monck, the crisis was a footnote among the many social events of the Quebec Conference. She blithely recorded that her brother-in-law received a telegram "that fussed him," adding that it made him eat his breakfast in some haste before leaving for Quebec.

Seward had also written to Francis Adams, the American ambassador to Britain, asking him to inform the British that the people of the Canadas were not displaying "good neighborhood" in permitting such raids.

Seward also took up the matter of Dix's inflammatory "pursue and destroy" order with Lincoln. It had been universally condemned in Canada, though hailed as more than acceptable in the U.S. The *New York Herald*, for example, demanded that the raiders be followed into Canada and shot on sight. If the raids continued Canada should be treated as a dangerous enemy.[98] Lincoln wisely rescinded it.

Sanders, meanwhile, had hired the best defence team possible for Young and his comrades. They were the renowned John C. Abbott, who would later become Canada's third prime minister, and Rodolphe Laflamme and William H. Kerr, two notable criminal lawyers in the city.

Abbott quickly concluded that the best and only defence was that the raid had been carried out as an act of war, the opposite of Monck's conclusion (he believed it was an act of piracy). Abbott felt that the proof lay in Young's commission from War Secretary Seddon. He nonetheless asked Clay to send a messenger to Richmond to provide a blanket letter authorizing the raid, which Clay did.

In the meantime in Quebec, the Canadians continued their deliberations, with the distant thunder of war adding all the proof they needed. In an extraordinary stretch of twenty-one days, they crafted and agreed upon a constitution for a new nation on the North American continent.

CHAPTER 12
Nation Builders at Quebec

"We all desire these provinces should be as great as possible. There is something better to be done, something greater to be attained."
Nova Scotia Premier Charles Tupper
October 1864

On the morning of October 19, as Bennett Young and his men were preparing for their raid on St. Albans, Canada's fathers of Confederation were hard at work in Quebec. Unlike the Americans a century earlier, who sought "life, liberty and the pursuit of happiness" in their Declaration of Independence, the Canadians wanted something more modest. They wanted independence within the strong confines of the British Empire, and settled for "peace, order and good government" over the more radical ideas chosen by the authors of the American Constitution.

It was their second week of deliberations aimed at forging a Canadian Constitution. Ultimately, the seventy-two resolutions agreed upon would become the basis of the British North America Act. This Act became, in effect, Canada's constitution until 1982, when Prime Minister Pierre Elliott Trudeau repatriated a "Made in Canada" document.

John A. Macdonald moved the resolution that would outline the powers of the new federal government. It was here that the disturbance caused by the St. Albans Raid could now be used to good effect. For here was another example of the complete breakdown of the United States. That one group of Americans should feel it necessary to burn down the towns of another group of Americans could all be traced back to the powers invested in Washington and the states a century ago. There the states had delegated certain powers to Washington while retaining the rest for themselves. That doctrine of state rights had led to the secession of the eleven Southern states in 1861. The argument was not about the morality of slavery, but the right of the states to enact the laws to impose institutions like slavery without interference from Washington.

For Brown, this states' rights was "a great evil" and so the Canadians should ensure that any "implied" power rested with the federal government. The Civil War had proved this all too well. In the Canadian model there could never be a civil war, because there would be no basis to secede: the federal government would control the whole nation. In Macdonald's view the Canadians must avoid what de Tocqueville had called "a source of radical weakness" in the American constitution. "It would ruin us in the eyes of the civilized world," Macdonald declared. In the end this resolution passed too.[99]

The thirty-three men seated around a battered, book-littered table in the reading room of an old post office saw their task as creating a future that held the prospects of greatness and the possibility of a transcontinental nation. The meeting in Charlottetown had revealed that it was possible, but it had been a whirlwind courtship, and now was the acid test of whether it could end in marriage. "We have arrived at the very crisis of our fate," noted the *Toronto Globe*, somberly.

If that first meeting had set out the broad areas of agreement, the proof lay in the details. What form should the union take, and how many seats in a new parliament should each province have? How would the Senate or Upper House be elected? What steps needed to be taken to ensure the new country could be defended? How would it all be paid for? And, what of the vast empty Prairies? Already they were slipping into the grasp of the Republic as its settlers moved west. The one thing favouring the future was that the past was not working. Beyond that, it required a leap of faith that could only be proven right or wrong after the fact, when it might be too late.

The men at Quebec had no polls to tell them what to think or speechwriters to polish their words. The most powerful medium of the age, newspapers, was excluded from the deliberations. Not all the contributions were lofty or noble, not all of the speeches fluid and inspiring. But there was a dignity and grandeur about the event, if only because everyone knew they were present at a moment of creation. It called upon them to give the deliberations their most serious and responsible thought. What followed has often been criticized as the product of men in a hurry. But these remarkable and variously talented people fairly represented the interests and occupations of their time.

While many among them were lawyers, Brown, Galt, Nova Scotia's Sam Tilley, and New Brunswick's Charles Tupper, though practical and experienced men, were not. Their views were less legalistic and more imaginative. Together the assembly contained the best and brightest minds of the day, and their task was extraordinary, all the more gratifying because as mere colonists they were proposing it themselves. That gave the conference a buoyant mood, a feeling that despite differences — and there were many — the majority of people gathered believed powerfully in a union of British North America, and that the belief was strong enough to overcome the differences. These were the Fathers of Confederation.

In the three weeks after Charlottetown, there was discussion of Confederation everywhere in Canada, and in anticipation of the events to come the public debate roamed over the possibilities in endless combinations. The *Globe* welcomed it all and saw it as a way to, among other things, open up the Northwest, force the Hudson's Bay Company to cede its control of those territories to a new sovereign state, and keep the rapacious and expansionist Americans at bay. There was no reason why the Canadians couldn't pursue westward expansion independently, but joining with the eastern section together first greatly enhanced the chances of achieving it.

As they gathered around the table on Monday, October 10, the Canadians and the Maritimers were brought together by common purpose, but with different motives. The Canadians felt the need for Confederation as a pressing solution to intractable problems. They couldn't turn back. George Brown's goal was to eliminate the stranglehold of French Canada on the province's affairs. As Brown told New Brunswick's Governor General Arthur Gordon during the Charlottetown trip, "We can't wait. We are not going to be tied to Lower Canada for twelve months more."[100]

John A. Macdonald had made a virtue out of necessity and resolutely pushed forward. Cartier had gambled both on the idea and on Macdonald, casting his eye forward and seeing an alliance that could keep him in power. If he could do that and protect the interest of French Canada then he was in. Galt, the financial genius, unstable, often depressed and then wildly happy, believed in the spirit and principle of what was to come. After all, he had first proposed the idea of Confederation six years earlier, and its ultimate shape would be very similar to his proposals. He was joined in his enthusiasm by D'arcy McGee.

The Maritimers were largely self-governing and free of the internecine struggles of the Canadas. What drove them forward was as powerful, if less tangible. Tupper, Tilley, John Hamilton Gray, William Pope, and Edward Whelan: they were all men of power and accomplishment, and their reputations suffered by supporting this grandiose scheme. But they had seen something others had yet to perceive and it was this: Confederation offered wider horizons and broader fields of play, an end to the smallness and pettiness of their limited provincial pastures, the impoverishment of their issues and their parochial concerns. Here was nationalism on a different scale, prestige and respect outside their own small borders, a recognition and awareness of them in the wider world beyond. This was why they gambled. What had John A. Macdonald called it in his great speech in Halifax, "the dreary waste of colonial politics"? Well, Confederation could change all that.

The delegates carried out their meetings in private. They had agreed to meet to decide the future of half a continent, not to fight old party battles nor to feel unable to discuss matters freely and change their opinions. Nor would there be any grandstanding for political gain. As John Hamilton Gray later put it, "Candor was sought for more than mere personal triumph."[101]

At eleven o'clock on October 10, as Bennett Young and his fellow Confederates were converging on Philipsburg for their pre-raid briefing, the conference formally convened. John A. Macdonald got up to move the fundamental resolution of the conference and said simply, "That the best interests and future prosperity of British North America will be promoted by a federal union under the Crown of Great Britain."[102]

Tilley for the Maritimes seconded the plan, and Cartier, representing the third bloc at the table — French Canada — stood and, in his rambling English, went over once more the main political and economic reasons for union. "We all desire that these provinces should be as great as possible," he concluded. "There is something better to be done, something greater to be attained."

Gray declared that it had been his life's dream to one day be "a citizen of a great nation extending from the great west to the Atlantic seaboard."[103] And that more or less set the tone for the first day, which included a round of speeches on the virtues of Confederation.

Throughout it all, Macdonald exercised control of process and procedure. During the first two days, when the delegates were still stiff and formal, he worked to loosen things up. It was essential that an atmosphere of friendly concord be maintained, for there were plenty of obstacles. The delegates would need all of their goodwill to overcome them.

That evening was the first of a round of dinners, balls, and other social events that characterized the two-week affair. As Islander Edward Whelan noted, "If the delegates will survive the lavish hospitality of this great country, they will have good constitutions — perhaps better than the one they are manufacturing for Confederation!"

If at night the delegates ate and drank away their tensions, by day they were hard at work. On the second day of the conference, Macdonald, in a persuasive and reassuring speech, emphasized the main themes: the need for a strong central government, and keeping British traditions and parliamentary government. The basis of Confederation must be a strong central government to withstand the shocks that divided the Americans. The provinces should not regard themselves as separate and distinct entities, as had the seceding Southern states, and all powers not strictly reserved for the provinces should lie with the federal government to ensure that would be so.

In this respect, Macdonald was no doubt preaching to the converted. The men gathered at Quebec, unlike those of the Thirteen Colonies a century earlier, had not the slightest intent of changing anything by revolution. They were mid-Victorian British colonials who valued their political system and their ties to the mother country. The American system, with its separation of executive, legislative, and judicial branches, seemed dangerously rigid and unwieldy and its constitutional checks and balances awkward. The parliamentary system avoided these defects, and as all could see, the American experiment had degenerated into a deadly civil war, which many saw as proof of the failures of that system. Macdonald's speech rambled on for three hours, and after a break for lunch the discussion continued. By the end of the day his general motion had passed unanimously with a burst of applause that could be heard outside the hall. It was the end of the second day and of the last easy piece of business.[104]

On the third day, as Bennett Young and his team infiltrated St. Albans, the meeting turned to the question of an Upper House, which, like the American system, would be called a Senate but which, unlike it, would be unelected. It proved to be the first real problem, because the issue was important to the Maritimers.

They knew that in the general legislature, to be called the House of Commons, they would be outnumbered, since its basis was representation by population. Their one hope of redressing the balance lay in the Upper House, and they had a precedent. The small American states had been protected this way during their constitutional talks in Philadelphia in 1776. John A. Macdonald was determined to avoid this at all costs and proposed dividing British North America into three equal parts: Canada West, Canada East, and the four Atlantic provinces, each having an equal number of senate seats. The Maritimers were dissatisfied, and Tilley countered with an amendment that would have given twenty-four seats each for the two Canadas and thirty-two for the four Atlantic provinces.

The deadlock broke on Monday, when Brown proposed a compromise. The two Canadas would have twenty-four seats each, the three Maritime provinces another twenty-four, and Newfoundland, four more. It was four less than the Maritimers wanted, but four more than the Canadians had proposed. The resolution passed.

The next problem was whether the Senate should be elected or appointed. Some wanted the chamber elected, while the smaller provinces wanted them appointed locally, so that they could control the voice they sent to it. Brown argued that it shouldn't be elected because it would be unlike the very active American Senate. In his eyes the Upper Chamber was merely a check and balance against too hasty legislation — a sober second look — and to elect its members would only give them a false sense of power. In this Brown won the day, and the conference moved on to the all-important Lower House.

On the morning of October 19, Bennett Young launched his raid and Brown introduced a series of resolutions to establish a House of Commons whose seats were allocated based on representation by population. It was the full embodiment of the principles that Brown had always craved. Canada West would have eighty-two seats, Canada East sixty-five, down to Prince Edward Island's five, the numbers to be adjusted according to a census every ten years. It ran into trouble right away.

The Islanders, painfully aware of their tiny numbers, asked for one more seat for no particular reason. They claimed it would be difficult to divide the Island's three counties into five seats and so wanted a sixth. "We could not justify it," Galt said later. Islanders, realizing how limited their role would be in Confederation, suddenly seemed to lose enthusiasm for the plan. They voted against the resolution and stayed largely in a disaffected gloom for the rest of the conference.[105]

As news of St. Albans washed over the Conference, at the end of the second week, it looked suddenly as if the whole scheme was foundering. The Newfoundlanders, though a part of the proceedings, showed little interest in being drawn into them. The Islanders were angry, and while the key players of New Brunswick and Nova Scotia were still there, they were less enthusiastic than when they'd started. As the conference entered its third week, it put the final touches to the powers of the local legislatures, which would look after strictly local matters. The provinces would have their own legislatures and a Lieutenant Governor appointed by the federal government. The last remaining hurdle was the financial arrangements for Confederation. Galt introduced resolutions to cover the transfer of all debts to the federal government and assets to the federal authority with grants and allowances to be made back in return. With some fine-tuning on the amount of the transfers, this too was done.

In the end there were seventy-two resolutions, each one formally adopted, which together constituted a plan for Confederation. It was a magnificent achievement in three rainy weeks, the consequence of able and earnest men, careful preparations, and an awareness, heightened by events around them, that the moment must not be lost.

Less than two months earlier the Canadians had set out as uninvited guests for Charlottetown. Now all the provinces, with the exception of Prince Edward Island, had agreed to the Canadian scheme for federation. This great union would embrace not only the existing provinces but, in the end, the whole of British North America, including the Northwest and eventually British Columbia and Vancouver Island as well. Brown was triumphant. In a hasty letter to Anne on that last day he wrote: "All right!!! Constitution adopted — a most creditable document — a complete reform of all the abuses and injustices we have complained of! Is it not wonderful? French Canadianism entirely extinguished!"[106]

Now the real work of making Confederation a success was about to begin. The delegates went on tour to unleash public celebrations of their achievement and persuade Canadians that an idea they had known about for a decade had suddenly taken form and shape and substance. For while the delegates had agreed to it, the people of the various provinces had not. The road ahead held Confederation, but not as quickly or as easily as the men at Quebec would have liked.

CHAPTER 13
Diplomatic Crisis

"The bane and curse of this country is the surveillance under which we work. Detectives and those ready to give information stand on every street corner."

Jacob Thompson
December 1864

The outcome at Quebec was welcome relief for Lord Monck from the diplomatic crisis surrounding the St. Albans raid. The quick Canadian action in rounding up the raiders had gone over well with the authorities in Washington, but Congress was angry. It wanted to re-arm the Great Lakes and end the Reciprocity Treaty, which allowed for the free flow of goods across the border. Lincoln's government had also imposed a passport law, which customs agents on both sides were enforcing. Trade was grinding to a halt. American papers were renewing their cries to annex Canada, and some even wanted an invasion to clear the rebels out. As the *New York Herald* noted: "Let the Canadian government look out, or the Green Mountain boys and the hardy lumbermen of Maine will take the law into their own hands. They will do justice on the robbers and murderers wherever they find them."[107]

In a letter to Colonial Secretary Cardwell, a few days after the end of the Quebec conference, Monck summarized its achievements, foremost among them that unlike the Americans ninety years earlier, the colonists had exhibited "feelings of loyalty to the Queen" and "the most earnest desire to maintain a connection with

England." Of the plan itself, its benefits were self-evident. "The advantages whether looked at from the point of view of administration, commerce or defence appear to me so obvious that it would be a waste of time to state them," Monck wrote.[108]

But if the movement toward Confederation was pleasing, the St. Albans affair was more vexing. John Abbott, who was acting for the raiders, sent a courier to Richmond urging the Confederate government to take responsibility for the raid. The prisoners, mean-

Clement Clay quickly distanced himself from the St. Albans raid, even though he authorized it and helped pay for it.

while, had been moved to Montreal, where they were treated more like heroes than criminals. The fourteen young men who had helped sack the Vermont town were so courteous and captivating they won the hearts of the people of Montreal, who flocked to their trial offering encouragement and to their cells offering food, drink, and money for their defence.

St. Albans lawyer Edward Sowles noted indignantly that prison meals were served on the European plan, with menus, table cloths, and a choice of wine or ale. The raiders were never short of luxuries like tobacco, newspapers, or writing paper. They were a self-assured bunch, more like university students than criminals and seemingly oblivious to the enormous consequences of their actions. They were for the most part the sons of leading families in Kentucky, well-spoken, well-educated, and barely in their twenties. It added to their charm and stacked sympathies heavily in their favour.

During one interval in the proceedings, Bennett Young dashed off a letter to the *St. Albans Messenger* requesting that two copies of the paper be sent to the jail, so that he could follow their coverage of the trial. "Your editorials furnish considerable amusement to me and my comrades," he wrote. Young also wrote to the manager of the American Hotel in St. Albans to square accounts. He did so with five dollars stolen from one of the banks. He asked that the manager forward a shirt he'd left behind and a bottle of Old Rifle Whiskey, which he'd intended to use "in case our ammunition was used up."[109]

George Sanders was doing his part to rouse sympathy for the Confederates and their cause. In a letter to the *Montreal Gazette*, Sanders reiterated the main theme of their coming legal defence, which was that they were all commissioned soldiers engaged in acts of war, none of which had taken place in Canada or injured Canadian laws. "This enterprise was conducted without unnecessary violence and by an open and public declaration that they were acting as soldiers under the orders of the southern Confederacy," Sanders wrote.[110]

The extradition trial opened on November 5 to a packed courthouse. The American case was simple. Young and the others were common criminals charged with robbery and murder. They should be extradited. Abbott, acting for the Confederates, said the case against them was flimsy and they were Confederate soldiers who had committed an act of war on American soil and had not broken any Canadian laws. In a letter to Clay on October 25, Abbott wrote, "The strength of our position consists in the documents establishing the authority of the raiders from the Confederate States government."[111]

For the next three days, fifteen witnesses from St. Albans told their stories of the bank robberies and the raid. Canadian police described rounding up the rebels. A week later, Young exhibited his commission and instructions from War Secretary Seddon. "Having heard the evidence do you wish to say anything in answer to the charge," Judge Coursol asked Young.

He stood and faced the court:

> I am a citizen of the Confederate States to whom I
> owe allegiance. I am a commissioned officer in the

Army of the Confederate States with which the United States is at war. I owe no allegiance to the United States.

Whatever was done at St. Albans was done by the authority and order of the Confederate government. I have not violated any laws of Canada or Great Britain. The course I intended to pursue in Vermont was to retaliate for the barbarous atrocities of Grant, Butler, Sherman and others, except that I would scorn to harm women and children, or unarmed defenceless and unresisting citizens, or to plunder for my own benefit.

Young asked for a recess of thirty days during which time he hoped to have important supporting documentation arrive from Richmond. Young's companions said more or less the same thing. At the end of the day, Coursol adjourned the hearings until December 13 to allow the prisoners to gather the material for their defence.

Clay was anxious to return home. "I do not see that I can achieve anything by remaining longer in the province; and, unless instructed to stay, shall leave here by the 20th for Halifax and take my chances running the blockade," he wrote to Benjamin on November 1. "I am afraid to risk a winter's residence in this latitude and climate."[112]

Clay sent the letter by courier, but also placed an ad in the personal columns of the *New York*, one of the many alternate communication the Confederates had.[113] It ran on October 29 and read: "To: H.L. Clay, Richmond — I am well. Have written every week, but received no answer later than 30th June. Can I return at once? T.E. Lacy."

The reply came on November 12:

Mr. T.E. Lacy: Your friends think the sooner you return the better. At the point where you change vessels you can ascertain if it's better to proceed direct or via Mexico. Your wife and all your relatives are well. Your letters and packages all received. I send you letters today by safe hands. H.L.C.[114]

By early December, Clay had wrapped up his affairs. He turned over the remainder of his funds to Thompson — a little over $32,000 — and on December 10 moved on to Halifax. He booked passage on a mail packet that left on January 13 and reached Bermuda five days later.

Jacob Thompson was working to keep Captain Cole from the hangman's noose. He was also fighting the Canadian authorities, who were trying to show their helpfulness in the wake of St. Albans by extraditing Bennett Burley for his part in the Johnson's Island affair. As well, with Clay's departure the defence of the St. Albans crew was his responsibility, and he ensured that there was plenty of money to do it.

Thompson had his hands full defending Cole. On the day after the raid on Johnson's Island, Cole's girlfriend, Annie, beat a hasty retreat to Toronto, where she obtained a letter from Thompson claiming that Cole was a soldier and not a spy. A few days later she was back in Sandusky with the letter, signed by both Thompson and Clay. She handed it to Colonel Charles Hill, who was in command of the prison at Johnson's Island.

They sent a letter to President Davis, calling on the Confederate government to intercede on Cole's behalf. They never received a reply. In the end it didn't make any difference. Cole was found guilty and sentenced to hang. His sentence was commuted, and in 1865 he was released.

Hines and Castleman had moved south in September, splitting their squad of twenty men in half, hoping to burn federal shipping on the Mississippi and otherwise harass their enemies. By October 2, Castleman was in Cell #3 at the U.S. Military Prison in Indianapolis, having been arrested after one of his squad got drunk and was picked up by the local provost marshal, prompting him to tell all.

Castleman had the good fortune to be related to the Breckinridge family of Kentucky, whose many members were well known in legal political and business circles.

His uncle John Cabell Breckinridge was vice-president of the United States between 1856 and 1860 and was a cabinet colleague of Jacob Thompson. Other branches of the family were solid Union sympathizers, and his sister Virginia had married a Yankee, who happened to be a judge in Indianapolis.

The authorities wanted to hang Castleman, but Judge Breckinridge went to Washington and received an audience with President Lincoln at the White House. The pair had known each other before the war, and according to a later account by Breckinridge, Lincoln welcomed the meeting as a respite from his official duties. They talked of many things and only briefly about Castleman. It was enough. Judge Breckinridge walked away with a letter that saved his brother-in-law's life.[115] It read:

Executive Mansion, Washington,
November 29, 1864.

Whomsoever may have charge: Whenever John B. Castleman shall be tried, if convicted and sentenced, suspend execution until further order from me and send me the record.

A. Lincoln.[116]

Thompson still believed that havoc on the lakes was possible. He envisaged a Confederate raider on lakes Erie and Huron being secretly rearmed at Canadian border points and sacking American ports from Buffalo to Detroit with impunity. It was openly belligerent and would surely either bring him a jail sentence or extradition.

Nevertheless, his captain was to be James Bates, a former Mississippi steamboat captain, and in late October, Thompson gave Bates $16,500 to buy the steamer *Georgian* from O.M. Smith and Co. in Toronto. The reason he gave for purchasing the ship was that it was to be used in the timber trade on Lake Huron and Georgian Bay. But Godfrey Hyams had already tipped off the U.S. Consul in Toronto, James Kimball, that the boat was to be fitted with a bow ram on Lake Huron, where she would also take on cannon, small arms, and other means of war. Her first task was to sink the *Michigan* and then proceed on a cruise of destruction along the lakes.[117]

Bennett Burley, who had accompanied Beall on the *Philo Parsons*, was supposed to be among the crew. In the intervening few weeks since the mid-September raid, Burley was putting his technical knowledge to work in Guelph, about sixty miles west of Toronto, where at a foundry he was making cannon and torpedoes as part of the armaments for the *Georgian*. He was confident his version of Greek Fire, which had met with limited success elsewhere, would work. In a letter to Bates, who was in Toronto, Burley asked for waterproof blasting caps for the torpedoes and inquired whether the Greek Fire mixture needed to sit for some time to blend its incendiary elements.

Burley's whereabouts became known to the authorities, who were looking for him in connection with the Johnson's Island affair. With help from the American Consul in Toronto, he was traced to a Guelph foundry. When local lawyer J.J. Kingsmith was sent to investigate, he learned that a fourteen-pound cannon had been shipped by wagon from the foundry to Collingwood on the south shore of Georgian Bay. At the Guelph railway station he found a carriage for the cannon, along with torpedoes and other small arms, awaiting shipment to the remote town of Spanish River at the top of Georgian Bay.

While Burley was busy making cannon, another rebel, Larry Macdonald, was using the basement of his Toronto home at the corner of Agnes and Teraulay streets to make torpedoes, hand grenades, and Greek Fire. A Confederate sympathizer later testified that when he visited Macdonald's home he was led to a trap door into the basement, where he saw large kettles for potash, a pile of torpedoes, a large quantity of cartridges, newly moulded bullets, and other things to supply the vessel Thompson would buy.[118]

On November 1, the *Georgian* was delivered to the mouth of the Welland Canal at Port Colborne on Lake Erie. Scarcely had the transfer taken place when the American newspapers began asking why it had been bought for a price so far beyond its actual value, at a season of the year when shipping was almost at an end. This heightened awareness on the American side came just two weeks after the St. Albans raid. Nerves were frayed, and the citizens of the border towns still expected an imminent invasion. As Thompson wrote to Benjamin: "The story went out that she had been purchased for the sinking of the *Michigan*. At Buffalo two tugs had cannons placed on board, four regiments were sent to guard the city, bells were rung at Detroit and broken up on Sunday. The whole shore was the scene of excitement."[119]

The tribulations of the *Georgian* had just begun. At Port Colborne the propeller came loose, and her first trip was across the lake to Buffalo for a new one. The ship returned to Port Colborne, and on November 3, after loading thirty cords of wood, it headed for Sarnia on Lake Huron.

During the passage up the Detroit River, the *Georgian* was boarded by Colonel B. H. Hill, the area's military commander. He could find nothing suspicious. At Sarnia on November 11 the boat was searched yet again. The ship moved on to Collingwood, where it was searched yet again, this time by Canadian officials. Meanwhile, two barrels and a large box, all marked "potatoes," had been shipped from Guelph to Sarnia to the *Georgian*. They were intercepted and, as expected, contained munitions. In Collingwood, Bates let anyone who cared to know hear that the *Georgian* was laying up for the winter. It had in fact been shadowed all along by the *Michigan*, whose new captain, Frank Roe, reported that while Bates had assured everyone he was engaged in the lumber trade, the *Georgian* "has not carried a pound of freight or earned a dollar since falling into their present hands."[120]

It was December, the beginning of a long Canadian winter, and the *Georgian* was stuck. Thompson wrote to Benjamin that the "bane and curse of carrying out anything in this country is the surveillance under which we work. Detectives and those ready to give information stand on every street corner."[121]

Thompson sold the *Georgian* to Lieutenant-Colonel George T. Denison, who aided Thompson's intrigues in any way he could. Denison paid $13,000 in promissory notes and told the papers that his intention was to make use of the *Georgian* in the timber trade. On April 7, 1865, it was seized by Canadian authorities on the instructions of John A. Macdonald. It lay in Collingwood for the rest of the year, and despite Denison's protests, it was turned over to the American government.

Most of it was Monck's doing. Monck was more eager than ever to block Confederate attempts to compromise the official neutrality of the provinces. On November 5, when Hyams told the U.S. Consul at Toronto, David Potter, about the sale of the *Georgian*, Potter also warned Monck and U.S. War Secretary Stanton. Stanton in turn told General Dix, who, ever ready to send troops across the border, suggested he might take steps independent of the Canadian authorities. Monck, fearing such an outcome, asked revenue collectors at the lake ports to examine the *Georgian* when it docked. It was those men who searched the ship at Sarnia and found nothing suspicious.

Secretary of State Seward took the unusual step of wiring Monck privately on November 7, when the mayor of Buffalo, alarmed that the *Georgian* might be used for an attempt on his city, indicated that fear to Seward. Monck would normally have frowned on such a breach of etiquette, but in the wake of St. Albans he wanted to speed up the normally triangular pattern of communications. He acted on Seward's suggestion that the ship be investigated by keeping the vessel under constant surveillance.

Another by-product of Monck's intention to improve relations with the Americans was the arrest of Bennett Burley in Guelph on November 17, where he had been making his cannon and Greek Fire. He was taken to Toronto and committed for extradition to the United States for his part in the raid. Thompson sent a letter to the Confederate Consul in London, James Mason, pleading with him to press the British government to withhold the warrant. Thompson's argument was that the Webster-Ashburton Treaty was intended to apply to murders and robbers, not political offenders or belligerents in the act of war.

When the appeal of the lower court's decision to extradite the raiders was heard in the Superior Court in Toronto, Thompson was in the courtroom every day. It made no difference. The court decided the hijacking of the *Philo Parsons* and what happened thereafter was not a legitimate act of war and committed Burley to be extradited. Worried that the Confederates might try to free Burley, he was taken by an armed escort of twenty British soldiers and ten more policemen to the suspension bridge at Niagara Falls and handed over to the Americans in early February. With all these distractions, Thompson still had one last operation in mind. He still believed that if enough pressure could be brought to bear, Lincoln might not be re-elected. The best way to do that, he reasoned, was to destabilize the federal government. This mission would be no St. Albans. That was minor in comparison to what Thompson had in mind. This plan called for nothing less than the firebombing of New York City.

CHAPTER 14
Firebombing New York

"We wanted the people of the North to understand there are two sides to this war and they can't be rolling in wealth and comfort while we in the South are bearing all the hardships."
Confederate Robert Kennedy, on the firebombing of New York City

As the St. Albans Raiders sat in jail waiting for the vital proof of their Army commissions, and as Clement Clay made his preparations to go home, Jacob Thompson turned his attention to the firebombing of New York. It was a project that he expected to strike terror in the hearts of the North, break their morale, and revive the flagging fortunes of the peace Democrats, whose voices had grown silent after the fall of Atlanta and Sherman's march to the sea in Georgia.

Thompson still held firmly to the delusion that there was an army of disaffected Americans ready to "resist the despotism at Washington and it may come at the presidential election," as he put it in a letter to Benjamin. He was still in touch with the Copperheads in Illinois and was now pouring money into the campaign of James C. Robinson, who was running for governor. Thompson had Robinson's firm pledge that once elected he would place the control of the state's militia in the hands of the Sons of Liberty. Regardless of how likely this might be, or, if done, whether the militia would follow the order of traitors, Thompson nonetheless made a $50,000 investment in Robinson's campaign. As the election drew closer, Thompson summoned Lieutenant John Headley and Colonel Robert Martin, both veterans of Morgan's Cavalry, and outlined his broad plan for an uprising on election day in Chicago and New York. Similar uprisings were planned in Cincinnati and Boston as diversions from the main thrust in New York.[122]

Hines would be in charge of the operations in Chicago, and his second-in-command would be the British adventurer Colonel St. Leger Grenfel. They were to team up with Charles Walsh, the leader of the Sons of Liberty in Chicago, and once again try to release prisoners at Rock Island and Camp Douglas to form the nucleus of an army around which the Confederates could rally. Camp Douglas seemed an easier target now, since the guard was only eight hundred men, all of them disabled veterans, and they stood guard over eight thousand prisoners.

In New York, Martin, with Headley as his second-in-command, would lead a small party launching an insurrec-

John Headley described his part in the firebombing of New York in his 1906 memoirs.

Colonel Robert Martin, another veteran of Morgan's Kentucky Cavalry, led the raid that firebombed New York.

tion there. In a now familiar refrain, the New York conspirators boasted of a force of twenty thousand well-armed and well-organized men, ready for the breakout. Incredibly, New York Governor Horatio Seymour promised to stay on the sidelines and not call out the militia once the uprising began. The plan was to set a number of diversionary fires on election day to occupy everyone's attention, while the Treasury building, arsenals, and other federal property were seized. Confederate prisoners in Fort Lafayette would be released simultaneously. The prisoners would be met by Martin and Headley and take up the fight again. Here in the heartland of the North, hundreds of miles from the nearest lines of supply, surrounded by the military might of the Union, these bedraggled, ragtag, half-starved, and ill prisoners were supposed to wage war. It was the stuff of schoolboy dreams.

Before long the word was out. As early as October 21, Benjamin Sweet, the commander of Camp Douglas, had been warned to expect some action around election time. On October 30, Sweet appealed to his commander for more troops. On November 2, Secretary of State Seward sent out the word that "information from the British provinces has been received of a great conspiracy afoot to set fire to the principle cities in the northern states on the day of the presidential election."

In Chicago everything was ready by November 5, and Hines was once again excited by the prospects of triumph. But at the prison camp, Sweet had heard rumours of a gathering of the Sons of Liberty and Confederate agents. He sent off a frantic telegram to the Brigadier General John Cook, in command of the District of Illinois, urging once again that more troops be sent. "My force as you know is too weak to guard between eight and nine thousand soldiers," he said. "I urge that we be reinforced at once."

Sweet employed an ingenious ruse to find the rebels and in the end betray them. He had won the confidence of a Confederate prisoner, Lieutenant John Shanks, who was in charge of the medical dispensary at the camp. Sweet's leverage was a young widow. The woman was a regular camp visitor, and he had encouraged Shanks to become friendly with her. Shanks had fallen in love with her, and she had convinced him the war was lost, the Confederate cause was unworthy, and it was time for him to look to a future that included her. Sweet believed that the woman had persuaded Shanks to change his allegiance to the Union and so sent the officer into the city, allowing him to escape by hiding in the back of a scavengers wagon, covered with camp refuse. Sweet made sure a camp guard followed.

At the Richmond House in Chicago, Shanks found Grenfel, who had registered without an assumed name. He told the British officer he was a loyal Confederate who had just escaped from the camp. Grenfel must have believed him, for he explained how he was to lead a portion of the raiders on an assault of the city, while Hines with the rest would raid the camp. Grenfel also injudiciously told how the commissioners in Canada were financing the campaign. Grenfel arranged to meet Shanks again in a few hours, by which time Shanks had relayed all to Colonel Sweet.

Sweet acted without delay. He launched a series of raids on the leaders of the conspiracy and in one swift action he rounded up Grenfel, Colonel Vincent Marmaduke (another former Morgan raider on the expedition), and a third rebel by the name of Cantrell. Hines escaped, but Sons of Liberty leader Charles Walsh was arrested in his home. Some hours later, Cook's detachment of militia arrived in Chicago and patrolled the streets for the next two days, rounding up 106 people and holding them without charges.

As the Canadians concluded their historic deliberations in Quebec, Colonel Martin and Lieutenant Headley slipped into New York. Martin and his team of eight split up, renting rooms in pairs in hotels while awaiting further orders. Martin and Headley met with James McMasters at the office of his paper, the *Freeman's Journal*; McMasters was to be part of the conspiracy. Headley's first impressions of the man were that he appeared "determined and very able and a true friend. Physically he was large without much flesh. His head was bald in front and he had a large rather Roman nose. Everything about him denotes strength of intellect as well as body." McMasters told them that a sympathetic druggist had arranged to make twelve four-ounce bottles of

Greek Fire, which would start the blazes. Martin and Headley were jubilant at the prospects and for the next few days spent time enjoying themselves, seeing the sights, going to plays, listening to campaign speeches, and spending one evening as dinner guests of the McMasterses.[123]

On November 4, General Benjamin Butler told the papers that ten thousand troops had arrived in the city to guard it until election day. He warned everyone to stay calm, adding that the government had been informed that raids similar to the one at St. Albans were planned for New York.

To the *New York Times*, Butler was the right man for the job. He had "scattered the howling rabble of New Orleans like chaff and reduced that city to order most serene." Nobody would dare try anything in New York.[124]

It was enough to persuade McMasters to call off the attack, true friend of the Confederacy or not. As long as Butler's troops remained in New York, it would be suicidal. Martin and Headley still wanted to go ahead, but since McMasters controlled the main manpower they could do nothing, as Headley observed, "but acquiesce." Darkening their moods the next day were the newspaper accounts of the arrests of Grenfel, Marmaduke, Walsh, and others in Chicago.

Martin and Headley pressed McMasters for a new date, but "the more we insisted the weaker, Mr. McMasters became," Headley wrote. In the end McMasters withdrew all his support and the rebels were left to their own devices. Once again, their well-paid allies had deserted them. So the only thing left to do, as he put it, was to "set the city on fire and give the people a scare if nothing else." And they did.

The little band was encouraged in their arson by the daily reports in the papers of Sherman's victories in Georgia and General Philip Sheridan's scorched earth raids in the Shenandoah Valley of Virginia. It fuelled their desire for revenge, as it had in St. Albans. As one of the New York raiders, Robert Cobb Kennedy, admitted, "We wanted the people of the North to understand that there are two sides to this war and that they can't be rolling in wealth and comfort while we in the South are bearing all the hardships and privations."

141

Headley was given the delicate task of retrieving the Greek Fire from the pharmacist. "I found the place in a basement on the west side of Washington Place," he later wrote. "The heavy-built old man I met there wore a long beard. All I had to do was tell him that Captain Longmuer had sent me for his valise and he handed it on to me without saying a word. I departed in the same silence."

The suitcase was about two feet long and heavy. Headley had to change hands every ten feet just to carry it. He boarded a street-car heading up Bowery Street to Central Park and soon began to smell a peculiar odour.

> It was the a little like rotten eggs and I noticed the passengers were conscious of the same presence. But I sat unconcerned until my getting off place was reached, when I took up the valise and went out. I heard one passenger say: "There must be something dead in that valise." When I lugged it into our cottage, the boys were glad of my safe return. We were now ready to create a sensation in New York.[125]

Butler had withdrawn his troops on November 15, a week after the election, and the plotters set their date for ten days later, November 25. All the leading hotels in the city were to be put to the torch. Headley bought a handful of cheap satchels that the raiders would pass off as their luggage. In the late afternoon of the twenty-fifth they met at the Central Park cottage to launch the raid. Two of the eight lost heart and failed to show. Nevertheless the remaining six divvied up the Greek Fire and set out for their evening's work.

The firebombing began a little after 7:00 p.m., led by Headley at the Astor Hotel. He piled all the furniture he could onto the bed, packed loose newspapers around it, and poured turpentine over that. Leaving the key in the lock lest the explosion force him to make a hasty exit, he uncorked a bottle of the noxious liquid and poured it on the mess on the bed. It burst into flames. He calmly retreated out the door, closed it, walked down the flight of stairs to the desk, left his key, and strolled out into the street.

His next stop was the City Hotel and then the Everest House. He had started on his fourth hotel, the United States, before he heard any alarms. As this last hotel, he received such an ugly look from the clerk that it sent shivers up and down his spine. The work done, Headley took a stroll down Broadway. He wrote:

> It seemed that a hundred bells were ringing, great crowds were gathering on the street and there was general consternation. I concluded to go and see how my fires were doing. The surging crowds were frantic. But the greatest panic was at Barnum's Museum. People were coming out and down the ladders from the second and third floor windows and the manager was crying for help to get his animals out.[126] People were getting hurt running over each other in the stampede. I could not help feel some astonishment for I did not suppose there was a fire there.[127]

Unknown to Headley, Kennedy had fired three hotels and had then wandered into Barnum's with some of his Greek Fire. He later recalled feeling an impulse to "play a huge joke on the Fire Department" and smacked a vial of the liquid on the stair as he would "crack an egg." A spectacular blaze bloomed, and moments later pandemonium broke out. Terrified visitors poured down the stairs, trampling the less able or less fortunate to get to the street, or they smashed windows to climb down fire escapes, with the show's large and small attractions bringing up the rear.[128]

Headley continued down Broadway, crossed over to the North River Wharf, and tossed his last vial of Greek Fire onto a barge carrying baled hay. It burst into a satisfying ball of flame, and he resumed his stroll to catch a streetcar for City Hall.

In all, the rebels started fires in nineteen hotels, most of which were put out in a very short time. But the panic was everywhere. Shortly after 8:00 p.m. there was an alarm at the St. James Hotel, where one of the band had registered as Dr. Schooler and thereafter applied his own prescription to the furnishings in his room.

Some minutes later at the St. Nicholas another alarm was sounded when someone noticed two rooms on the fourth floor ablaze. At half past nine, fire was spotted at the LaFarge. At 10:00 p.m. the Metropolitan was on fire and there one of the team also spread the Greek Fire in the adjoining Metropolitan Theatre. In the panic that followed an innocent bystander was nabbed as the arsonist. When the fire was put out there, the police found a pair of old boots by the bed. They were taken as evidence to the police station, and when dropped on the floor they burst into flames.[129]

On it went until well past midnight and into the early hours, with guests fleeing their rooms in their nightclothes and firefighters and police not knowing where to turn next. Adjoining the LaFarge Hotel stood the Wintergarden Theatre. There the Booth brothers, Edwin, Junius Brutus, and John Wilkes, the third already known to the Confederates in Canada, were appearing together for the first time in a benefit performance of *Julius Caesar*. The two thousand people there were helping raise money for a statue of Shakespeare in Central Park. Fear rippled through the crowd at the sound of the alarm next door, and cries that it would spread to the theatre turned the fear to hysteria. As the crowds surged for the exits, Junius Booth took the stage and assured the house that the fires were under control. The play resumed.

There was the "wildest excitement imaginable," reported the *New York Times* the next morning where crowds had come to view the scene of the previous night's attacks.[130] The word was spread that Confederate raiders were the arsonists, and lynch mob threats echoed in the crowds. By midnight most of the fires had been put out. Some had burned briefly, while other smouldered. The raiders had bungled — by leaving windows and doors closed they had deprived the fires of oxygen. Damage everywhere was slight.

As Headley stepped off his streetcar, he caught sight of a man up ahead and recognized him as Kennedy. He walked up behind him and slapped him on the back. Kennedy, without turning, dropped to one knee and drew a pistol. "I laughed and then he knew me," Headley recalled. "He laughed and said he ought to shoot me for giving him such a scare."

By about 2:00 a.m. the group had split up, finding new lodgings and agreeing to meet later in the morning. By midday, Martin and Headley were eating breakfast at 12th Street and Broadway, reading the papers and shocked to find their little adventure dominating the news. The clerk at the United States Hotel gave a good description of Headley, recalling his empty satchel and the fact that he'd stayed there for two days without eating a meal in the hotel. Other interviews revealed that clerks recognized most of the six members of the party. Headley and Martin spent the rest of the day loafing in Central Park and in the late afternoon decided to pick up their baggage, which had been stored in a piano shop owned by an ally of McMasters. As the streetcar stopped and Martin stepped down, he noticed the storeowner's daughter. "The moment she saw Colonel Martin, she shuddered and putting her palm upward, motioned him away," Headley wrote. "Martin turned instantly, running to overtake our car. I halted it and he came in, looking pale. He sat down without saying a word, but looked casually back."[131]

The evening papers reported that two of the gang had been picked up. Martin and Headley decided it was time to leave, and meeting for one last time at the Central Park cottage, they were delighted that none of the party had been arrested. The papers were wrong.

They found a train leaving for Albany at 11:00 p.m. Two of the men bought tickets on sleepers for the rest of the team. They spotted detectives at the station, but nobody approached them or searched the train. Even so, they slept in their clothes and mapped out an escape route to the rear of the train they need it. At 6:00 a.m. it pulled into Albany, and after catching some rest at local hotels they boarded their connection for Niagara Falls and Toronto. More than a month after they'd left, they pulled into what is now Union Station, crossed the road to the Queen's Hotel, and reported in to Thompson.

Thompson had followed it all in the Canadian press and was exhilarated by the raid's outcome. As he later reported to Benjamin, he had proudly sanctioned the attack in retaliation for federal atrocities in the Deep South. "A most daring raid has been made to fire the city," he wrote. The only disappointment was with the Greek Fire, which had failed virtually every test so far in the campaign, including this one. Thompson assured Benjamin he would never use it again.[132]

Two days later in the middle of an early snowfall, Thompson came to Headley's boarding house to tell him that American detectives had come to the Queen's looking for Headley and Martin. He advised them to lay low. The pair moved to a small cottage in the outlying suburb of Mimico. The others did likewise at various safe houses in the Toronto area. Headley and Martin prepared for the eventuality of capture and hired a local lawyer, John Macdonald, to represent them if needed. Macdonald seemed not at all upset by their larceny. "We rode in a sleigh to his residence," Headley wrote. "He greeted us cordially and we discussed our case fully until a late hour. But it happened that the time never arrived when his services were required."[133]

CHAPTER 15
The Confederation Road Show

"We were much disgusted with the squalid look. The streets were so rough, like dirt roads. I wondered how we could ever live there."
Lady Monck's first impression of Ottawa

The Canadians were meanwhile busy preparing to sell the idea of Confederation to a half-interested electorate. On October 28, the Quebec Conference adjourned and moved on to Montreal, where the city declared the day a public holiday.

It was the beginning of a tour that was part sales pitch and part triumphal procession. It continued for several weeks and impressed upon the Maritimers, if nothing else could, the prevailing excitement in the provinces over the idea of Confederation. Brown had hurried home to Toronto to prepare celebrations there, and Macdonald was chosen to lead the charge during the delegation's stopover in Ottawa. In Montreal, it would be Cartier.

The Montrealers had prepared an elaborate outdoor celebration that included a steeplechase, a military review, fireworks, and a dinner and ball at the St. Lawrence Hall for one thousand people. But the rains continued, accompanied by blustery gale-force winds from the east. As the delegates moved west, it pounded down on their train windows, which rattled with its driving force. In the end, much to the disappointment of the Montrealers, it was all called off but for the ball, immune to the vagaries of the weather and a fitting honour for the occasion.

St. Lawrence Hall was the main meeting place of Confederates in Montreal.

Courtesy of the National Archives of Canada

By half past eight long lines of carriages, black and gleaming under the yellow gas lamps, were moving slowly down Craig Street towards the hotel portico. Once there, the Montrealers moved inside, anxious to dance and to meet with and talk to their guests about the conference, Confederation, and the future of a great new nation.[134]

The surroundings themselves couldn't have been grander. The hotel was considered by many to be British North America's finest. The Hall, as it was known, was situated in the heart of the old city, near the magnificent Notre Dame Cathedral and the wide-open square of the Champ de Mars, chief parade ground of the British garrison. It was close to the financial centre of the city, near its theatres and its best restaurants, and not far from the mile-long sprawl of

Montreal's dockland. It stood some five storeys high, with a mansard roof and a facade that stretched the length of an entire city block, on this night protecting the guests and their finery from the rain.

The hotel boasted a huge ballroom, two dining rooms, a telegraph office, a reading room, and a circulating library. On the ground floor there was a post office, a barbershop, a saloon, and two newsstands carrying the latest American and European papers. Past that, a sweeping staircase rose to a high-ceilinged salon with a piano in its centre and anterooms where guests received visitors. Past that was the main dining room, with its wide corridors and elaborate gilt mouldings, the crystal pendants of the chandelier flashing in the gaslight. Beyond that was the ballroom.

The party lasted well into the next morning, with the last of the revellers departing at two o'clock in the morning for their beds. But by mid-morning the delegates were back at work for their last official session. The delegates pored over the proofs of the seventy-two resolutions that had been printed in Quebec on Friday and brought up to Montreal on the night train. They were revised and corrected, and three supplementary resolutions were passed, the last of which was to ask the Queen to name the new nation. After the briefest of intermissions came luncheon, the *dejeuner* so famous at the St. Lawrence. It was a majestic process of consumption, stretching out over six hours of eating, drinking, and speechmaking. Here in Montreal, and later in Ottawa and Toronto, these lavish affairs followed a precise and carefully arranged pattern. The Maritime delegates were toasted by the Canadians. Members from all three Maritime provinces would rise, thank their hosts, and discuss once more the merits of Confederation. At some point, usually towards the end, the chairman would propose a toast to the Canadian cabinet, and then a senior minister would launch into his views of the greatness of the union to come. It was an utterly effective public relations campaign, feeding the public's need for as much information about the scheme as they could find. A good deal of detail had already appeared in the papers, but the public seemed to have an insatiable appetite for more.

By most recollections the speeches at that Montreal luncheon were magnificent, the honeyed rhetoric flowing easily and grandly from the lips of speakers like McGee and Brown. The *Montreal Gazette* had four stenographers there to catch their words. It is hard to say how these men took hold of their audience that day, because the subtle and silent things that move people — gestures, tones, delivery — can never be captured on a piece of newsprint. Even the *Gazette* remarked that the most surprising thing of all was that the pettiness of thought, action, and attitude, which had prevailed among politicians of all stripes for so long, was gone. "These men, all bred in small communities and raised to positions of influence amid the contests of petty jarring factions, spoke as they acted at Quebec with a patriotism that warmed one's heart to witness," the paper reported.[135]

Each took his turn at describing this noble destiny: Whelan was followed by the voluble Cartier, New Brunswick's John Hamilton Gray, and then D'Arcy McGee. McGee was not on the list as part of the program, but the crowd demanded him and took up a chant of "McGee, McGee!" Finally, the curly-haired Irishman got to his feet and, without notes, gave a magnificent address. He dealt not with what they had done, but why they had done it, a sweeping summation of those rainy weeks when the thirty-three men had cloistered themselves in the legislative library, not intending to invent some new system of government, but to consult in reverent spirit "the oracles of the history of their race ... to build upon the old foundation, a piece of solid British masonry, which would bear the whole force of democratic winds and waves and resist the effect of our corroding political atmosphere, consolidate our interests and prove the legitimacy of our origin." When it was over and he sat down, everyone else rose to their feet and cheered.

After a day's rest, the visitors were up early and on the road for a visit to the new capital at Ottawa. The rain had stopped, but it was still cloudy and cool as the steamer carried them up the Ottawa River. Yet even though the hour was late and the weather brisk, they received a welcome from the citizens worthy of a conquering army. They were met by hundreds of people with torches who followed their procession to the Russell Hotel. As William Henry, Attorney General of Nova Scotia, remarked the next day, "We were received like conquerors, like warriors returning home from a great victory..."[136]

The next morning the boat took them on a sightseeing visit past the unfinished parliament buildings, rising in their Gothic splendour in the center of the town. The only room in the central block large enough for lunch, and with a roof, was the Picture Gallery, and it was there that they were feted on that November first.

The excitement that the delegates felt about the visit to their new national capital was not shared by Lady Monck, who, in a vice-regal party including British ambassador to Washington Lord Lyons, had visited the city just three weeks earlier. Arriving in the same torrential rain that blanketed the Quebec Conference, the party was shepherded to the Russell House, which Lady Monck described as "clean, but third rate" with food that "looked and tasted uncivilized." Of the city itself: "We were much disgusted with the squalid look, though we only saw it by lamp-light which was scarcely any light, such wretched gas. The streets were so rough, like dirt roads. I wondered how we could ever live there."

But even Lady Monck conceded that the legislative buildings "will be very magnificent," built as they were of grey stone with a good deal of pink mixed in, the architecture sort of French Gothic.[137]

On November 2, early in the morning, the delegates moved by train to Kingston. John A. slipped quietly away for home. The train moved on, stopping in Belleville, briefly again at Cobourg, and after that nonstop to Toronto, which it reached at a little after 10:00 p.m. It was dark, it was cold, it was late, but the reception that awaited the delegates there overwhelmed them. It went beyond anything in Montreal and anything they could have hoped for or dreamed of. It was breathtaking.

The crowd overflowed the station platform. In fact they jammed the station and its approaches. York Street, Front Street, and a large part of the Esplanade were thronged with people. The delegates were greeted with cheer after cheer; they could barely make their way to their carriages, and once there the carriages could hardly move. In the air all around them was an explosion of fireworks, roman candles, and falling rockets, and the chords of pipe and drum were heard as the band of the Queen's Own, the 10th Royals, welcomed the delegates. Behind them were three hundred members of the fire department carrying torches. For those staying at the Queen's Hotel, it was only across the street, but it took half an hour or more to get there. The crowd waited. "Speech," they cried.

Shortly, on the balcony of one of the first floor, one figure emerged, and then more. It was George Brown, who was leading Tupper, Tilley, Gray, and others out. It was then that they could see the full force of the demonstration below them. The shower of fireworks, the shimmering flames of the torches, and the thousands of faces looking up, waiting, eager, expectant. It was the culmination of the tour. In the distance was Charlottetown, the mid-summer meeting so informal and effective. Then Quebec and drafting the words of Confederation. But in Montreal, and now here in Toronto, were the people whom it would all affect, whose faith and determination would be the mortar of a new nation's foundation.

The cry for a speech became deafening and irresistible. First was Tilley, who pointedly thanked his "fellow countrymen" for their welcome; next came Whelan, with his words about the great national future before them. Then Tupper stepped forward. This great union would provide strength to meet and withstand the incredible military transformation of the United States. Brown proclaimed a new commercial and political renaissance for Toronto, as the capital of the new province of Ontario. The crowd was silent, faces upturned, listening carefully to the words. The speeches were short, with Brown's the last. He closed it quickly and effectively, by leading three rousing cheers for the Queen.[138]

CHAPTER 16
John Wilkes Booth

"Abe's contract is near up and whether re-elected or not, he will get his goose cooked."
> John Wilkes Booth, in a Montreal bar
> October 1864

On the morning of October 18, the day before the St. Albans Raid, while the Fathers of Confederation were hard at work in Quebec, a brooding and intense twenty-six-year-old Shakespearean actor named John Wilkes Booth, a zealous believer in the Southern cause and a man who already had murder on his mind, checked into the St. Lawrence Hall in Montreal.

Historians have speculated for more than a century on the connection between Abraham Lincoln's assassin and the Confederates in Canada. At the trial of the conspirators in 1865 there was no conclusive proof that any of the Commissioners in Canada were linked to the crime of that century. Attempts to link Confederate president Jefferson Davis to the assassination also failed.

Yet for eight days in October 1864, and again briefly in January 1865, Booth was in Montreal, where he met Confederate agents. The city was a haven to hundreds of Confederates who were well received and popular. Some were wealthy enough to live in rented homes with their families, others in hotels, like the St. Lawrence Hall or Donegana's. The less fortunate flopped in rooming houses. There were escaped prisoners of war, refugees, and official agents of their government like Thompson, Clay, and Holcombe.

How many of these people met Booth and why will never be known. Perhaps the visits were only the courtesy calls of fellow travellers in a foreign land. Maybe Booth, who was known to have been involved in clandestine Confederate secret service, was passing on a message or planning to take one back to the South. Possibly, he was arranging to smuggle badly needed drugs back through the blockade, something that a handful of Thompson's agents could easily have arranged. Or maybe the conversations turned on pleasantries, including Booth's recent theatrical performances, his scheduled readings in

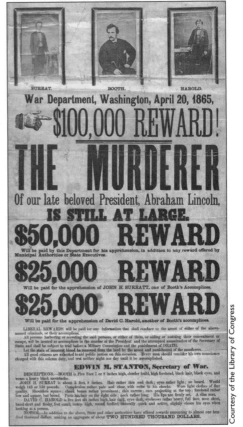

War Department, Washington, April 20, 1865,

$100,000 REWARD!

THE MURDERER

Of our late beloved President, Abraham Lincoln,

IS STILL AT LARGE.

$50,000 REWARD

Will be paid by this Department for his apprehension, in addition to any reward offered by Municipal Authorities or State Executives.

$25,000 REWARD

Will be paid for the apprehension of JOHN H. SURRATT, one of Booth's Accomplices.

$25,000 REWARD

Will be paid for the apprehension of David C. Harold, another of Booth's accomplices.

EDWIN M. STANTON, Secretary of War.

Courtesy of the Library of Congress

In the fall of 1864, John Wilkes Booth was a frequent visitor to Montreal, where he was renowned as a Shakespearean actor.

Montreal, and plans for a November appearance in New York.

On October 14, four days before Booth arrived, both were in Quebec, hoping to gain an audience with Monck. But Monck, deeply disturbed by the raids on Johnson's Island and a misguided bank robbery in Calais, Maine, refused to see them. Clay wrote to Beverly Tucker in St. Catharines that the visit was waste of time, "a fool's errand," and both he and Thompson had been snubbed and humiliated. "Not a call or a card in response to ours," he sniffed. "We will leave here sadder and wiser tomorrow." He regretted following George Sanders' advice to go to Quebec, adding, "Jake is even more mortified and disappointed than I am."[139]

Both would pass through Montreal on the way to their respective residences in Toronto and St. Catharines. Clay was back in St. Catharines on October 19, and Thompson was in Toronto on October 21. Thus for six days, Thompson's whereabouts are unknown. If he met Booth in Montreal, they didn't rendezvous at the St. Lawrence Hall. They would have been noticed, because the hotel was under constant surveillance by the detectives of Union General Lafayette C. Baker's secret police.

Booth stayed in Montreal for ten days, leaving just as the Canadian and Maritime delegates arrived on the first leg of their post-Quebec road trip. Perhaps they even passed each other in the lobby of the hotel. By all accounts, Booth electrified Montreal audiences with his reading of Shakespeare's *Merchant of Venice* and Tennyson's "Charge of the Light Brigade" at Corby's Hall. It was over a game of billiards in the hotel's saloon that Booth told a fellow guest that the outcome of the November presidential election didn't matter, "For Abe's contract was near up and whether re-elected or not, he would get his goose cooked." The guest wrote a letter to the *Hamilton Times* relating the conversation shortly after Lincoln's death; the letter was reprinted in the *New York Times* on May 15, 1865. Unfortunately for Thompson, while there is no proof that he and Booth met in Montreal, many made the assumption that they did. It forced Thompson to flee to Europe soon after the assassination, fearing his arrest as an accomplice in the affair.

John Wilkes Booth was born in 1838 on his family's farm in Bel Air, Maryland, a town about twenty-five miles northeast of Baltimore, the ninth of ten children. His father was the famous actor Junius Brutus Booth, a man of passion and compassion, a man who left one family in England to form another one in America, drank too hard and too often, and appeared at some times to be quite mad. He was periodically overcome with black moods of despair and heavy drinking.[140] In the fall of 1852, Junius Booth died while on tour.

The younger Booth, John Wilkes, was an indifferent student, but excelled at sports.[141] He was a fine swordsman and a dead shot on foot or on horseback. Temperamentally, he was at times his father's son, melancholy and moody and usually able to get his way with the women of the house. Later in life, he would draw female company to him, but he never formed lasting relationships. In one of the many tragi-comedic episodes of his short life, one lover tried to kill him in his sleep during a tour of Albany, New York, in 1861. She managed to inflict a small flesh wound on his face, before falling on the dagger herself. In the best acting tradition, she too was barely wounded.

By the age of seventeen he had begun his acting career. Booth's first successes were in Southern cities, but as the South moved towards secession, Booth spread his wings and went North. One reviewer saw Booth's style as "raw, crude and much given to boisterous declamations." A critic from the *Baltimore Sun* called him the "Gymnastic Actor." At one time he accidentally knocked a fellow actor into the orchestra pit and overzealously slashed another during a mock duel. Booth jumped over scenery, leaped off balconies, and displayed an energy yet another observer called a natural "dashing buoyancy."[142]

By the outbreak of war, Booth was a diehard secessionist and a member of the Knights of the Golden Circle, a Copperhead group. He was fascinated by the audacity of John Brown's raid on Harper's Ferry, Virginia, in October 1859, in which Brown hoped to trigger a slave uprising. It fired Booth's imagination.

Two and a half weeks after the raid, a regiment of Virginia Militia was ordered to stand guard duty pending Brown's execution. Booth temporarily deserted his acting company and appears to have borrowed part of a uniform and conned his way aboard the train even though he wasn't a member of the unit. When he arrived at Harper's Ferry he was given duties and allowed to remain. The execution was a moment he savoured.[143]

By the war's third year, Boothe had played throughout the North, in Boston, New York, Philadelphia, Cincinnati, and St. Louis. He was usually advertised as "J. Wilkes Booth, tragedian," which meant that Shakespeare was a large part of his repertoire. Booth was drawn into Confederate secret service, in part to gather

John Wilkes Booth despised John Brown and Brown's cause of freeing slaves.

intelligence about Northern morale and attitudes to the war, but also to run much-needed drugs to the South. His ability to move in and out of northern cities and his access to society and men of power made him a natural spy.

In August 1864, as Captain Charles Cole was organizing the Johnson's Island raid, Booth was not far away. He was in Meadville, Pennsylvania, which authorities argued later was the first clue of his intention to assassinate Lincoln. At the McHenry House, someone had used a diamond to cut an inscription into the windowpane of Room 22. It said: "Abe Lincoln Departed this Life August 13 1864 By the Effect of Poison." At the trial of the Lincoln conspirators, the windowpane was carefully cut out, a piece of velvet placed behind it, and the whole thing mounted on a wooden frame. Booth's hotel signature in the registry book was cut out and placed on the glass under the inscription. Experts testified it was in the same hand.[144]

In July, Booth was in Boston and made his first Canadian connection. Godfrey Hyams, Thompson's courier and a double agent, had been sent to Boston as part of a plot devised by Dr. Luke Blackburn, who believed that in the face of the total war being waged by the Union, the South should retaliate in kind. In what became known as the Yellow Fever Plot, Blackburn infected clothes with the disease and shipped the trunks to Boston and other Northern points, where Hyams was to collect them and deliver them to Union hospitals as a deadly act of charity. At the last minute Hyams had a crisis of confidence and refused to deliver the trunks.[145] But Hyams met Booth there, and a check of hotel registers found that Booth had stayed at the Parker House in Boston along with Hyams, a man registered as H.V. Clinton, and two others giving false names and Canada as their address. "H.V. Clinton" was also registered at the St. Lawrence Hall in May and August. The Hall by then had become a rendezvous for Confederate agents.

In August, Booth found two recruits to "his enterprise," as he called it: Samuel Arnold and Michael O'Laughlin, two former schoolmates, both discharged from the Confederate Army. The trio devised a plan to capture or kidnap the president in Washington, spirit him south to Virginia, and then exchange him for enough Confederate prisoners to win the war.

At 9.30 p.m. on Tuesday, October 18, as Bennett Young and his men spent an uneasy night in St. Albans, Vermont, Booth checked into the St. Lawrence Hall. Dr. Blackburn registered a few lines below him. Booth had lined up his appearances and readings and planned to leave Montreal on October 28. In and around his performances, there were important details to attend to, last-minute arrangements for his trip to Washington, and of course personal and social obligations to fulfill. He visited a photographic studio and stood at stiff Victorian attention wearing his foxskin cap. The day before his departure, he opened an account at the new Italian-style Bank of Ontario on Place D'Armes, where the spacious banking hall was backlit by three huge Venetian windows and the bank manager lived on the top three stories of the building.

This was the Confederate bank in Canada, where Thompson's small fortune, exceeding $400,000, was held for safekeeping. The teller, Robert Anson Campbell, recognized Booth. It was a moment he wouldn't forget. An actor of Booth's calibre didn't walk into his bank every day. Booth took out a roll of bills and cheques worth $455, and once the formalities were complete he was handed a passbook. Booth told Campbell he planned to run the blockade and asked whether the money order issued in pounds could be used by anyone else should he be captured. Campbell said not unless he signed it first. Booth seemed satisfied and took a sterling bill for $300, which came to 61 pounds and some odd shillings.[146]

In Montreal, Booth did meet Patrick Charles Martin, a New York native. An 1862 letter in Federal War Department files recommended that the government end any dealings with Martin because he was "an uncompromising rebel." Another unconfirmed report said he was forced to leave Baltimore in a hurry because of an act of piracy on Chesapeake Bay.

Martin arrived in Montreal in the late summer of 1862 and set up a business brokering contraband goods for shipment to the South via Halifax. He chartered vessels at Montreal that took the goods to Halifax, where they were transshipped onto blockade-runners that continued on to Wilmington or Charleston.

Booth arranged with Martin to ship his trunks and wardrobe. Martin's chartered vessel, the seventy-three-foot *Marie Victoria*, left Montreal in mid-November. Some days later, the ship foundered in a storm in the Gulf of St. Lawrence and ran aground near Bic, Quebec. It is believed all hands were lost, including Martin. The ship was salvaged in the spring of 1865 and among the goods was the theatrical wardrobe of John Wilkes Booth: silks, velvet, ermine, plumes, caps, mounted swords, and pistols. It was all sold for $500.[147]

But Martin and Booth had more to talk about. Martin had been given, by a group of Southern planters, the task of kidnapping the President, and it is here that the two plans might have become one. It may also explain Booth's meeting with the Canadians in Boston in July and why he arranged to have a reason to come to Montreal — a combination of business and pleasure. And Martin, who had come from southern Maryland, had contacts in the Confederate underground and an intimate knowledge of the many coves and inlets where the kidnappers could hide the President and then spirit him across the Potomac River. He gave Booth a letter of introduction to William Queen, an elderly doctor who lived on the edge of the Zekiah Swamp in southern Maryland. The hope was that Queen would help Booth by organizing escape routes through the swamp and manpower to move the President along a pipeline.

In Montreal, Booth was also known to have met George Sanders. They had a common hatred of Lincoln, a love of Republican government, and a devotion to the Southern cause. Sanders was also very bitter. His son, Captain Reid Sanders, who had spent part of the summer in St. Catharines, was captured on his return trip and imprisoned at Fort Warren, near Boston, where he died that fall.

In the meantime, Booth let slip the few drunken words that later led American authorities to believe that Confederates in Canada had a part in the killing of the President. One night after drinking more than usual, Booth went down to the billiard room and was soon playing pool with another guest. His remarks would only make sense six months later. His opponent was good and had made a run on the table. It prompted Booth to say, "Do you know, I have the sharpest play laid out ever done in America. I can bag the biggest game this side of ... just remember my address ... you'll hear of a double carom one of these days."

The conversation turned back to the game and then the upcoming presidential election. "It makes little difference head or tail," he said. "Abe's contract is near up and whether re-elected or not, he will get his goose cooked." Then, relaxing slightly, he said: "I like your Canadian style. I must post myself in Canuck airs for some of us may have to settle here shortly."[148]

By early November, Booth was back in Washington, staying at the National Hotel. He carefully watched the President, observing in particular his theatre-going habits. It was an easy thing for Booth to do. He was well known at the theatres in the city, and Ford's, where the assassination would take place, was one place where he directed his mail. He knew every entry and exit, every door, every hall, and every lobby. He came and went as he pleased. That month he is also known to have made repeated rides on horseback south of Washington, studying the roads and paths that he might use as an escape route.

He sent a letter to his sister Asia, which included some stock and oil certificates. The letter in part referred to a plan for making "a prisoner of this man, to whom the South owes so much misery." The letter talked in general terms of a mastermind controlling a band of schemers. It referred to the cabal Booth had now collected and who lived at a boarding house in Washington on H Street between Sixth and Seventh. They included a twenty-year-old drug-store clerk named David E. Herrold, a carriage maker from Port Tobacco, Virginia, named George Atzerodt, and a tall, broad-shoul-dered, twenty-year-old giant and veteran of three years of war named Lewis Paine.

When Booth found Paine, he was penniless, in rags, and beg-ging for food. Booth fed him, clothed him, gave him somewhere to sleep, and brought him into the conspiracy. Months later, while Booth was slipping into President Lincoln's box at Ford's Theatre, Paine was breaking into the home of Secretary of State William Seward, who was bedridden and recovering from a fall that had broken his leg. He would stab five people, including Seward, who missed a fatal wound by inches.

The crew filled the boarding house of Mary Surratt, whose son John, a tall, sandy-haired youth of twenty, was a Confederate couri-er known to Jacob Thompson in Canada. John Surratt brought into this group Louis Weichmann, a school chum with a clerk's job in the federal bureaucracy.

While Surratt's mother would hang for her part in sheltering the Lincoln assassins, John Surratt would flee to Canada, begin-ning a two-year odyssey that saw him hidden in the Canadian bush by sympathetic French Canadian priests, smuggled to Europe, and later enlisted in the Papal Guards in Rome. He was captured in Italy by American authorities and brought home in chains for a trial, which vindicated him.

In 1870, Surratt gave a lecture in Rockville, Maryland, on the Lincoln conspiracy and assassination. The speech shed some light on Booth's movements soon after he left Montreal. Surratt claimed to have met Booth sometime in the fall of 1864. Booth knew that Surratt worked as a courier and wanted to know the best routes in and out of the city to the Potomac. Surratt knew them all. He had ridden them with dispatches hidden in his boots, sewn into the lining of his clothes, or in between planks in his buggy. He says Booth tried to pump him for information, while not revealing any-thing of his own plan. It aroused Surratt's suspicion. They met several times and finally Surratt said if Booth didn't explain what he wanted and why he wouldn't help.

"Well, sir, what is your proposition?" Surratt asked. He explained:

> He [Booth] sat quiet for an instant and then before answering me, arose, looked under the bed, into the wardrobe, in the doorway and the passage, and then said: "We have to be careful, the walls have ears." He then drew his chair close to me and in a whisper said: "It is to kidnap President Lincoln and carry him off to Richmond." I confess I stood aghast at the proposition and looked upon it as a foolhardy undertaking. To think of successfully seizing the Mr. Lincoln in the capital of the United States surrounded by thousands of his soldiers and carrying him off to Richmond, looked to me like a foolish idea. I told him as much.

But as Booth outlined the minutest details of his plan, Surratt recalled feeling "amazed, thunderstruck at the unparalleled audacity of this scheme." And so he joined the group.

Some months later they got their chance. They learned on short notice that Lincoln would be visiting a downtown hospital. The team moved quickly to the location and readied for action, only to be disappointed to learn that at the last minute Lincoln had been replaced by Secretary of the Treasury Salmon Chase. They called it off.

Soon after, Surratt left Washington for Richmond, where in the dying hours of the war he met Confederate Secretary of State Judah Benjamin, who gave him dispatches and $200 in gold as travel money and told him to deliver the papers to Jacob Thompson. Surratt arrived in Montreal on April 6 and registered at the St. Lawrence Hall. His name again appears in the register on April 18. The register notes that Surratt arrived from New York on the midday train. He said he had nothing more to do with Booth.[149]

The links between Booth and the Confederates in Canada don't stop there. It was discovered some months after the trial of the conspirators that Colonel Robert Martin, Lieutenant Headley's commander during the firebombing of New York, met Booth and knew well in advance of the plans to kidnap Lincoln. If Martin knew, presumably so did Headley and so did Thompson. This all came to light in October 1865, when Martin was arrested in Kentucky and taken to a military prison where he was put in the same cell as two Union soldiers. Martin bragged about a handful of exploits, including the raid on New York and the fact that he knew of a plan to kidnap Lincoln.

The prisoners informed the commandant, gave sworn statements of what they had heard, and Martin was moved to New York to await a trial. It dragged on inconclusively, and he was finally pardoned in 1866. What it does prove is that Booth was well known to the Confederates in Canada and involved some of them in his plot to kidnap, if not assassinate, President Lincoln. It might also explain the enthusiasm for Thompson's final, desperate act of war in March 1865, which was a no less audacious plot to kidnap Vice-President Andrew Johnson.

In the meantime, the Confederate commissioner had other things to think about. The trial of the St. Alban's raiders was set to resume, and they needed his financial and moral support. Thompson was also still wedded to the belief that Confederate prisoners of war could be freed from Northern camps and used as a foraging army to wreak havoc behind Union lines. This theory would persuade Thompson to turn to a train in Buffalo as a means to this dubious end. And for Booth there were still some months to go before his act of madness and revenge changed the course of history.

CHAPTER 17
That Stupid Judge

"When the dinner was nearly over, the G.G. was mysteriously called out. Soon he came back. That stupid Judge in Montreal had ... let out the raiders and they were at liberty to scamper about the country and attack the Yankees."
Lady Monck in her diary

The morning after their triumphal reception at the Queen's Hotel, the delegates were treated to a welcome not seen since the 1860 visit by the Prince of Wales. Flags hung from lampposts on King Street, Yonge Street, and as far north as Queen Street. Banners, buntings, and streamers draped storefronts and awnings. The visitors were met by a cavalcade of carriages, which ferried them first north to Upper Canada College, where headmaster George Cockburn waited to show them the raw material to be moulded into the next generation of Canada's ruling elite. The procession turned next to the law school at Osgoode Hall, then to the University of Toronto, followed by the Toronto Normal School, where Egerton Ryerson, who dreamed of a province-wide system of standard education, waited with more good wishes and words. A brief stop at the Queen's and then another of the famous lunches, this time at Toronto's Music Hall. The Hall, like the rest of the city, had been carefully prepared. Huge silk Union Jacks draped the walls, and behind the podium was a portrait of the Queen. Mirrors had been strategically placed in the arched recesses of the room to give the illusion of more space and people.

Hanging from the gallery in gothic letters were the names of all the British Canadian colonies.

It began at 2:00 p.m. with the delegates piped in by the band of the 16th Regiment and ended at 7:00 p.m. after an afternoon of food, fine wine, and expansive speeches. The delegates explained the merits of the great Confederation that lay ahead, with the keynote address saved for Brown. After all, it was his city, the source of his political power and the locus of his aspirations for the future.

Brown ranged over the ground with eloquence as he described the structure of the new government, the division of powers between Ottawa and the provinces, and how it would all be financed. He covered the major steps it would need, including the completion of the Intercolonial Railway, something he had long opposed, but now saw as necessary to tie the new nation together. Furthermore, the rail system would have to be expanded into the wilderness of the North West, a largely empty territory stretching from Northern Ontario to the Rocky Mountains and British Columbia. This was vital to keep this Canadian space from the orbit of the expanding Union.

This American menace was part of a related matter, and that was defence. The delegates at Quebec had unanimously decided that the united provinces should address this always-troubling issue as quickly as possible. Brown didn't believe the Americans would invade — "I cannot doubt they have plenty of work on their hands for years to come," he said. "I have faith in the good sense and good feelings of our neighbors." But one could never be sure. Canadians had to be prepared.[150]

He continued, "I speak for every man in Upper Canada when I say that the first hostile foot placed upon our shores would be the signal and the summons for every man to meet the enemy on the threshold of our country."

"Hear, hear," roared the crowd.

His fellow countrymen would show the same mettle now that they had shown in arming themselves against the Yankee invaders in 1812. Northerners must be made to believe that Canada was strong and resolute. While the Northern press concluded their powerful armies could overcome the provinces, Brown and the other delegates knew differently. That is why the issue of defence and ensuring it was of paramount concern to his government.

Beyond the threat of invasion, if Canada wished to take its place among the nations, it could no longer depend on Britain for protection, or expect Britain to pay while Canada looked on. It was a matter of pride. No more, no less. Among the responsibilities of a new nation was to put itself in "such a position of defence that we may fearlessly look our enemies in the face," Brown said.

Brown's paper, the *Globe*, covered every word, devoting the entire front page and more inside to the delegate's every move and word. Other papers picked most of it up. As Brown wrote to Anne in Scotland somewhat immodestly: "They say it was the best I ever made."[151]

That next morning, some of the delegates moved on to Niagara Falls and the last leg of the tour. Brown returned to Quebec, where the cabinet was meeting to discuss a highly important document prepared by Lieutenant Colonel William Jervois, who had been sent out by the Colonial Office for the second time in three years to report on strategies to defend the colonies. It was a problem that taxed the Imperial authorities and always boiled down to the same thing: British naval superiority could defend coastal cities in the Maritimes and possibly Quebec and Montreal, but the rest of the country was virtually impossible to defend. The best option was a series of key fortifications, supported by gunboats on the lakes, which might enable a small force to resist a huge army, at least until reinforcements could arrive. The strategic price to be paid was abandoning most of Canada West to an invading force. The document called for a militia of 110,000 men and huge fortifications at Quebec, Montreal, and Kingston. The financial cost of this containment plan was still staggering — £1.75 million.

The Canadian cabinet went to work preparing their recommendations for the Colonial Office. The problem seemed overwhelming. On the one hand the fact that the Canadas were already carrying a large debt, and were adding more to it, was unlikely to push public support for Confederation their way. Yet in the wake of the St.

Albans Raid, tensions with the Americans had reached their most worrisome since the Trent Affair. The same edition of the *Globe* that covered the delegates' visit to Toronto also carried a story about the continuing alarm along the frontier. The good citizens of Ogdensburg, New York, turned the arrival of a few hunters on the islands at the head of Lake Ontario into a new Confederate invasion force. Militia patrolled the streets, and grain merchants were busy shipping their stores east and west for safekeeping in case the town was plundered like St. Albans. In the face of this inflamed Northern anxiety it would be difficult indeed to sell Confederation to the Imperial authorities without providing a strategy for Canadian defence of its soil.[152]

The task fell to Brown. He had been selected to go to London and meet with the Colonial Office and the Prime Minister. After long debate, the cabinet decided on a two-pronged strategy that was practical and subtly persuasive. The costs of defence would be shared until Confederation took place. The colonists would show their willingness to pay — something that always rankled the authorities in London — and at the same time give the Colonial Office good reason to approve their plan, if only to rid themselves of the problem. In the meantime, as a gesture, the Canadians agreed to spend $2 million fortifying Montreal, if Britain would do likewise at Quebec and supply the arms for both cities. The cabinet would also vote to spend another $1 million on the militia in the next parliamentary session.

On November 15, as Colonel Martin and Lieutenant Headley passed the time sightseeing in New York, Brown and Colonel Jervois arrived in the city. The next day, they boarded the *Persia* bound for Liverpool. Eleven days later, Brown was reunited with his wife, Anne, in Edinburgh in time for their second wedding anniversary. They spent a week together before Brown's official business took him to London and pivotal interviews with the British government.

On Saturday, December 3, Brown met with Colonial Secretary Edward Cardwell, who had already read in Monck's November dispatch the details of the Confederation plan. Cardwell kept Brown for the full day, going over the minutest details. He gave his approval. Brown was elated.

Writing to Anne on December 5, he described Cardwell's attitude as "a most gracious answer to our scheme. It outdoes anything that ever went to any British colony — praises our statesmanlike discretion, loyalty and so on." The Colonial Office would be happy to back the plan for union, for as the colonists had hoped, it offered the Imperial government two solutions to the problem of defence. Unity brought strength of numbers and also a commitment to shift the burden away from the mother country.

Brown turned to the most admired British politician of the Victorian Age, William Gladstone, to settle the last remaining question, the issue of the vast North West territory, which belonged to the Hudson's Bay Company. On December 6 he met with Gladstone, whom he described as "the ablest man in England." He told Anne that their ninety-minute discussion went well and Gladstone agreed with the colonists' strategy of westward expansion, with its two related planks of settlement and containment of American expansion. Brown was in awe of Gladstone and a little surprised that he was not the intellectual giant he had expected. "He did not by any means drag me out of my depth," Brown wrote.[153]

Thereafter it was a continuous round of meetings with undersecretaries and other members of the bureaucracy. There were more meetings at the War Office and with members of cabinet. They wanted to hear that Confederate operations in Canada were being contained and how it was affecting relations with the Americans.

In the end the talks were inconclusive. The government would decide on the defence proposal in January. On the subject of the Hudson's Bay territories, the government had been negotiating with the company for the better part of a year, laying the framework for a financial settlement that would turn more than a third of the continent over to a future Canadian government. The Company didn't oppose the plan, or the idea of a transcontinental railway linking east with west; the issue was how much it would be paid in compensation. The Company's governor was well known to Brown. He was none other then Sir Edmund Head, who had been Monck's predecessor as Governor General of Canada.

But Head was no soft touch, and his latest proposal called for the sale of all the lands for £1 million. The colonists argued that the territory belonged to Canada by right of the original French possession of New France. The subsequent claim by the Company and the charter granted to it by the British Crown were therefore invalid. What it all boiled down to was that Canada wanted the West but didn't want to pay, while the Hudson's Bay Company stood behind its title and wanted compensation to give it up. The British government was the mediator, arguing neither side and not interested in paying for any of it.

Brown tried to lean on colonial authorities for support, shrewdly claiming that the Hudson's Bay Company had no right to sell Crown land it did not own for an exorbitant price and that the British government should put an end to such a pretence. Furthermore, it was enormously unfair to ask Canadians to pay for a monopoly they hadn't created nor recognized. In exchange for British support to break open the Company's hold on the North West, a Canadian government would agree to encourage settlements, roads, railways, and telegraph links and so serve Imperial geopolitical ends on the continent. Again there was no firm answer, but at last the cards were on the table.

Brown's official business was finished by mid-December, but he was much in demand as a dinner guest. He dined with Colonel Jervois and partied with Colonial Secretary Cardwell and Attorney-General Sir Roundell Palmer. MP John Bright, the statesman and Victorian radical, offered another dinner, and noted economist and free trader Richard Cobden invited Brown to his home at Midhurst. The crowning engagement of the trip was a weekend with Prime Minister Lord Palmerston at his home, Broadlands.

Just before Christmas, Brown was back in Edinburgh with his family, with less than two weeks left before their departure for Canada. There the pressing issue was a full debate on Confederation awaiting the legislature when it was recalled in mid-January. On New Year's Eve 1865, the Browns left Liverpool aboard the *China*, arriving thirteen days later at New York. The next night they were comfortably back in Toronto.

If Brown rightly felt he achieved a great deal by his visit to the Imperial government, he returned to a heightening of the crisis created by the St. Albans raid. On December 13, as he wrapped up his official business in England, a Montreal judge dismissed the case against the raiders. The decision angered the Americans and utterly dismayed the Canadian government. While some of the raiders had been rearrested, the bulk of the loot stolen from the banks had gone missing, handed over to the raiders by the Chief of Police, Guillaume Lamothe. It would cost the judge and police chief their jobs.[154]

The Montreal courtroom was hushed and filled to capacity that morning as prosecution and defence took their seats. The trial of Bennett Young and his band was resuming after the three-week delay to allow a courier to be sent to Richmond for proof of their army commissions. Rumour had it the courier had not returned.

The lawyers acting for the United States and State of Vermont believed it all to be a simple matter. They hoped to prove that the raiders were common thieves and therefore subject to extradition. The men on trial contended they were soldiers engaged in an act of war and though they had escaped to Canada they had not broken any Canadian laws.

All rose while Judge Charles Coursol entered and sat down. Defence lawyer William Kerr stood immediately on behalf of the prisoners and challenged Coursol's right to hear the case, arguing that because the law under which they were being charged had not received Royal assent, he could not try them. Kerr maintained the raiders could only be arrested on a warrant issued by the Governor General and not by a local magistrate, which Coursol was.[155]

John Devlin, acting for the Americans, said that was nonsense. After a delay of more than month, the court had reconvened to hear evidence, not legal arguments. Coursol paused and then observed that Kerr had raised "knotty questions" and adjourned the court until 2:00 p.m., when he would announce his decision.

A rumour began spreading through the courtroom that the raiders might be released. It built throughout the intervening hours and brought a huge crowd to the court. Coursol returned at 3:00 p.m. and began reading a lengthy decision.

The Americans were astonished. They couldn't believe that Coursol, having only heard these complex arguments a few hours earlier, could have managed to produce such a detailed, written judgment in so short a time.

Coursol cited precedent and statute, leading as everyone could now see to dismissal. He summed up by saying: "I declare that having no warrant from the Governor General, I possess no jurisdiction. Consequently, I am bound in law, justice and fairness to order the immediate release of the prisoners upon all charges brought before me. Let the prisoners be discharged."[156]

Pandemonium ruled in the courtroom. St. Albans lawyer Edward Sowles later recalled that the crowds behaved in a way "never before heard or known in a court of justice."

Chairs and tables were overturned in the mad rush for the doors. Under cover of the chaos, Police Chief Lamothe quietly slipped out back with the prisoners, who were quickly bundled into waiting sleighs where they made their way to homes of refuge in the city. A day earlier, Police Chief Lamothe had gone to the Ontario Bank and asked that the $58,000 on deposit there that had been stolen from the St. Albans banks be made available should the raiders be released. As soon as that happened, the cash was promptly withdrawn. That day, Clement Clay, who had appeared in court to offer his testimony on behalf of the raiders, departed for Halifax and the South.

In the meantime, the lawyers for the Americans swarmed the bench, bitterly protesting Coursol's action. Devlin complained the prisoners had been charged on seven counts, yet Coursol had only heard one. He urged Coursol to reconsider.

"Would you discharge a criminal on six indictments because he was acquitted on one?" he pressed the judge.

"Having no jurisdiction in the one case, I would certainly have none in the others," Coursol shot back.

Finally, John Rose, another lawyer for the Americans, told the judge: "With all due respect, I dissent from the soundness of the judgment."

"Not another word of this," Coursol roared. "I am bound to do what my conscience and duty direct, without regard to influence, feelings or consequences."[157]

He turned and left the room.

After a brief conference, two of the lawyers for the Americans — Edward Sowles and Thomas Ritchie — prepared a fresh warrant for the arrest of the fugitives. They were joined by George Edmonds, another lawyer who was acting for the State of Vermont, and hurried to the offices of two superior court judges who refused to swear them out, unfamiliar with the details of Coursol's decision and reluctant to interfere.

They were luckier at the home of a third judge, James Smith, but by then it was late evening. Next the lawyers made for Police Chief Lamothe's home, where they found him asleep on a couch. Lamothe had no interest in executing the warrant and asked for forty-five minutes to think it through while he had something to eat. Without waiting for an answer the lawyers went in search of Adolph Bissonnette, one of Montreal's high constables, who agreed to execute it. Back they went to Lamothe's home, where the police chief and Bissonnette held a private conversation for fifteen minutes. They all piled into a sleigh and made for Coursol's home, where the judge gave a verbal order that the chief of the city's water police was to give any help he could. At one point in the adventure Edmonds was asked whether he would ever return to Montreal, to which he replied: "Only at the head of a regiment." There was not much to be done until morning.[158]

The thunder of American anger once again darkened Canadian skies. John A. Macdonald was disgusted with Coursol, "this wretched prig of a police magistrate," who was plainly out of his depth in the complexities of the affair.

The *St. Albans Messenger* wondered next day whether Coursol had been "bought" from the beginning, since it had been widely rumoured the rebels would be released. A day later in even

greater fury, the *Messenger* said that Coursol "has not only written himself down as an ass, but laid himself open to the very serious charge of being bribed." The paper pointed the finger at Police
Chief Lamothe, "another actor in this disgraceful affair."

The other larger and leading newspapers in the Northeast
echoed the *Messenger*'s sentiments. One story was that Lamothe
had been paid off by Confederates, another that Coursol had told
a justice of the Vermont Supreme Court that a gift of $10,000
would ensure the right verdict. Canadian papers too were embarrassed by Coursol's decision. The *Montreal Gazette* observed that
the Vermonters "had a right to expect different treatment from us
than they have received." The *Toronto Globe*, in reviewing what
it called the "extraordinary conduct of the magistrate," wondered
why a mere justice of the peace without any knowledge of constitutional law would make such a hasty decision without consulting
better legal minds. The *Globe* concluded that Coursol "betrayed
his trust" and was a man "unfitted to his position." The paper
urged an official inquiry.[159]

The hotheaded General John Dix heaped a little more fuel on the
fire. He reissued his inflammatory search and destroy order,
rescinded by Lincoln shortly after the St. Albans Raid. John A.
Macdonald termed the measure "most unfortunate and uncalled
for and an insult to Great Britain, conceived in a moment of irri-
tation." When news of it reached London, the *Times* called it "a
declaration of war against Canada."[160]

In Washington, Michigan Senator Zachariah Chandler read
news of the prisoners' release aloud in the Senate and predicted
that while Vermont might allow towns to be burned, the
Northwest would not. He went on to predict retaliatory raids
into Canada. Within days a resolution went from Congress to
the President giving notice to the British government that the
United States intended to terminate the Reciprocity Treaty, which
had made Canadians so prosperous for a decade. By December
17, Secretary of State William Seward had announced tight

passport regulations, a measure that would stay in force until the following March.

The Canadian authorities moved swiftly to lower the tenor of the debate. The fugitives were ordered rearrested, and the cabinet decided to make examples of Coursol and Lamothe. As well, the government agreed to indemnify the plundered banks for some of their losses.

Monck learned the news as he finished dinner on the evening of December 13. John A. Macdonald, George-Étienne Cartier, whose portfolio included Attorney General for Canada East, and two other cabinet ministers, William Macdougall and Hector Langevin, all converged on Monck's home, Spencerwood, on the outskirts of Quebec.

It was a little bit of excitement that Lady Monck savoured:

> When the dinner was nearly over, the G.G. was mys-teriously called out. He said: "I suppose this is an invasion of the Yankees." I longed so to listen at the door. Soon the G.G. came back. That stupid Judge in Montreal had on his own hook let out the raiders and they were at liberty to scamper about the coun-try and attack the Yankees. The fuss was great fun.

The next day, Monck wrote to Hume Burnley, the British Chargé d'Affairs in Washington, with a message for Secretary of State Seward. He told Burnley that the raiders had been released on "grounds so absurd that I cannot account for it." He asked Burnley to personally "convey my annoyance at what has hap-pened with reference to the Vermont raiders; and inform him that I shall do everything I can to remedy the effect of Judge Coursol's proceedings.[161]

On December 15, Monck wrote to Colonial Secretary Cardwell that he had been advised by the best Canadian lawyers that Coursol's decision "was not well founded in law." The raiders had been ordered rearrested, and if released by another court, Monck would ensure he made the charges stick.

It was at Monck's urging that the Canadian government ordered an investigation into the conduct of Coursol and Lamothe. The Executive Council recommended that Coursol be suspended.

At a hearing convened by Montreal city council, it was revealed that Lamothe and George Sanders had met a day before the prisoners were released and had made the arrangement to turn the money over to the Ontario Bank to conceal its whereabouts. The committee found no evidence of dishonesty, but accepted Lamothe's resignation on the grounds "of rank indiscretion and an unwarranted haste in relinquishing the booty in his care."

But where had the raiders gone? That night, in the outskirts of Montreal in a number of safe houses, they celebrated their releases. In the words of L'Abbé Henry Casgrain, a French Canadian priest who later wrote a detailed chronicle of the raiders' escape, they "soon fell asleep in delusive security, little conscious of the new danger they were soon to face."

For three precious days they stayed put, reasoning that since Lamothe was their friend there was little worry. But Edward Ermatinger and another constable, Adolph Bissonnette, were less sympathetic and had already thrown a net over the expected routes of escape. Guessing rightly that the raiders would make for the safety of New Brunswick, where no warrants could hold them, the pair had alerted every set of eyes and ears to that possibility.

At the first light of dawn on December 16, Bennett Young and two comrades stumbled out of their hideaway and hailed the first cab to come in sight. It turned out to be a rude and disgruntled Irishman driving a dilapidated rig, pulled by an equally ancient nag. In this dubious comfort they set out along the north shore, reasoning that any pursuers would be looking on the more travelled routes on the south side.

It became apparent that the Irishman knew little about the country through which they were travelling and even less French than they did. They passed through the villages of Terrebonne, Mascouche, and L'Assomption and were forced to make many stops at farmhouses where neither the driver nor his passengers could make themselves easily understood. At each spot they left another telltale sign of their route.

By the end of the second day, the cold chicken and hard bread was all gone and the brandy was no longer keeping the chill of a Canadian winter at bay. Horse feed for the nag was impossible to find and the exertion of his journey required frequent rests. Late that evening they arrived in Trois Rivières, ninety miles east of Montreal, where they found a new, younger driver and a fresher horse. They pressed on through the night, reaching Levis, on the south shore opposite Quebec, a little after dawn on December 19. They changed horses and sleighs again, always moving east and closer to New Brunswick. They spent that night in a hotel in the village of Rivière-Ouille. In the morning, the skies opened and a blizzard descended on the south shore, forcing the horse to wade through belly-deep drifts of snow with visibility at times only a few yards. They had no choice but to press on. To stop would mean death.

At daybreak on the twentieth they arrived in Rivière-du-Loup, the junction of three roads leading back to Quebec further to the west, deeper into the South Shore to the east, and south to the New Brunswick border. They may have been tired, cold, and hungry, but Young and his two comrades were jubilant.

They turned south, and at the tiny hamlet of St. Francis, twenty miles from their destination, they stopped at a tavern. There they came face to face with the wily constable, Colonel Edward Ermatinger, who had wisely decided to make his stand here. After a hazardous three-hundred-mile journey through the teeth of a Canadian winter, just miles short of freedom, the young Confederates faced imprisonment again, with sinking hearts.

"Ah, well, I am your prisoner," Young said.

On Christmas Eve, Young and his companions were again lodged in the comfort of Payette's Hotel. Here they found two other of their comrades who had been captured several miles above Quebec. Four more would be arrested on December 27 in West Lebanon, New Hampshire, trying to enlist in the Union Army. Another four would spend a winter snow- and icebound on the North Shore of the St. Lawrence, before making a daring break in the early spring through the ice floes of the Gulf of St. Lawrence. They escaped from an almost certain death more than once before ultimately making safe passage back to the defeated South.

But if the disheartened St. Albans raiders sadly pondered this, their fourth Christmas away from home, their commander Jacob Thompson, in equally low spirits, was nonetheless enjoying his Christmas Eve. In Toronto, Thompson enjoyed wine, a traditional goose with all the trimmings, and a blazing fire in the hearth at Hayden Villa, the home of Lieutenant Colonel George Denison, a Canadian whose Southern sympathies Thompson found useful.

CHAPTER 18
Soldier of Empire

"... We are satisfied that so close an espionage is kept upon you that your services have been deprived of the value which is attached to your residence in Canada. The President thinks that it is better that you return to the Confederacy."
                                   Judah Benjamin to Jacob Thompson
                                   December 1864

If there was one family that embodied the essence of the mid-Victorian Canadian identity with all its certainties and apprehensions, it was the Denison family of Toronto. They were wealthy, well educated, and members of the military and political elite. Not unlike Governor General Monck, whose class they aspired to, the Denisons held nothing but contempt for American political and social institutions and had an abiding loyalty for the monarchy and mother country. They personified the evolution of Canadian attitudes and aspirations from the small group of Loyalists who had fled the American Revolution to the restless colonists of the 1860s, eager for nationhood and to buttress the interests of the British Empire on the continent.

The Denisons also represented the fundamentally conservative nature of life in Upper Canada, with it views that wealth and status derived from land and power from politics. It explained in part their sympathy for Jocob Thompson and the Southern cause, seeing Southerners as being like themselves. The Denisons also believed that with reasonable men like themselves governing and providing

wise and ordered administration, the colony would prosper
and be protected from the agitation beyond its borders.
While the Americans might
crave liberty and justice,
Canadians like the Denisons
sought law and order.

George Taylor Denison III was
born in August 1839, the same
year that Jacob Thompson was
first elected as a Mississippi
congressman. Denison's father,
George Taylor Denison II,
was a magistrate and landowner, wealthy enough to build
a baronial estate called
Rusholme amid open fields and

George Taylor Denison III was
descended from United Empire
Loyalists. He was pro-Southern and an
important Jacob Thompson ally.

stands of pine and cedar on the western edge of Toronto. George
would later build his own estate, Heydon Villa, near his father's
home.[162] The family represented the rising energy of entrepreneurs
and businessmen who were building the fortunes of Canada West.
They were involved in farming, owned office blocks, and invested in
mining and insurance companies. They were patrons of the arts and
sciences, local aldermen, and captains of the militia.[163]

George was one of nine children and enjoyed all the advantages
that his father's wealth could provide.[164] In 1861, George, then
twenty-two, received his law degree from the University of
Toronto. He was never much interested in law, believing himself to
be a soldier. That year, he took command of the 1st Toronto
Volunteer Cavalry, a regiment raised and supported by his family.
Like many of his peers, he was sympathetic to the South. He saw
danger to Canada in Southern defeat and empathized with the
Southern way of life with its rigid class structure. Southern politi-

cal ideology tended to be conservative, and of course, Denison admired the myth of the Southern cavalier — a man better bred, better trained, and more likely to be gentlemen, although tragically outnumbered by the might of the conscripted Union Army. The South seemed to be fighting the same fight as Canadians — trying to preserve its identity against the overwhelming pressure of Yankee expansionism. Denison's Northern antipathy was so strong that in April 1865, when Toronto's City Council moved a resolution expressing sympathy with the people of the United States over the assassination of Lincoln, the only vote against it was his.

A closer tie to the South was his Uncle George Dewson, who had moved to Florida in 1850, taking his Yankee prejudices with him. When war broke out, Dewson joined the Confederate secret service, rising to the rank of colonel. Dewson arrived in Toronto in September 1864, on the instructions of Confederate Secretary of State Judah Benjamin, to evaluate and report on Jacob Thompson's activities. Dewson somewhat overenthusiastically told Benjamin that Canadians wished the Confederacy "God Speed."[165]

Dewson's presence at Heydon Villa and Rusholme was an invitation to any and all Confederate sympathizers and agents to come calling. Jacob Thompson was there; so was William Cleary, Thompson's secretary, and William "Larry" Macdonald, who was making hand grenades and Greek Fire in Toronto and Guelph. Heydon Villa became a transit point for Confederate couriers, including those who would try to bring back vital evidence for the second trial of the St. Albans raiders in Toronto.

Denison's position as an alderman for St. Patrick's Ward, his commission as an officer, and his zeal for the cause made him a perfect Thompson ally. As the purchase of the *Georgian* showed, Thompson was more than willing to take the offered assistance. Denison's diary, kept from May 1864 until his death in 1925, shows increasing contact with Thompson from the time his uncle arrived in Toronto on September 13, until Thompson's departure the following May.[166]

There are a handful of entries where Denison and Dewson called on Thompson at the Queen's together, but never any men-tion of what was discussed or who else was there. The diary is barren of all but the most mundane details, but by early December the meetings with Thompson appear more frequently. On December 13, as the St. Albans raiders were being released in Montreal, Colonel Dewson boarded the train in Toronto for Montreal, Halifax, and the South. Denison, however, maintained his close contact with Thompson.[167]

By early December, Thompson was feeling more than the chill of a Canadian winter and was in desperate need of allies. Canadian and American authorities were working closely together, passing information back and forth in an effort to foil Thompson's plans. The Canadians had no wish to be drawn into the war and resented Thompson's harassing actions from bases on their shores.

After seven months of covert operations, key members of the team, like the St. Albans raiders, were in jail. Others, like Hines, Eastin, Castleman, and the team that had firebombed New York, were on the run. The other commissioners, Clay and Holcombe, were gone. Canadian authorities were angry enough at Thompson's abuse of their neutrality that they pondered jailing him. Traitors in Thompson's inner circle had been in the pay of the U.S. government for months. Just a few floors beneath his suite, detectives staked out the main bar of the hotel. Across the street at Toronto's main railway station, more men noted the coming and going of sympathizers, couriers, and Thompson's military aides. The signs of failure were everywhere.

"I had hoped to have accomplished more," Thompson mused bitterly in a letter written December 3 to Benjamin. "But the bane and curse of this country is the surveillance under which we act. Detectives, or those ready to give information stand on every corner."

Just a few days earlier William Fargo, the mayor of Buffalo, New York, had received a message in the mail. The letter is among records in the Public Archives of Canada relating to Confederate activities in the country during 1864 and 1865. A Canadian informant identified only as "Fides," who gave the edgy mayor an update on Thompson's plans, wrote it. Fides's report describes Thompson's purchase, the *Georgian*, and an overview of Thompson's plan. Thompson bought the *Georgian* to make a second attempt at capturing the *Michigan*, which still stood guard in Sandusky Harbour. Fides describes a conversation with James Bates, the former Mississippi steamboat captain hired by Thompson to buy the ship.

"He [Bates] is a determined old fellow, an old maniac," Fides wrote. "His Captain knows the lake well and is a man to succeed. It behooves the people of Sandusky to keep a good lookout."

Fides also named some of Thompson's couriers as well as their routes south. Some went by rail from Toronto to the Suspension Bridge at Niagara Falls. Others preferred to go to Windsor and then Detroit, or via Sarnia and across Lake St. Clair to Michigan.

"There is something on foot [sic], the precise nature of which I have not yet been able to determine, but will find out," Fides concludes.

Monck was at his most diplomatic in his attempts to mollify the Northerners in the wake of the St. Albans and *Georgian* affairs. While Fargo heard about the *Georgian* at the end of November, an informer told the U.S. Consul in Toronto, John Potter, about it on November 5. Potter warned Monck and War Secretary Stanton. Stanton wired the news to General Dix, who had energetically wished to pursue the St. Albans Raiders across the border; he indicated that he wished the freedom to do the same with the *Georgian*. Monck, fearing such an outcome, ordered the ship examined by Canadian revenue inspectors when it put in at Sarnia in mid-November. Fargo, meanwhile, had contacted William Seward with his intelligence from Fides. Seward passed it on to Monck, bypassing the normal channels, which would have been through the British Ambassador to Washington.[168]

It became increasing difficult for Thompson to communicate with his superiors at Richmond. Couriers, which were his main form of communication with Richmond, were followed and captured when they crossed the border. While we live in a world of instant communication with cell phones, fax machines, and e-mail, it took Thompson's couriers weeks to take an overland route home and a month or more if they went by sea. That assumed they arrived at all. Both Clay and Holcombe were shipwrecked. Events moved far faster then the messages. Replies and requests for instructions were out of date before they were received, a fact of life that gave Thompson huge leeway in how he conducted his affairs.

In this climate of uncertainty, Thompson turned to Denison for help. Thompson stood alone as the sole Confederate commissioner in North America and saw his duty clearly. He paid for the continuing defence of the St. Albans raiders and provided ongoing moral support by his daily appearances in court. A key part of their defence was whether these men were bank robbers or soldiers of the Confederate States engaged in acts of war. The proof of their commissions lay nine hundred miles south in Richmond, with the Department of War. Thompson needed to get a courier to Richmond to bring back those documents, which was why he turned to Denison. While Thompson's every move was observed, nobody was watching Denison's house or his comings and goings.

On the morning of January 5, 1865, in the pre-dawn darkness, Denison and Lieutenant Sam Davis, a Confederate courier who had been hidden in his house for several days, moved quickly and quietly across an open field covered with a crust of new snow. Minutes before, the two men had said goodbye to Jacob Thompson. Thompson gave Davis, who was no relation to the Confederate president, final instructions and wished him "God Speed." The pair headed across the field to the home of Denison's father, where they hitched a horse to a sleigh, threw extra furs over their laps, and set off for Mimico train station in a suburb of Toronto. They went over the details of Davis's route through the northern states and rehearsed what Davis would say if captured and what he would do with the second set of dispatches he carried.

While Davis carried the official request for the enlistment papers of the St. Albans raiders from Thompson to Seddon, he also carried other letters to Judah Benjamin. These messages were written on five small squares of silk, which Denison's wife had sewn into the elbows and collar of Davis's coat.

"The plan was carefully considered," Denison wrote. As he recalled in his memoirs, *Soldiering in Canada*:

> Federal officers had learned nearly every trick. Boots and collars were cut open and folds of cloth everywhere examined. Buttons were taken to pieces and carefully scanned under magnifying glasses. An idea struck me which I explained to Col. Thompson. It was to write the dispatches on thin white silk in pencil and sew them in the back of the coat and in the sleeve near the elbow. The silk could not be felt, nor would it rustle and we found that an ordinary wetting would not wash out the pencil writing.

If Davis was captured and searched, the messages would be almost undetectable. They could also be easily destroyed.

"I left him in the dark about 100 yards from the station so that no one should see us together," Denison recalled. He continued:

> He got off safely, escaped all the spies on the frontier and in the trains. He was rapidly approaching the border of his own country when as ill luck would have it he was recognized. He was arrested, carefully searched, his clothes and boots cut open, his buttons examined and nothing found but his passport. He was locked in a room and at once took out the dispatches and burned them.

Davis was captured at the Newark, Ohio, train station. Union soldiers recently freed from Andersonville Prison in Georgia spotted him. Davis had spent a brief time at Andersonville as an aide to the commandant, while recovering from wounds he'd received at Gettysburg. Davis was tried as a spy and sentenced to death.

When Thompson learned of his capture, he made a plea to Abraham Lincoln for clemency. Lincoln responded by commuting Davis's sentence.

It was apparent to the authorities at Richmond that Thompson's usefulness in British North America was at an end. On December 6, Benjamin wrote to Thompson that General Edwin Lee was being sent to replace him, should Thompson wish to return home. Lee, the second cousin of Robert E. Lee, had resigned his command because of ill health. In a subsequent letter, written December 30, Benjamin used much stiffer language, ordering Thompson to turn everything over to Lee.

Benjamin wrote: "From reports which reach us from trustworthy sources, we are satisfied that so close an espionage is kept upon you that your services have been deprived of the value which is attached to your residence in Canada. The President thinks that it is better that you return to the Confederacy."[169]

Thompson, however, had no plans to retire. He was still convinced that if he could free the many Confederate prisoners held in Northern prisons, he could create a foraging army that would fight its way back to the South. They would need leaders, and this fit nicely with a piece of intelligence he had received from Johnson's Island. The news was that several imprisoned Confederate generals were to be transferred to Fort Lafayette in New York on December 15. They included Major General Edward Johnson, who inherited Stonewall Jackson's brigade at Gettysburg; Major General Issac Trimble, who lost a leg and was captured during Pickett's charge at Gettysburg; Brigadier General John R. Jones, wounded at the second Battle of Bull Run and again at Antietam, only to later be accused of cowardice at Chancellorsville where he was captured; and General John Frazer, a Tennessean captured in late 1863 during a raid in the eastern part of the state.

Thompson turned to Colonel Robert Martin and Lieutenant John Headley, who had led the raid on New York. He proposed that Martin and part of the team board the train at Erie,

Pennsylvania, and when it reached Dunkirk, New York, just to the west of Buffalo, those on board would be joined by a party waiting at the station. They would derail the locomotive, overpower the guards, and spirit the Confederates across the border.

Headley recalled the incident in his memoirs:

> Col. Thompson directed that after taking the train we should immediately arm the generals and use our judgment after that time, until Captain Beall with a few men should secure all the money in the express safe.
>
> He and Martin would at once give a reasonable amount to each of the generals and each member of the party, for we might be obliged to scatter in Ohio and New York. It was distinctly understood that nothing should be taken that belonged to passengers, but if passengers interfered, we should shoot them.[170]

Headley recruited John Beall, who had been in hiding since the failed Lake Erie Raid, and seven others. On Saturday and Sunday, December 13 and 14, the party crossed the border at Fort Erie, Ontario, and booked into hotels in Buffalo. They met that evening at the Genesee Hotel. The next morning the party made their way to Dunkirk, with Martin alone continuing on to Erie, about eighty miles west along the lake, just over the New York state line. Headley wrote in his memoirs that:

> [We would] capture the train between Sandusky and Buffalo by surprising the guards and taking their arms. We would then leave the passenger coaches behind on the track between the two stations. After cutting the telegraph wire we would run to Buffalo, if near that place, otherwise scatter. We intended to have the generals change clothing with passengers of the same size.

When the second train through Dunkirk arrived, Martin was on it, but not the generals. The team returned to Buffalo, where Martin ordered a close watch that day and the next at the Buffalo train station. By midday Tuesday, when there was no sign of any Confederate prisoners, the team moved a few miles outside of Buffalo and came up with a scheme to stop the train by putting an iron rail on the track.

They hid in the bushes and a train hit the rail, tossing it fifty yards in the air. The impact persuaded the engineer to stop the train two hundreds yards down the track, and two members of the crew came to investigate, but instead of capturing the men, the Confederates fled like mischievous school boys after a prank. It was back to Buffalo and then by pairs across the border by train. While seven of the ten returned safely to Toronto, Beall and two others were captured while they napped in a restaurant near the international bridge between Buffalo and Fort Erie. They had waited for a train, while Headley and others had walked across.[171]

And so with a whimper, Confederates in Canada retreated in failure from their last raid across the frontier. A day earlier, on December 15, Governor General Monck, outraged by the release of the St. Albans raiders, had issued an Imperial warrant for their rearrest.

CHAPTER 19
Winter Debates

"We are seeking by calm discussion to settle questions ... hardly more momentous than those that have rent the neighbouring Republic.... Have we not great cause for thankfulness that we have found a better way?"

George Brown during the Confederation debates
February 1865

The release of the St. Albans raiders in December cast a pall over relations between Canada and the United States, heightening tensions to their most dangerous level since the Trent Affair of 1861. The release of the raiders was universally condemned. The *St. Albans Messenger* said it "smelled a rat" in the decision and called Coursol "an ass." General Dix ordered American troops to pursue any suspected raiders across the border, an order that was quickly rescinded by Lincoln. John A. Macdonald, not sure if he was more angry at Coursol or the American reaction, called Dix's decision an "unfortunate insult to Great Britain."

As all of this unfolded, George Brown was in London selling Confederation to the British government.

On December 15, Monck issued warrants for the rearrest of the St. Albans raiders. To further mollify the Americans, he ordered the creation of a special secret police force to patrol the border. Troops at border points were put on high alert. Monck wrote another letter to Burnley, asking him to pass on to Seward "my annoyance at what has happened with the Vermont raiders and inform him that I will do everything that I can do to remedy the effect of Judge Coursol's proceedings."[172]

Almost immediately, the Americans applied political and economic pressure to the Canadian authorities. On December 17, the Lincoln administration imposed passport controls, signalling that the normally easy coming and going across the border was to end. Every person crossing into the U.S. required a passport. The *Globe* suggested that Canada introduce its own passport controls in retaliation. The *Toronto Leader* called it expedient and vindictive. The *Detroit Free Press* argued that the law would be hard on the hundreds of people in Windsor who worked in Detroit and that the effect would be to make life difficult for ordinary citizens, not criminals and raiders. The *Free Press* argued quite sensibly that the border was too long and too porous, with numerous lake and land crossings, to stop any determined efforts to slip across the border.[173]

Monck, meanwhile, called a meeting of the Executive Council — the Canadian cabinet — to look into the conduct of Coursol, who had been suspended. These measures seemed to mollify the Americans. Toronto's consul, David Thurston, had been working closely with lawyers for the U.S. in the St. Albans affair. Seward wrote, on Christmas Eve, that in his opinion, the Canadians were doing all that they could.

"The government has acted promptly and decidedly to remedy the effect of Judge Coursol's decision," Thurston wrote.[174]

The effect of the passport controls was to paralyze cross-border traffic. The lineups were long, tempers were short, and the disruption in the normal flow of people and goods was enormous. In early January 1865, Frank Brown, an exasperated citizen of Massachusetts, wrote to Toronto Consul Thurston, asking for the return of the two dollars in gold he had paid Thurston for a "certificate." Brown had been visiting friends in Toronto over Christmas and after visiting Thurston's office was assured that the certificate would be enough to get him across the border. At Niagara Falls, an American customs official turned Brown away, claiming the certificate wasn't enough proof of the man's citizenship.

He retraced his steps by train to Hamilton, where he roused an American acquaintance. Together, the pair went in search of the local judge so Brown's friend could swear an affidavit as to Brown's U.S. citizenship. Then it was back to the border, where the customs officer "was so drunk it took three hours to make out my passport and then only by me sitting with him and prompting him." There were eight other people in line, and as Frank Brown noted: "You cannot conceive of the disgust and wrath at the consul's office. At one time I did not know but that blood would be shed." Some six dollars later, Brown was on his way.[175]

While the Consuls were the first to admit that a passport law was more nuisance then sound policy, Seward had another goal in mind when he pressed for the law's introduction. He wanted to put pressure on the Canadians to pass a Neutrality Act, a bill that would make it tougher for Confederates to mount cross-border raids. The passport law was the stick. In this he was successful.

Monck asked that the Canadian parliament reconvene on January 19, a month early, to deal with such a law. With John A. Macdonald leading the way, the "Frontier Outrages Bill" was quickly passed, although its official name was the Alien Act. The law called for the expulsion from the Canadas of any foreign person suspected of engaging in hostile acts against a friendly nation. Judges could levy a $3,000 fine and seize arms and vessels intended for such use. The Act was to remain in force for one year and would have serious consequences for Denison and his purchase of the *Georgian*. The passport laws were lifted by the end of March.

Meanwhile, the extradition case against the St. Albans raiders had begun. Most of the raiders had been rounded up and the hearings were underway in Montreal. Unlike Coursol, the new judge ruled he did have jurisdiction to hear the case. The hearings started in late December, but were soon remanded for thirty days to await the documents from Richmond that Lieutenant Sam Davis had been sent to retrieve. On January 13, the investigation into the behavior of Coursol and Lamothe wrapped up, concluding that both were stupid, or worse, but recommending no further action.

Late December and January found Thompson undeterred by the failure at Buffalo, but keenly aware of constant surveillance and the hardening Canadian attitudes towards his adventures. He had one last plan in mind. It called for General Lee to abandon the South and move north and west through West Virginia and Pennsylvania. Lee would create a foraging army that would free Confederate prisoners along the way and form a new government at Wheeling, West Virginia.

The strategy called for Lee to break out of his defensive position around Richmond and Petersburg and move his armies north, threatening Washington and then swinging west to capture Pittsburgh and south to Wheeling. In the meantime, part of his army would split off, freeing the up to one hundred thousand Confederate prisoners in Northern jails. In the midst of all this havoc the North would sue for peace. Lieutenant John Headley, whose turn-of-the-century book described the plot, admitted that in hindsight it was absurd, but within the context of the times, it had a certain appeal.

Headley wrote:

> The South was exhausted. It appeared to us that nothing could be lost and everything could be gained. Of course, this change of base would leave the South absolutely at the mercy of the enemy, but the Northern people and their property would be equally in the power of the Confederates, who would be unopposed in marching west.
>
> None of us could see the propriety of making the last ditch in the impoverished South when the gates to the North and West stood wide open. We felt certain that the South could afford to have the seat of war transferred to the North, where we could win or lose at the expense of the enemy.[176]

On February 2, Headley and two companions made for Windsor and walked across the frozen Detroit River. They easily evaded passport controls and any scrutiny at all, as the *Free Press* had suggested criminals might.

By the first week of February, the Canadians had put the issues of St. Albans and Confederate incursions aside to begin a nightly ritual that would last for two months and become known as the Confederation Debates. While it was a time of excitement and expectation, they could not escape from the shadow cast by the raids from Canada across the border. In a sign of the times, the *Chicago Tribune* suggested the United States should dispose of Canada "as a St. Bernard would throttle a poodle pup." Washington had given notice it intended to put gunboats back on the Great Lakes. The Americans had also given similar notice that the Reciprocity Treaty would expire in one year.

The threats brought on by Jacob Thompson's actions, fears of invasion, real or imagined, and the economic and political fallout of the raids created a sombre and fearful mood. The positive side for the men who were committed to seeing Confederation become a reality was that it was all first-hand evidence of the American menace. In fact, during the debates, no less than sixty members of the assembly spoke about the dangers to Canada from the United States.

Montreal Consul John Potter catalogued the anti-Northern sentiment in his regular communications with Washington. Two weeks into the debates, Potter told Seward that many Canadians favoured Confederation as a way to avoid annexation by America, and that Canadian support for the South stemmed from the same fear. "This [sympathy] arises not from any particular regard or affection for the rebels, but from a desire to see our government weakened and these provinces thereby relieved from what they regard as the imminent peril in which they are placed by their proximity to a powerful neighbour."[177]

The Confederation debates opened on February 3. Étienne Taché, Minister of Militia, moved the seventy-two resolutions passed at Quebec and noted that if Canadians passed up this opportunity for union, they would one way or the other fall into the American orbit, either by force or gradual absorption.

The next day, John A. Macdonald recapped the reasons why the proposal offered Canada's only hope for the future. Macdonald had carefully crafted the proceedings so that the resolutions proposed on the opening night were an all-or-nothing affair: accept or reject. There was nothing in between.

Macdonald touched on the themes of defence and strength in numbers as a bulwark against American expansionism. He pointed out how the Canadian plan included a division of powers between the central government and the provinces that would ensure a civil war could never occur in Canada. He emphasized that the Canadian way would avoid the weaknesses that the Americans had built into their political system:

> If we are not blind, we must see the hazardous situation in which the interests of Canada stand in relation to the United States. I am no alarmist. I do not believe in the prospect of immediate war. I believe that the common sense of the two nations will prevent a war; still we cannot trust to probabilities.

Macdonald also played to the theme of the lessons of the American experience:

> It is in fashion now to enlarge on the defects of the Constitution of the United States, but I am not one of those who look upon it as a failure ... I think it is one of the most skillful works that human intelligence has ever created; is one of the most perfect organizations that ever governed a free people. We can now take advantage of the last 78 years, during which that Constitution has existed. I am

strongly of the belief that we have, in great measure, avoided the defects which time and events have shown to exist in the American Constitution.

They commenced at the wrong end. They declared that each state was a sovereignty in itself. Here we have adopted a different system. We have strengthened the general government. We have expressly declared that all subjects not distinctly and exclusively conferred upon the local governments shall be conferred upon the general government. We have thus avoided the great source of weakness which has been the cause of the disruption of the United States.

On February 8, it was George Brown's turn. "I cannot help feeling that the struggle of half a life time and the strife and discord and abuse of many years are all compensated by the great scheme which is now in your hands," he said.

Here is a people composed of two distinct races, speaking different languages, with religious, social and municipal institutions, totally different; with hostilities of such a character as to render government for many years well-nigh impossible. And yet, sir, here we sit, patiently and temperately discussing how these hostilities can be justly and amicably swept away forever. We are striving to do peacefully what Holland and Belgium, after years of strife, were unable to accomplish. We are seeking by calm discussion to settle questions that Austria and Hungary, Denmark and Germany, that Russia and Poland, could only crush by the iron heel of armed force. We are striving to settle forever, issues hardly more momentous than those that have rent the neighbouring Republic and are now exposing it to all the horrors of civil war. Have we

not then, great cause for thankfulness that we have
found a better way?

The House erupted in applause with shouts of "Hear, hear."
Brown continued:

> Could the pages of history find a parallel to this? One
> hundred years has passed since these provinces
> became by conquest part of the British Empire. I
> speak in no boastful spirit — I desire not for a
> moment to excite a painful thought — what was the
> fortune of war of the brave French nation might have
> been ours on that well-fought field. I recall those
> times merely to mark the fact that here sit today the
> descendants of the victors and the vanquished in the
> fight of 1759, with all the differences of language,
> religion, civil law and social habit nearly as distinct-
> ly marked as they were a century ago. Here we sit
> seeking amicably to find a remedy for the constitu-
> tional evils and injustice complained of by the van-
> quished? No, but complained of by the conquerors.

"Look at the map," he urged. There was Newfoundland the
size of Portugal, Nova Scotia as big as Greece, New Brunswick as
big as Switzerland and Denmark combined; here was Canada East
as large as France, Canada West larger than the British Isles, and
the North West greater than all of the Russian Empire. He went on:

> The scheme in your hand is no greater than to
> gather all these countries into one — to establish a
> government that will seek to turn the tide of immi-
> gration into this northern half of the American
> continent. Does it not lift us above the petty poli-
> tics of the past and present to us high purpose and
> great interests that may well call forth all the abil-
> ity and all the energy and enterprise among us?[178]

196

Brown spoke with a mixture of hope and vision, talking for four hours before sitting down to thunderous applause.

The next night was the turn of the gifted orator D'Arcy McGee, Minister of Agriculture and a member for Montreal East. McGee chose to launch his speech with humour, playing on the many different attempts by newspapers to pick a name for the new country, beyond the obvious and popular choice of Canada. "I would ask any member of this House how he would feel if he woke up one fine morning and found himself instead of a Canadian, a Tuponian, or a Hochelagander." But McGee soon became far more serious in his support of Confederation, and, like Brown and Macdonald before him, he played the American card:

> The policy of our neighbours has always been aggressive. There has always been a desire among them for the acquisition of new territory. They coveted Florida and seized it; they coveted Louisiana, and purchased it; they coveted Texas and stole it; and then they picked a quarrel with Mexico, which ended by their getting California.

"Hear, hear," came the cries from the floor. McGee went on:

> They sometimes seem to despise these colonies as prizes beneath their ambition; but had we not had the strong arm of England over us, we should not now have had a separate existence. The acquisition of Canada was the first ambition of [America] and never ceased to be so, when her troops were a handful and her navy scarce a squadron. Is it likely to be stopped now, when she counts her guns afloat by thousands and her troops by the hundreds of thousands?

But for every inspired orator like Brown or McGee, there were many more who were dull, tedious, and ill-informed. Often the benches were empty. When John A. Macdonald spoke, the crowd was thin. Finance Minister Galt drew a better crowd, for a short speech.

But, wrote the *Hamilton Spectator*:

> ... even in his case, the number of empty seats was a curious commentary upon the professed interest which is felt in this subject. I cannot help feeling that the number of members who have given the subject any serious consideration at all is very small, and that the members are drifting into this new state of political existence with a blind reliance on the soundness of their leaders.[179]

There were many speakers who objected to Confederation. Some French Canadians saw it as a plan that set them on the slippery slope toward assimilation. It was only George-Étienne Cartier, whose Conservative alliance with Macdonald had allowed the plan to get this far, who carried the day. He gambled his political life and won, carrying with him a slim majority of French Canadian members. The opposition's difficulty was that their objections weren't held together by common interest, so they could not mount an effective bloc of opposition. As author P.B. Waite has noted, "Such a motley opposition did not have much of a chance and they probably knew they had not; but their comments on Confederation are by no means without point. The scheme was not perfect; even its supporters admitted that."

As the debate dragged on through the end of February, the people of New Brunswick were going to the polls in a process that, because of the distances and difficulties in polling, lasted for two weeks. On the weekend of March 4, the shocking news for the Canadians was that Sam Tilley, the incumbent premier and pro-Confederation ally, had gone down to defeat. His government was now finished and so, it seemed, was the drive for Confederation. Without New Brunswick, it would be difficult for Nova Scotia to come aboard.

The last day of debate was set as Friday, March 10. The talks continued into the small hours of Saturday. Members waited to vote, lying around on benches in antechambers and the corridors.

The bell rang at last at 4:15 a.m. The motion carried by 91 to 33, a margin of almost three to one. French-Canadian members also voted for it. Their margin was smaller — 55 percent for to 45 percent against.[180]

As the Speaker left the chair, the members of the house cheered and sang, stumbling out into the pre-dawn darkness and their waiting beds. Obstacles remained, but nothing could stop the Confederation train.

CHAPTER 20
Assassination

"... There were some so ... depraved, as to exult over this great crime. I am more grieved to say that these persons — I cannot call them men — were but a short time since citizens of the United States ... Treason has transformed them to brutes."
U.S. Consul in Montreal David Thurston
April 1865

On January 13, Clay left Halifax for Nassau. As his mail boat left the harbour, George Brown was tying up at the wharf in the port of New York. Not even a two-week voyage on the stormy North Atlantic could change his buoyant mood.

It would take Clay more than three weeks to reach his home in a voyage that was more terrifying and fraught with misadventure than the one that had carried him to Canada nine months earlier. His blockade-runner, the *Rattlesnake,* could not make for Wilmington because the union blockade was now complete: nothing could get in or out of the port. On the thirteenth, as Clay left Halifax, a Union naval fleet began bombarding Fort Fisher, in whose shadow the *Thistle* had patiently waited nine months earlier. For the next two days the fifty-nine ships kept up an assault that, at the time, was the greatest concentration of naval firepower in history. The fort fell two days later and so did Wilmington, leaving Charleston, South Carolina, as the only open Southern port on the eastern seaboard.

On January 31, the blockade-runner *Rattlesnake* left Nassau for Charleston. Three days later in a violent storm, the *Rattlesnake* ran aground. Clay, carrying what he could, boarded a lifeboat, which got him within a few dozen yards of the beach.

"I waded to shore carrying what I could in my hands," he wrote in his diary. "Lost a trunk and much of my own baggage which was in the hold of the ship — all being burned in it."[181]

A friend took Clay to Charleston, where he spent a day drying out before moving on in search of his wife. He went first to Columbia, South Carolina, where he left a large trunk in the care of friends. He then hired a carriage to take him to Augusta, Georgia, where he destroyed a number of papers relating to his Canadian stay. Finally, on February 10, as the Canadians debated Confederation and warned about the dangers of the American "experiment," Clay and his wife were reunited in Macon, Georgia.

It would be two more months before Clay reported to his superiors in Richmond. By then, it was irrelevant. On April 2, when he arrived in the Confederate capital, the government was abandoning the city. They had no time or inclination to listen to his explanations about the raid on St. Albans or the failure of the Canadian mission. It didn't matter. The war was over.

In February and March, as Clay recovered from his near drowning, Thompson was tying up loose ends in Canada, defending the St. Albans raiders, and interceding on behalf of his many jailed comrades.[182]

On February 2, Thompson learned that the courier Lieutenant Sam Davis had been captured and was to be hung as a spy. That day, Thompson wrote to Abraham Lincoln asking for clemency.

"This young man's life is in your hands," Thompson wrote, as he outlined the reason for Davis's travels through the Northern states in search of documentary evidence from Richmond to help with Bennett Burley's extradition. Thompson explained that Davis had been sent by the fastest route possible and that while he could be tried as a Confederate courier, he was not a spy — a charge that upon conviction drew the death penalty.

"I know that however much you desire to crush out the Confederate States Government, it must be repugnant to your sense of right to pursue individuals with undue harshness," Thompson wrote. "As one private citizen speaking to one clothed with authority, I ask you to spare this young man's life. You have a right to retain him as a prisoner of war, but I declare on my honour, he is not a spy." Ten days later, Lincoln commuted Davis's death sentence.[183]

On February 3, as Clay waded ashore near Charleston, Bennett Burley had been taken under armed guard from Toronto aboard a special train to Fort Erie, where he was handed over to American authorities in Buffalo. He was moved to Port Clinton, Ohio, and formally charged with the robbery of the *Philo Parsons*. Burley produced his Confederate commission, and while his lawyer tried to have him freed on a technicality, he escaped from jail by bribing a guard. Burley made his way to Detroit and from there Windsor with the aid of friends.[184]

Meanwhile, in New York, the trial of John Yates Beall continued. After Beall's arrest in December at the Buffalo Suspension Bridge, Beall was charged with spying and piracy in connection with the Lake Erie raid. Thompson tried to procure proof from Richmond of Beall's commission as an acting master in the Confederate Navy. By the end of January, the courier had not returned. Beall was executed on February 24, 1865.

"I have been styled a pirate, a robber etc.," Beall wrote. "When the United States authorities, after a 'trial', shall execute such a sentence, I do earnestly call upon you to officially vindicate me, at least to my countrymen. With unabated loyalty to our cause, I remain truly your friend, John Yates Beall." Beall was executed three days later.

Throughout February, the extradition trial of the St. Albans raiders continued in Montreal. On at least one occasion Thompson was present in the courtroom, with George Sanders and Colonel Denison. The main thrust of the defence was that the men were commissioned Confederate soldiers who had not broken any Canadian laws. Any depredations had been carried out on American soil.[185] On February 20, the case was adjourned for two weeks when the judge fell ill.

Even so, Thompson was busy. On March 15, he wrote to Hines, replying to a letter Hines had written about the impact of his acts of arson and sabotage along the higher reaches of he Mississippi. Thompson asked Hines to use the "considerable unexpended balance" of money Thompson advanced him for the Chicago uprising to look after the legal bills of Colonel St. Leger Grenfel, who had been captured and was being tried a spy for his role.

On March 21, the raiders' trial resumed, and after six days of testimony, Justice James Smith rendered his decision in a two-day summation. The Americans could sense from the judge's tone and words that another defeat was imminent. Consul Potter had sent a telegram to Seward warning that the case for their extradition might fail. Potter confirmed his worst fears in a telegram received at the War Department in Washington at 4:15 p.m. on March 29, the day the decision was rendered: "Judge Smith discharged the prisoners and declared the raid justifiable and even commendable. Opinion received with applause in court. They are rearrested on other charges. John Potter."[186]

In a letter next day to Seward, Consul Potter appended a synopsis of Smith's decision. Potter declared the judgment was "loose, dogmatic, illogical and evinces the illiberal and hostile feeling toward the Government of the United States for which the bench and bar of Lower Canada are distinguished." Potter was galled by the fact that Smith's decision "was cheered most vociferously both in the courtroom and in the street, indicating the pressures, both in the courtroom and vicinity of a large number of the same class of villains. The decision removes all barriers to similar outrages and their repetition is now highly probable."[187]

Smith determined there were no grounds to extradite the St. Albans Raiders. He concluded that they were commissioned officers in the Confederate States army, that the United States and Confederate States were in a state of war, that the St. Albans raid was an act of war, and that since no crimes had been committed in Canada, there was no reason to extradite Young and the other Confederates. However, Monck had prepared for the eventuality and made sure the raiders were remanded in custody to face new charges of breaching the new Neutrality Act. They were taken to Toronto on April 6, but by then the war was over and there was little point in continuing the prosecution. On April 10, all the raiders except Young were discharged. A few days later Young was freed on a bond of $10,000 posted by Colonel Denison. The charges against him were dropped six months later in October, a little over a year from the date of the raid.

During a hiatus in the extradition trial of the raiders, Thompson received his last dispatch from Judah Benjamin. It was dated March 2 and ordered Thompson to return to Richmond. He was told to keep enough cash to cover his expenses and deposit the rest with Fraser, Trenholm and Co. in Liverpool, England. Fraser, Trenholm and Co. had acted as financial agents for the Confederacy throughout the war. The dispatch was hand delivered by General Edwin Gray Lee when the two met in Montreal, where Thompson was staying pending the resumption of the trial of the St. Albans raiders.

Thompson was ordered to turn over $20,000 to Lee and to wire the remainder of his funds, less a sufficient amount to travel south, to Fraser, Trenholm and Co. The sum to be remitted should have been about $400,000, according to Benjamin.

Benjamin realized how little time remained for the Confederate States, because he told Thompson not to send a reply via courier, but to place an ad in the *New York Herald*. The ad was to say that a number of acres of land were for sale in Illinois, with the number of acres representing the amount in pounds sterling Thompson was remitting to the company. The amount of money that Thompson remitted — or didn't — would later become a sore point with the Confederate leadership in exile. As Thompson spent the immediate post-war years in Europe, living in high style, Confederate government debts went unpaid and former cabinet ministers, including Benjamin, were hounded for their repayment.

In the end, Lee received only $10,000 from Thompson, who resented the fact that Lee, a twenty-nine-year-old second cousin of the famous general, wouldn't divulge the nature of his plan. In his book *Confederate Operations in Canada and the North*, Oscar Kinchen speculates that Lee planned to attack the prison at Elmira, New York, and free Confederate prisoners there. Kinchen speculates that Lee sent courier John Surratt, whose mother was later executed as part of the Lincoln assassination conspiracy, to reconnoitre. Kinchen says the fact that Surratt was in Elmira at the time of Lincoln's murder supports the theory.

Meanwhile, Hines, whose small band had been burning federal boats along the upper Mississippi, was ordered by Thompson into Kentucky to begin creating a guerrilla command. When news came of Lee's surrender, Hines disbanded his team. He made for Detroit, and crossed over to Windsor.

Shortly after 10:00 p.m. on Good Friday, April 14, 1865, John Wilkes Booth killed President Abraham Lincoln, shooting him in the back of the head

It had been a full day for Lincoln, including a cabinet meeting attended by his commanding general, Ulysses S. Grant, during which the president related a recurring dream he had of a ship "moving with great rapidity toward a dark and indefinite shore." The cabinet discussed the problems of reconstruction and how to treat Confederate leaders. At 8.30 p.m. Lincoln left for Ford's Theater to see a comedy, *Our American Cousin*. Grant declined an invitation, saying he needed to spend time with his children.

At the theatre, the crowd cheered when Lincoln entered his box overlooking the stage. The play had just resumed when a pistol shot rang out. Everyone turned to the President's box, for that was where the sound had come from. Thinking, however, that it was part of the play they turned back to the stage, until John Wilkes Booth jumped down waving a long knife. Booth broke his leg in the fall, but he quickly jumped up and shouted, "Sic semper tyrannis [thus always tyrants], the South is avenged," before hobbling out of the theatre.

The President was taken across the street to a house where he was laid out on a table. The bullet was lodged near his eye, and he died the next morning. Outside, a cordon of troops kept the multitudes back. Many wept. Soon the house was full of doctors, cabinet ministers, and congressman. News arrived of another incident. Secretary of State William Seward, recovering at home from a carriage accident, had been stabbed by an assailant who had broken into his home. Only the heroics of his son and a plaster cast on his left arm saved him from death. He had managed to raise the arm, deflecting a potentially fatal knife thrust. Washington, still celebrating the surrender of the Confederate armies at Appomattox five days earlier, suddenly turned to mourning.

In Toronto, the *Globe*'s editor, John Robertson, who would later go on to own the *Toronto Telegram*, carried the news to George Brown's home. Brown wrote the lead editorial next day, condemning the assassination, praising Lincoln, and wondering what these momentous events might mean for reconstruction and relations between Canada and its southern neighbour. The pulpits of city churches and the editorial pages of newspapers greeted the assassination with sorrow. David Thurston, the U.S. consul in Toronto, wrote to his superiors that the spontaneous outpouring was unlike anything he had seen in his dozen years in Canada:

> The assassination was received with the profoundest exhibition of sympathy and indignation by all classes of citizens. By noon of Saturday [April 15], the streets were crowded with men and women, anxiously inquiring the news. The news offices were thronged and crowds collected in the streets. Business was literally suspended. There was a general manifestation of reverence and respect, especially gratifying to an American residing here. The flag of the Customs House was floating at half mast and on almost every vessel in the harbour, the same gesture of respect was observed. One univer-

sal feeling of horror seemed to wipe away all the differences of opinion between Northern and Southern sympathizers. The whole city presented the appearance of mourning and sorrow. The general expression of sympathy has afforded me much satisfaction and I have great pleasure in communicating it to the department.[188]

In Montreal, Consul John Potter noted the same sympathetic reaction, telling Seward in a letter on April 24 that on the day of the funeral, "business in the city was generally suspended and many buildings were draped in mourning. The expression seemed spontaneous and sincere."

But Potter was also aware of more hostile reactions among the large Southern exile community in Montreal. In the same dispatch, he said:

I am sorry to say there were some so devoid of all feeling, so wicked and depraved, as to exult over this great crime. I am more grieved to say that these persons — I cannot call them men — were but a short time since citizens of the United States, born under its flag and participants in its government. Treason has transformed them to brutes and eradicated all sense of moral sight.[189]

Two days after Potter wrote his letter, the Canadian connection to Booth became public. In the early morning of April 26, at a farm near Port Royal, Virginia, about forty miles south of Washington, Booth was trapped in a barn and fatally wounded. He died the next morning. Among the possessions found in his Washington hotel room was a Bank of Ontario pass book showing a credit of $455. Montrealers were well aware of the connection, and the *Gazette* reminded its readers of it on Monday, April 17, three days after the assassination:

He was in Montreal last winter, attempting to make an engagement with Mr. Buckland [owner of the Theatre Royale] He expressed himself as a southern sympathizer. While here, his expenditure was profuse and reckless and his habits intemperate. According to all accounts, he was a man capable of committing any wickedness for the sake of its notoriety.

In his letter to Seward on April 24, Potter pointed out Booth's Montreal connection. Potter also recorded the comings and goings of Thompson's courier John Surratt and his registration at the St. Lawrence Hall on April 6 and again on April 18.

"Booth was here in the latter part of October and probably under an assumed name at a subsequent date," Potter wrote. "J Wilkes Booth name appears in the register at the St. Lawrence Hall Oct. 18th 1864."

Potter added that detectives sent by the U.S. government were scouring the city for Surratt, who had disappeared. The detectives were interviewing everyone from porters at the St. Lawrence Hall to the taxi driver who had driven him to the hotel. Porter says Surratt simply disappeared, having told the hotel clerk he was taking an evening train to Quebec. Potter wrote, "He did not get on the train ... Detectives started for Three Rivers by boat, but failed to find any trace of him."

Thompson left Montreal for Halifax on April 14, the day of the assassination. He chose the overland route from Montreal, via Quebec and then south from Rivière du Loup, through the St. John River Valley. On May 2, while U.S. detectives were still hunting for Surratt, Thompson learned that President Andrew Johnson had charged him and the other Canadian commissioners with complicity in the Lincoln assassination.

The news prompted Thompson to write his last official communication of the war, one that he wanted to be as public as possible. The message was several thousand words long and was written as a letter to the editor of the *New York Tribune*. It was published May 22 and declared that the Lincoln's murder was "most unfortunate" not only for himself but also for the people of the South. It proclaimed Thompson's innocence (and ignorance) of any plot to assassinate Lincoln and denied that there was any link between Booth, Confederate President Davis, and the Canadian commissioners. (The conspiracy theory had been bolstered by the news that Booth had been a frequent visitor in Montreal in the fall of 1864. It is likely, though not confirmed, that Booth met Thompson there.) Thompson noted that there was about as much evidence to connect the Canadian Commissioners to the assassination as there was to connect it to President Johnson himself.

With that final blast, he sailed for England, ending his career as a soldier, diplomat, and spy.

EPILOGUE:
The Dominion of Canada

"We dined at public places together, played euchre in crossing the Atlantic, and went into society in England together. And yet on the day after [George Brown] resigned, we ceased to speak."
John A. Macdonald in his memoirs

In Ottawa and Toronto in the first week of July 1867, Canadians were celebrating. For George Brown and John A. Macdonald, it was the realization of a dream they had cherished in their different ways. It was a release from Macdonald's "dreary waste of colonial politics," and for Brown it offered "larger meadows and wider fields of play." The two had managed to overcome personal antipathy to build the most unlikely coalition in Canadian history; one that had worked with single-minded purpose towards this momentous day. Each basked with pride in the achievement. They had not spoken a word civilly in the ten years prior to the coalition, and nor would they once it collapsed. But for now, they were partners in a magnificent venture.

In Toronto, the church bells pealed "God Save the Queen" at midnight on June 30. Bonfires blazed in downtown streets as the city erupted in a carnival, with showers of fireworks lighting up the night, mingling with the clatter of small arms and dancing to greet the birth of a nation. George Brown arrived at his newspaper office just before midnight and began writing the next day's lead article. At dawn, as a twenty-one-gun salute boomed from the city's garrison, he was still at it. At 7:00 a.m., with a crowd waiting outside to buy the *Globe's* first edition, Brown was done writing a nine-thousand-word treatise that occupied the entire front page of the paper and most of the next.

"We hail the birthday of a new nationality," he wrote. "A United British America, takes it place this day among the nations of the world."

In Ottawa, Macdonald watched troops parade past Parliament Hill in a spectacular procession of colour and precision. The guns boomed 101 times as the crisp ranks of red-coated soldiers wound through the capital. Beside him sat an eminently satisfied Viscount Monck, whose quiet diplomacy had hastened the Confederation train along, kept American tempers from boiling over, and maintained a quiet and effective diplomacy during the trying final year of the war.

Americans watched the celebrations with mixed emotions. Few knew much about the vast land on their northern border, and most saw the new Dominion as a benign development. In the previous two years, Americans had focussed on healing the wounds of war and expanding westward across the Great Plains to California. Yet Americans were perplexed at the other celebration that saw Jefferson Davis treated as a hero during his visit to Canada. The *New York Times* was indignant when news of the raucous welcome at Toronto reached that city. How could such an "arch criminal" be received like a hero? *The New York Tribune* declared that the fuss made over Davis "proves that the Canadians are in a very bad condition of mind. They won't recover their equanimity until they are formally annexed."[190] These angry words were familiar to Canadians and had been the trump card played by Macdonald, Brown, and others during the Confederation debates. The Americans were always threatening to invade. Nationhood offered economic and military security.

Davis spent the first three days of June 1867 at Niagara-on-the-Lake, Ontario, among the gathered exiles. He played games with James Mason's grandchildren and attended an agricultural fair, where the talk was of May's heavy rains and June's hot weather. He helped Mason gather the eggs that his chickens carelessly laid around the small garden. It was cathartic and restorative, helping Davis purge the demons that had followed the South's defeat. Some months later he described to Robert E. Lee the humiliation of being "hooted at and jeered" at train stations throughout the Northern States, and yet he had been so thoroughly welcomed in Canada.

"For the first time since his capture two years before, he averred, he drew a full breath, feeling that he was breathing free air," Lee recalled. "He said that he instantly felt better and told me he believed it saved his life."[191]

Courtesy of the Ontario Archives

The mail steamer *Rothesay Castle* carried ex-Confederate President Jefferson Davis and his party from Toronto to Niagara-on-the-Lake.

Exchanges of letters that followed his Niagara visit show Davis also tried to determine what had become of the Confederate funds in Europe and those advanced to Thompson. Through Mason and Charles MacRae, at one time the Confederacy's chief business agent in England, Davis confirmed there was no money, only debts.

On the morning of June 3, his fifty-ninth birthday, Davis returned to Toronto. The next day, he was a guest at the wedding of William Hyde, editor of the *St. Louis Republican*, at St. James Cathedral. The *New York Times* reported that when Davis was recognized, he "was loudly cheered," and that "the event created quite a sensation."

Davis left Toronto for Montreal on June 6. More Canadian hospitality awaited him there. John Lovell, a wealthy local publisher, rescued the family from a boarding house and rented a narrow, three-storey home for them on Mountain Street near McGill University. It later became the home and office of noted Canadian poet William Drummond. The Davis family moved into the house in mid-June. Varina Davis, summing up the situation in her memoirs, referred to the family as "threadbare, great folks," unable to see a clear path forward. Her family had no money. Brierfield and Davis's brother's plantation, Hurricane, had both been destroyed. Her two young brothers were jobless and also in Montreal. The uncertainty about Davis's trial was a constant psychological weight.

In effort to rouse Davis from his lethargy, Varina suggested he begin work on his memoirs. In the vaults of the Bank of Montreal's main office in Place D'Armes in the heart of the old city, personal and official correspondence, letter books, and other dispatches had been gathering dust for two years. Varina had smuggled them out of Richmond at the end of the war, hiding them in a false bottom of a trunk. They had accompanied her mother and children on their journey to Canada and freedom in August 1865.

The trunk was sent to their home. At first, Davis read quietly. Soon, he came across a telegram from General Lee from April 9, 1865, the day Lee surrendered at Appomattox. In a moment Davis came to life. "All the anguish of that last great struggle came over us," Varina recalled.

We saw gaunt, half-clothed and half-starved men, their thin ranks a wall of fire around their homes; we saw them mowed down by a host of enemies, overcome, broken in health and fortune, moving along the highways to their desolated homes, sustained only by the memory of having vindicated their honor. He walked up and down distractedly, and then said, "Let us put them by for a while, I cannot speak of my dead so soon."[192]

Davis would not write his memoirs for another fifteen years.

Davis kept away from public places, declining most invitations, preferring solitude to the roar of the crowd. He appeared at one gala event that summer, a performance of Sheridan's comedy *The Rivals* at the Theatre Royale on the evening of July 18 — the same theatre where John Wilkes Booth had performed to a full house in the autumn of 1864. Friends insisted he appear, because part of the proceeds was destined for the Southern Relief Association, a charity that provided aid to Southerners.

The *Montreal Gazette* reported that Davis wore a simple black suit and carried a broad-rimmed white hat and thin cane. He was accompanied by one son and three female members of his household. As the party quietly took its place, murmurs ran through the audience, "and within moments the entire crowd from pit to box was on its feet cheering lustily."[193] The orchestra struck up "Dixie" and Davis, unsmiling, rose to his feet, acknowledging the reception.

Afterward, as Davis waited for his carriage, cheers rang out on the street. As he entered the carriage a man pushed forward and shoved a piece of paper in his hand. Reading it later at home, Davis saw it had only one word: "Andersonville." In that dreaded Confederate prison in Georgia, more than thirteen thousand Union prisoners had died of starvation, exposure, or disease.

It was Davis's last public appearance. In September, his family moved to Lennoxville, Quebec, so his sons could attend Bishop's College, frequented then by the children of other Confederate exiles. It was also cheaper than maintaining a house in Montreal.

In mid-November, Varina's mother, while visiting a sick friend in Vermont, became ill and, after returning to Montreal, she died. She was buried anonymously in Mount Royal Cemetery. It wasn't until 1959 that a headstone was erected.

Davis's doctor recommended that he not spend the winter in Canada, and so in late November the family left for Baltimore and from there for Havana, Cuba, and New Orleans. They returned to Lennoxville in the spring and early summer of 1868, before setting sail for England, "searching for their place in the world" and some means of support. As Varina wrote to a friend: "There must be relief from the wretched sense of idle dependence which has so galled us." Davis returned to Montreal in 1881, revisiting the places and people who had shown him kindness so soon after his release from prison. By then, he was settled in comfort, writing his memoirs at a plantation called Beauvoir on the shores of the Gulf of Mexico in Biloxi, Mississippi. And although he visited Toronto, he never did return to the town of Niagara.

Jacob Thompson's conduct has received mixed reviews. Either he was a scoundrel who absconded at war's end with hundreds of thousands of dollars entrusted to him, or he was a man of honour who looked after his friends long after Clement Clay and James Holcombe had abandoned their mission and cause.

By July 1865, Thompson was living in a Paris hotel with his wife, Kate. It was the beginning of an idyllic two-year meander through Europe and the Middle East during which the Thompsons travelled first class without any visible means of support. It is true that he was a wealthy man before the war, but much of that was in land and businesses destroyed by the conflict. The only other source of funds would have been sums held outside the country and the money advanced by Benjamin for the Canadian mission, a portion of which Benjamin allowed him to keep while in exile.

In August 1866, Thompson described his travels in a letter to a friend. He said the journey was being undertaken for pleasure and education. It began in Paris, where Kate had been educated, then Switzerland in the fall of 1865 and on to Rome for Christmas that year. From Rome they went to "delightful Naples," and as winter set they moved to Egypt, "the cradle of letters and learning," and Palestine, "to tred the ground our Savior trod. From here I came away a better man." By spring of 1866, the Thompsons were moving by steamer through the Greek Isles, up the Adriatic to Venice, "a most singular place, with a most marvelous history," then to Munich, Frankfurt, Cologne, Brussels, and Paris again. There, Mrs. Thompson left for Mississippi in early 1866 to be near to their son, Macon.

Author William C. Davis uncovered some clues to the missing money during his research of a biography of John C. Breckinridge, the Confederacy's last Secretary of War. Breckinridge was U.S. Vice-President in the administration of James Buchanan, the same government in which Thompson was Interior Secretary. After the war Breckinridge lived in Niagara-on-the-Lake, Ontario, where he was joined by Bennett Young and Tom Hines. Davis has made the case that Thompson absconded with hundreds of thousands entrusted to him for his secret mission. The basis of his belief came from letters that Davis found in a trunk in the possession of one of Breckinridge's descendants.[194]

Just days after Clay reported to Benjamin in Richmond, the Confederate capital fell and the war ended. Benjamin, Breckinridge, and Captain John Taylor Wood, the commander of the Confederate privateer *Tallahassee,* managed to escape through the Carolinas to Florida and from there to Cuba. Wood made his way to Montreal, while Breckinridge and Benjamin sailed for England. In July 1865, Wood wrote to Breckinridge relaying details of a meeting he'd had in Montreal with George Sanders and Beverley Tucker. The pair complained that Thompson had left for Europe with a $300,000 purse, leaving little if anything for them. Breckinridge turned the matter over to Benjamin, because Benjamin had been Thompson's superior during the Canadian adventure.

On September 3, Benjamin asked for the balance of the money Thompson was to have paid to Fraser, Trenholm and Co., as ordered by a letter hand-delivered by General Edwin Lee in March. Thompson had deposited £103,000, a portion of the requested sum.

Benjamin's letter was reprinted in Castleman's memoir *Active Service* and says in part: "I beg that you will make up your account with the department, so I can make use of any balance in your hands. I recognize in advance your right (and the propriety and justice of your exercising it) to retain such an amount as shall be necessary to your own maintenance."

Ten days later, on September 13, the men met in Paris and Thompson gave Benjamin £12,000. In return, Thompson received a letter saying the sum released him from all further claims by the Confederate government. The next day, Thompson wrote to Breckinridge explaining why he had kept the money and why he gave Benjamin the £12,000. William Davis found the letter in the course of his research. In it, Thompson says the Confederate government owed him money for his service in Canada and privations suffered. Thompson says he gave Benjamin the £12,000 after being informed that Benjamin had promised twice that sum held by Thompson to other Confederate creditors. Thompson gave Benjamin the cash "rather than have any difficulty that would lead to unpleasant consequences to me."

What could the Confederate authorities do? The leaders were broke and hounded by creditors. They seemed to believe that Thompson should have given them far more than he did. Yet Thompson believed he was entitled to compensation for living expenses, the destruction of his home and property, and the consequences of charges stemming from the Lincoln assassination. Thompson reasoned that since these charges related to his Confederate service and meant he must live in exile, he should be able to do so in reasonable comfort. The Confederate leadership did not have the money to sue Thompson, nor would that have been appropriate. The disgrace would stain the government and the cause at a time when the South had little else to sustain it. In those circumstances, £12,000 pounds was better than nothing. Davis concludes in his article that Thompson absconded with an unknown amount that was worth a small fortune at worst and a large one at best. "Just how much of his government's money Thompson embezzled is unknown. Documentary evidence shows that he stole at least £23,000 pounds which at the 1865 exchange rate was worth $113,780."

Two years later, in the summer of 1867, Thompson was living in Halifax with his wife and mother-in-law. Whatever the view of the Confederate leadership about his handling of his Canadian expenses, it appears that relations were cordial. He met at least once with Davis in the summer or fall of 1867, likely when Davis was in Montreal. In October 1867, Thompson wrote to a friend in Oxford, Mississippi, that he was living in a rented house in the city where his Canadian adventure had started.

"I live cheaply but pleasantly," he wrote to James Howry on October 8. "My only objection to the place is that I am too far removed from my old friends. Next spring, I sometimes think, I will go up to Canada and I will buy where I shall be within two days communication with Mississippi." He added, "I saw President Davis not long since. His health was fair and he seemed to be cheerful as usual."[195]

In May 1868, Thompson left Halifax for Montreal. A year later he was back in Oxford, but he moved to Memphis, Tennessee, where he died in March 1885 at the age of seventy-five. By then, he owned ten thousand acres of land in Mississippi, Missouri, Tennessee, and Long Island, New York. In Mississippi he had two plantations and a home in Oxford. His net worth exceeded $500,000 and included $100,000 in Bell Telephone stock. Davis does not think he could have amassed all this wealth in the sixteen years since the end of the war. He argues, "After the passing of a century, the evidence strongly indicates that part, if not all of this 'fortune', actually belonged to the Confederacy. It is safe to say that the character of the 'scrupulously honest' Mr. Thompson left something to be desired."

Judah Benjamin was left with his wits and his eternal optimism. This remarkable man, known as the Jewish Confederate, became a penniless exile at the age of fifty-five. His biggest asset was a law degree, which was useless in Great Britain. He joined a British firm as an articling student and within a year was called to bar. He went on to have a distinguished legal career in England, and his treatise on the sale of personal property, known as "Benjamin on Sales," became the benchmark treatise on the subject in British common law. It is still taught to students in Britain and Canada.

Benjamin died in May 1884 at the age of seventy-three. An obituary in the *Times of London* noted that Benjamin had "carved for himself by his own unaided exertions not one, but three ... histories of great and well-earned distinction."

In December 1865, George Brown resigned from the coalition government he formed with Macdonald. As Macdonald wrote in his memoirs, Brown's resignation returned their relationship to the status quo. "We acted together, dined at public places together, played euchre in crossing the Atlantic, and went into society in England together. And yet on the day after he resigned, we resumed our old positions and ceased to speak."[195]

Brown was defeated in Canada's first national elections in 1867. He gave up politics and returned to journalism, turning his hands to editing his newspaper and raising his three children together with his wife, Anne. He remained a power in the inner circles of the Liberal party. In 1874, he was appointed a senator from Ontario. Brown died in 1880 at the age of sixty-eight. A disgruntled employee shot him during a struggle and the minor leg wound became infected. His paper merged with the *Mail and Empire* in 1936 and survives today as Toronto's *Globe & Mail*. Brown's Liberal voice is now a Conservative one.

Conservative Party chieftain John A. Macdonald became Canada's first prime minister. He oversaw the expansion of the country from sea to sea, surviving scandals to dominate Canadian politics for half a century. He set the policy goals by which future generations of political leaders would govern, including an overriding caution when dealing with the United States. During Macdonald's first administration between 1867 and 1873, he was a nation builder, adding Manitoba, Saskatchewan, and Alberta (then know as the Northwest Territories), plus British Columbia and Prince Edward Island, to Confederation. The enormous cost of these plans, a scandal involving the Canadian Pacific Railway, and Macdonald's personal problems, which included bouts of heavy drinking, contributed to his defeat in 1873. In 1878 he returned to power, and he died in office in 1891 at the age of seventy-six.

Lord Monck remained in Canada until 1868. The British government extended his term by one year as a special favour, so he could become the country's first Governor General. Monck was well-respected and liked by Canadian government officials, though considered aloof and stiff by most ordinary Canadians. In a letter to Nova Scotia's premier Charles Tupper, just before Monck left, Macdonald said: "I like him amazingly and shall be very sorry when he leaves as he has been a very efficient and prudent administrator. He has managed the relations between Canada and the United States with great discretion, [when] the slightest mistake might have created a war."

In 1868, Monck returned to Ireland, where he served as lord lieutenant of Dublin County between 1874 and 1892. He died in 1899 at the age of seventy-five.

In May 1865, Clement Clay surrendered to American authorities in Macon, Georgia, to face charges in connection with his Canadian activities and complicity in the assassination of President Lincoln. He was taken to Fortress Monroe, near Washington, where he was imprisoned with Jefferson Davis. Clay was released in April 1866, after eleven months in prison. He settled on his plantation in Jackson County, Alabama, and devoted himself to agricultural pursuits and the practice of law. He died on January 3, 1882. He was sixty-six.

James Holcombe returned to Virginia and opened a private school that attracted students from prominent Southern families. A combination of failing health and a natural ineptitude for business caused the school to fail, even though enrollment had increased from 43 students in 1866 to 101 in 1870. Holcombe died in August 1873. He was fifty-three.

After his release from jail in the fall of 1865, Bennett Young remained in Toronto, where he tutored John C. Breckinridge's children. Young spent some time in Europe with Breckinridge and studied for a time at Queen's University in Belfast. He felt unable to pursue his theological studies and started at the University of Toronto in 1863, instead taking up law, perhaps as a consequence of his own brushes with the legal system in 1864 and 1865. He returned to Kentucky in 1868 and became a prominent lawyer and judge.

In 1911, at the age of sixty-eight, Young paid a visit to Montreal, the scene of his imprisonment all those years ago. "I have not been here since April, 1865 and I thought I would come once more and see the old town," the *Montreal Gazette* quoted him as saying in a report on July 20. The article brought a stream of visitors to Young's suite at the Ritz Carlton hotel. Among them was Jack Abbott, whose father, John Abbott, had defended him and had gone on to become Canada's third prime minister. An aging Adolph Bissonnette, one of the Montreal policemen who had pursued Young after his release by Judge Coursol, also paid a visit. Eight days later, a group of prominent St. Albans citizens made their way to Montreal. The *Gazette* reported that it was an extraordinary function where Young and the Vermonters relived the events of forty-six years earlier. Oscar Kinchen captured the event in his book *Daredevils of the Confederate Army*. Kinchen described how Young recalled his raid as "a reckless escapade of a youth of 21 years, steeped in patriotism for the South, and on reflection wondered that he undertook it at all." Young died in 1919. He was seventy-six.

Tom Hines remained in Canada until March 1866, when, together with his wife, Nancy, he also returned to Kentucky. Hines, like Young, became a successful lawyer and eventually became Chief Justice of the Kentucky Court of Appeals. He died in 1898, aged fifty-seven.

John Headley went into the tobacco wholesaling business and prospered. He was Kentucky's Secretary of State between 1891 and 1896. In 1906, he published his memoirs, *Confederate Operations in Canada and New York*, which described his exploits, including the firebombing of New York.

John Castleman stayed in Canada after the war, sharing a house in Toronto with Hines and George Eastin. Castleman studied French at the University of Toronto and received law tutoring from Breckinridge. In the spring of 1866, he joined the Thompsons, then touring England and Ireland. Later that year, Castleman was pardoned and returned to Kentucky. He too studied law and set up a thriving practice in Louisville. In 1883, he was appointed adjutant general of the state militia, and during the Spanish-American War in 1898 he served as a brigadier-general. The unit saw service during the invasion of Puerto Rico, and Castleman served as military governor of that island. His many varied careers included two stints as Kentucky's adjutant general, as well as founder and first commissioner of Louisville's park department. His memoirs, *Active Service*, were published in 1917, a year before his death at the age of seventy-seven.

George Denison maintained his anti-Northern feelings to the end. In 1866, his regiment, the Governor General's Bodyguard, saw action during the Fenian invasion. He founded the Canada First party in 1871. The party sought closer ties to Britain and portrayed the United States as the chief threat to Canada. He wanted a federation of the British Empire with Canada as an equal partner. Denison believed this would give Canada the prestige and security it needed to achieve greatness.

Ever restless, George sold his law practice to his brother. He became an internationally renowned military historian, and his work on cavalry tactics — drawing heavily on the experience of the American Civil War — won a prize sponsored by Russian Czar Nicholas I. In 1870, George was part of the expedition to put down Louis Riel's rebellion in the North West. In 1877, he became a Toronto police court judge, a position he held for forty-three years.

Denison maintained his close ties with Civil War–era Southern leaders. He corresponded off and on with Robert E. Lee, whom he described in his memoirs, *Soldiering in Canada*, as "one of those men that made the ancients believe in demigods." Cavalry General Jubal Early was a frequent guest at Hayden Villa, as were Breckinridge and Generals John McCausland and John Bell Hood. In 1882, Denison visited Jefferson Davis at Beauvoir. Denison died in Toronto in 1925 at the age of eighty-six.

And what of the three-hundred-day Confederate campaign in Canada? It was a desperate gamble at a time when the Confederate States were running out of options. It was led by a divided set of commissioners, with unrealistic expectations and little practical experience to effectively organize and implement their plans. The schemes brought Canada, Great Britain, and the United States the closest to war since the Trent Affair of 1861. For a brief moment, the commissioners grabbed headlines and caused panic, diverting attention from the slow suffocation of the Confederacy.

Jacob Thompson's guerrilla war did not change the outcome of the conflict, nor did it create or carry Confederation. Yet for Canadians it served as a catalyst: a poignant reminder of the perils of existence so close to a large and unruly neighbour. Coming as it did at a time when they had decided to secure their own future, it could be said that the final days of the embattled states of Dixie did in a small way help the Canadians form their own Dominion. In one of those serendipitous twists of fate, Jefferson Davis and Jacob Thompson were both present on Canadian soil to witness the official birth in 1867. But the real legacy is the one that has developed since then, the one Prime Minister Chrétien alluded to on Parliament Hill. It is that in the 130-plus years since the war, Canada and the United States have woven a richly embroidered, shared cloth of friendship that has seen the two countries live side by side on the northern half of the continent as friends, neighbours, and family.

A NOTE ON SOURCES

Scholars on both sides of the border have examined the events of 1864, but usually from only one of the two points of view. There are many accounts of the Northwestern Conspiracy, from the 1906 first-person account of John Headley, *Confederate Operations in Canada and New York*, to John Castleman's *Active Service*, published in 1917, to Oscar Kinchen's *Confederate Operations in Canada and the North*, published in 1970. There is also James Horan's 1954 popular account, *Confederate Agent*, with its focus on the exploits of Captain Tom Hines. All four were used as a resource for *Dixie & the Dominion*. On the Canadian side of border, several works touch on the impact of the war on Confederation. Notable among them are J.M.S. Careless's two-volume set *Brown of the Globe*, published in 1959 and 1963 respectively. Historian Donald Creighton's two-volume study of Canada's first prime minister, beginning with *John A. Macdonald: The Young Politician*, published in 1952, is also an invaluable resource. *The Road to Confederation: The Emergence of Canada*, Creighton's 1964 work, puts many of the events in a broader perspective, as does W. L. Morton's *The Critical Years: The Union of British North America*. Brian Jenkins's two volumes, *Britain and the War for the Union*, published in 1974 and 1980, provide an authoritative look at Anglo-American relations throughout the period.

The one work that stands out is Robin Winks's *Canada and the United States: The Civil War Years*, an exhaustive treatise that examines every nuance of the war's impact on Canada. Not coincidentally, Winks, a professor of history at Yale University, is the first non-Canadian to win the Governor General's Award for Canadian Studies. His book was originally published in 1960. The scholarship has proved so enduring, it was reprinted in 1988. Those interested in the details surrounding the St. Albans raid and its aftermath may wish to take a look at Dennis K. Wilson's *Justice Under Pressure*, a 1992 work that is a thorough and compelling look at that event.

For those wishing to look at the raw archival material, there is plenty of it, if you have the time and inclination. Some, like the Official Records of the War of Rebellion, are online, and you can browse them from the comfort of your home.

Here are archival collections visited by the author:

* The George Brown Papers in the Public Archives of Canada (PAC) in Ottawa contain Brown's correspondence, including letters written to his wife. The letters offers insights into his personality, portraits of key Confederation players, and views of the progress of the war. They also provide the flavour of the politics, attitudes, and social conventions of the time.

* Governor General Viscount Monck, papers and records, PAC Record Group 7 is divided into twenty-three series, numbered from G1 to G23, each sub-divided into volumes. They contain thousands of official dispatches, letters, and documents that round out the North American diplomatic relationship. The collection includes letters from Monck to Colonial Secretary Edward Cardwell and vice versa, from Monck to Lord Lyons, head of the British Legation in Washington, and from Monck to U.S. Secretary of State Seward. The correspondence relates to the American Civil War period.

* Governor General's Secretary, papers and records, PAC. This is a selection of material about the St. Alban's Raid and the organization of the Confederate spy ring in Canada. It is made up mainly of letters between Monck and Colonial Secretary Cardwell, letters between Monck and U.S. Secretary of State Seward, and papers relating to the extradition of the St. Alban's raiders.

* Governor General's numbered files, PAC. These files contain correspondence between Canadian, British, and American officials, primarily about Confederate activities in Canada, including the St. Albans Raid. They also contain a letter from Clement Clay to Confederate Secretary of State Judah Benjamin, describing the effect of the raid.

* Commander of the British Army in Canada, letter and files, PAC. Starting with Series C, Volume 696, these bound manuscripts include the original correspondence received in the office of the military secretary to the commander of the British forces in Canada and some drafts of outgoing correspondence. The papers relating to the Civil War are collected in Volumes 696–9 and are arranged chronologically. Volume 698 relates to 1864.

* Guillaume Lamothe Papers, PAC. Lamothe was Montreal's police chief in 1864 and a Southern sympathizer. Lamothe helped the St.

Albans raiders escape to Nova Scotia before a second set of charges could be laid. His papers contain a handwritten account of those events. They also offer insights into local views of the Southern cause.

* John A. Macdonald Papers, PAC. John A., Canada's first prime minister, was militia minister throughout most of 1864. His papers, organized in volumes, include special compilations about the St. Albans Raid, defence, the militia, and the border police. Letters are also organized by correspondent, including John S. Macdonald, Governor General Monck, and George Brown.

* John Sandfield Macdonald Papers, Ontario Archives, Toronto Papers. Letters and clippings relating to the life and times of John S. Macdonald, premier of the province of Canada between 1862 and 1864 and Ontario's first premier, 1867-71. Also includes JSM-Langlois papers, and JSM-Waggaman papers. Waggaman is the surname of Macdonald's wife, Christine. Her family were Louisiana planters, and her brother Eugene was a colonel in the 10th Louisiana Infantry.

* Clement C. Clay Papers, Duke University Library, Chapel Hill, N.C. This large collection of papers of the Clay family of Alabama is found in the Records of Ante-Bellum Southern Plantations from the Revolution through the Civil War. Series F. Part I relates to the Clays. The material includes letters and fragments of a diary of Clement Clay, second-in-command of the Canadian mission between May 1864 and January 1865

* Clement C. Clay Jr. Papers, National Archives (NAUS), Washington, DC. Record Group 109 is a collection of papers and letters sent by Clay to the government at Richmond relating to his adventures in Canada. It includes papers seized by federal troops after the fall of Richmond in April 1865 and those intercepted by federal agents. It includes dispatches from Clay to Secretary of State Judah Benjamin, Clay to President Jefferson Davis, notes passed between Commissioner Jacob Thompson and Clay, and letters to Clay from prominent Northern politicians.

* Thomas Hines Papers, University of Kentucky, Lexington; Filson Club, Louisville. Hines was largely responsible for carrying out the Northwestern Conspiracy plans. The University of Kentucky collection contains his notes on the conspiracy, written after the war as part of an extended article that appeared in *Southern Bivouac* in 1886–87. It also contains letters, newspaper clippings, and other printed matter. The Filson Club material (not seen by the author) contains miscellaneous letters.

* U.S. Consuls in Toronto and Montreal, 1864–65, (NAUS). This rich source of correspondence between the consuls and

the Secretary of State provide a uniquely Northern perspective on Confederate activities in the Canadas throughout 1864. Consular dispatches from agents in Toronto and Montreal to William Seward are the sources primarily used in *Dixie & the Dominion*. The reels are T-491 and T-222.

BIBLIOGRAPHY

Manuscripts

Gould, Ernest. "The United States and Canadian Confederation." M.A. Thesis, University of Toronto, 1934.

Holmes, John W. "Border relations between Canada and the U.S. during the American Civil War." M.A. Thesis University of Toronto, 1933.

Oldham, Dorothy. "Life of Jacob Thompson." M.A. thesis. University of Mississippi. 1930.

Overholtzer, Harry. "Nova Scotia and the United States' Civil War." M.A. Thesis, Dalhousie University, 1965.

Whyte, George H. "Confederate Operations in Canada during the Civil War." M.A. Thesis, McGill University, 1968.

Contemporary Books

Baker, Lafayette C. *History of the United States Secret Service.* Philadelphia: L.C. Baker, King & Baird printers, 1867.

Benjamin, L.N. *The St. Albans Raid; or investigation into the charges against Lieut. Bennett H. Young and command for their acts at St. Albans, Vt.* Montreal: John Lovell, St. Nicholas St., 1865.

Bett, F.P. (ed.). *Memoirs of Susan Sibbald, 1783–1866.* London: 1926.

Borrett, George T. *Letters from Canada and the U.S.* London: 1865.

Castleman, J.B. *Active Service.* Louisville: Courier Journal, 1917.

Claiborne, J.F.H. *Mississippi as a Province, a Territory and a State.* Jackson, Mississippi:1880.

Colquhoun, A.H. *The Fathers of Confederation: A Chronicle of the birth of the Dominion.* Glasgow: Brook & Co., 1916.

Davis, Jefferson. *The Rise and Fall of the Confederate Government*, 2 vols. New York: 1882.

Davis, Varina H. *Jefferson Davis, Ex-President of the Confederate States* of America. A Memoir by his wife. 2 vols. New York: 1890.

Day, S.P. English America: Or Pictures of Canadian Places and People, Vol. 1 and II. London: 1864.

Denison, George. Soldiering in Canada. London: Morang & Co., 1901.

Headley, John. Confederate Operations in Canada and New York. Neale, 1906.

Lovell, Sarah. Reminiscences of Seventy Years. Montreal: John Lovell & Son, 1908.

McGee, D'Arcy. Speeches and Addresses chiefly on the subject of British-American Union. London: 1865.

Official Records of the Union and Confederate Armies, 70 volumes. Washington: 1880-1901.

Official Records of the Union and Confederate Navies, 30 volumes. Washington: 1904-22.

Pitman, Benn. The Assassination of President Lincoln and the Trial of the Conspirators. New York: Moore, Wilstach and Baldwin, 1865.

Russell, W. H. Canada: Its Defences, Conditions and Resources. Boston: 1865.

My Diary North & South. London: 1865.

Scadding, Henry. Toronto: Past and Present. Toronto: 1882.

Seitz, Don. Horace Greeley. Indianapolis: Bobbs-Merrill, 1926.

Trollope, Anthony. North America. De Capo Press (reprinted from Alfred A Knopf), 1951.

Wolseley, Sir Garnet. The Story of a Soldier's Life, Vol. II. London: 1904.

Secondary Sources

American Dictionary of Biography, 12 Volumes. New York: Scribner, 1986.

Bakeless, John. Spies of the Confederacy. Philadelphia: J.B. Lippincott Co., 1970.

Beck, Murray. Joseph Howe: Voice of Nova Scotia, Toronto: McClelland & Stewart, 1964.

Bradford, Gamaliel. Confederate Portraits. Ayer Co., 1914. Reprinted New York: 1968.

Butler, Pierce. Judah P. Benjamin. American Crisis Biography. Philadelphia: George W. Jacobs & Co., 1907.

Callahan, J.M. American Foreign Policy in Canadian Relations. New York: 1937.

Careless, J.M.S. Brown of the Globe, Vol. II: Statesman of Confederation 1860–1880. Toronto: Macmillan, 1963.

Careless, J.M.S. Canada: A Story of Challenge. Toronto, 195e.

Careless, J.M.S. (Ed.). The Pre-Confederation Premiers: Ontario Government Leaders, 1841–1867. Toronto: University of Toronto Press, 1980.

Catton, Bruce. *Terrible Swift Sword*. Garden City, NY: Doubleday, 1963.

Collard, Andrew C. *Montreal Yesterdays*. Toronto: Longmans Canada, 1962.

Collard, Andrew C. *Call Back Yesterdays*. Toronto: Longmans Canada, 1965.

Commager, Henry S. *The Blue and the Gray*. New York: Bobbs Merrill Co., 1950.

Cottrell, John. *Anatomy of an Assassination: The Murder of Abraham Lincoln*. New York: 1966.

Creighton, Donald G. *John A. Macdonald: The Young Politician*. Toronto: Macmillan, 1952.

Creighton, Donald G. *Dominion of the North: A History of Canada*. Revised Edition. Toronto: Macmillan, 1957.

Creighton, Donald G. *The Road to Confederation: The Emergence of Canada 186–67*. Toronto: 1964.

Dabney, Virginius. *Richmond: The Story of a City*. New York: Doubleday, 1976.

Davis, William C. *Breckinridge: Statesman, Soldier, Symbol*. University of Louisiana Press, 1976.

Davis, William C. *Jefferson Davis: The Man and His Hour*. Toronto: Harper Collins, 1991.

Duberman, Martin (Ed.). *The Anti-slavery Vanguard: New essays on the Abolitionists*. Princeton: 1965.

Evans, Eli. *Judah Benjamin: The Jewish Confederate*. New York: The Free Press, 1988.

Fermer, Douglas. *James Gordon Bennett and the New York Herald: A Study of Editorial Opinion in the Civil War*. Boydell Press, 1986.

Fremantle, Lieutenant Colonel Arthur. *Three Months in the Southern States, April–June 1863*. University of Nebraska Press. 1991.

Gagan, David. *The Denison Family of Toronto 1792–1925*. University of Toronto Press, 1973.

Gougeon, Gille. *A History of Quebec Nationalism*. Toronto: James Lorimer & Co., 1994.

Gray, Clayton. *Conspiracy in Canada*. Montreal: L'Atelier Press, 1959.

Hanna, A. J. *Flight into Oblivion*. Ayer Publishing Co., 1936.

Hanson, M.L. *The Mingling of the Canadian and American Peoples*, vol. I. New Haven: 1940.

Haythornthwaite. *Uniforms of the Civil War*. New York: Sterling Publishing Philip Co., 1990.

Hendrick, Burton. *Statesmen of the Lost Cause: Jefferson Davis and his Cabinet*. New York: Literary Guild, 1939.

Hodgins, Bruce W. *John Sandfield Macdonald*. Toronto: University of Toronto Press, 1971.

Horan, James D. *Confederate Agents A Discovery in History*. Fairfax Press, 1954.

Jenkins, Brian. *Britain and the War for the Union*, vol. 1 & 2. McGill-Queens University Press, 1974, 1980.

Jenkins, Kathleen. *Montreal: Island City of the St. Lawrence*. New York: Doubleday & Co., 1966.

Jones, John B. *A Rebel War Clerk's Diary at the Confederate Capital*, vol. I. New York: Old Hickory Bookshop, 1935.

Kinchen, Oscar. *Confederate Operations in Canada and the North: A little known phase of the American Civil War*. North Quincy, Massachusetts: Christopher Publishing House, 1970.

Kinchen, Oscar. *Daredevils of the Confederate Army*, 1959.

Kirby, William. *Annals of Niagara*. Toronto: Macmillan, 1927.

Kirkland, H.C. *The Peacemakers of 1864*. New York: 1927.

Landon, Fred. *Western Ontario and the American Frontier*. Toronto: McClelland and Stewart, 1967.

Lehmann, Joseph. *All Sir Garnet: A Life of Field Marshall Lord Wolseley*. London: Jonathan Cape, 1964.

Long, E.B. *The Civil War Day by Day: An Almanac 1861–1865*. New York: Da Capo Press Inc, 1971.

Lonn, Ella. *Foreigners in the Confederacy*. University of North Carolina Press, 1965.

Luvaas, Jay. *The Education of an Army*. University of Chicago Press, 1964.

Luvaas, Jay. *The Military Legacy of the Civil War: The European Inheritance*. University of Chicago Press, 1959.

Macdonald, Helen. *Canadian Public Opinion on the American Civil War*. New York: 1926.

Marden, James. *Historic Niagara Falls*. Lundy's Lane Historical Society, 1932.

Martyn, L. Booth. *Toronto: 100 Years of Grandeur*. Toronto: Pagurian Press, 1978.

McPherson, James M. *Battle Cry of Freedom: The Civil War Era*. New York: Oxford University Press, 1988.

Marr, W.L. *Canada: An Economic History*. Toronto: Macmillan of Canada, 1980.

Meade, Robert D. *Judah P. Benjamin, Confederate Statesman*. Ayer Co., 1943.

Milton, George. *Abraham Lincoln and the Fifth Column*. New York: Viking Press, 1942.

Morrison, Neil F. *Garden Gateway to Canada*. Toronto: Ryerson Press, 1954.

Morton, W.L. *The Critical Years: The Union of British North America, 1857-1873*. Toronto: 1964.

Morton, W.L. *The Kingdom of Canada*. Toronto: McClelland and Stewart, 1968.

Nichols, Roy F. *The Disruption of American Democracy*. New York: Collier, 1962.

Nuremberger, Ruth. *The Clays of Alabama*. Lexington: University of Kentucky Press, 1958.

Parish, Peter J. *The American Civil War*. New York: Holmes & Meier, 1975.

Pope, Sir Joseph. *Memoirs of the Right Honourable Sir John A. Macdonald*. Toronto: Oxford University Press, 1930.

Raddall, Thomas H. *Halifax Warden of the North*. New York: Doubleday, 1965.

Rawley, James A. *Turning Points of the Civil War*. Lincoln: University of Nebraska Press, 1966.

Rawls, Walton (Ed.). *Great Civil War Heroes and their Battles*. New York: Abbeville Press, 1985.

Report of the Earl of Durham, second edition.

Robinson, W.M. *The Confederate Privateers*. New Haven: 1928.

Ross, Ishbel. *First Lady of the South: The Life of Mrs. Jefferson Davis*. New York: Harper & Bros., 1958.

Rolland, Unbar (Ed.). *Jefferson Davis Constitutionalist. His Letters, Papers and Speeches*. Ten Volumes. Jackson, Mississippi: 1923.

Sandburg, Carl. *Abraham Lincoln: The Prairie Years and The War Years*. One-volume edition. New York: Harcourt, Brace & Co., 1939.

Singleton R.G. *John Taylor Wood: Sea Ghost of the Confederacy*. University of Georgia Press, 1979.

Shippee, L.B. *Canadian-American Relations, 1849–1874*. New Haven, 1939.

Sisson, C. B. *Egerton Ryerson: His Life and Letters*, vol. II. Toronto: Clarke, Irwin & Co., 1947.

Skelton, O.D. *The Life and Times of Sir Alexander Tilloch Galt*. Toronto: 1920. Reprinted Carleton Library, 1966.

Slattery, T.P. *The Assassination of D'Arcy McGee*. Toronto: Doubleday Canada, 1968.

Starr, Stephen Z. *Colonel Grenfell's Wars*. Baton Rouge: Louisiana State University Press, 1971.

Stern, Philip. *Secret Missions of the Civil War*. New York: 1959.

Tidwell, William. *Come Retribution: The Confederate Secret Service and the Assassination of Abraham Lincoln*. University Press of Mississippi, 1988.

Todd, Richard C. *Confederate Finance*. Athens: University of Georgia Press, 1954.

Trollope, Anthony. *North America*. New York: De Capo Press, 1951.

Waite, P.B. *The Life and Times of Confederation*. Toronto: University of Toronto Press, 1961.

Waite, P.B. (Ed.) *The Confederation Debates in the Province of Canada, 1865*. McClelland & Stewart, 1963.

Weichmann, Louis. *A True History of the Assassination of Abraham Lincoln and the Conspiracy of 1865*. (Floyd Risvold Ed.) Vintage Books, 1975.

West, Bruce. *Toronto*. Toronto: Doubleday Canada Ltd, 1967.

Wheeler, Richard. *Sword Over Richmond: An Eyewitness History of McClellan's Peninsula Campaign*. New York: Harper & Row, 1986.

Wilson, Dennis K. *Justice Under Pressure: The Saint Albans Raid and Its Aftermath*. University Press of America, 1992.

Winks, Robin W. *Canada and the United States: The Civil War Years*. Baltimore: John Hopkins University Press, 1960.

Wise, Stephen. *Lifelines of the Confederacy*. University of South Carolina Press, 1988.

Wise, S.F. & L. Brown. *Canada views the United States: Nineteenth Century Political Attitudes*. Seattle and London: University of Washington Press, 1967.

Woodward, Vann (Ed.). *Mary Chesnut's Civil War*. New Haven and London: Yale University Press, 1981.

Articles

Baird, Nancy D. "The Yellow Fever Plot." *Civil War Times Illustrated*, November, 1974.

Chitty, Arthur B. "Enduring Memorial: A brief history of the University of the South." Sewannee, Tennessee.

Creighton, Donald G. "The United States and Canadian Confederation." *Canadian Historical Review*. 39:209-222. September 1958.

Davis, William C. "The Real Mr. Thompson." *Civil War Times Illustrated*, May 1970.

Downer, Edward T. "Johnson Island." *Civil War History*. Vol. VIII, 202-217, 1962.

Frohman, Charles E. "Piracy on Lake Erie." *Inland Seas*, XIV, 172-80.

Gagnon, Paul. "Why Study History?" *The Atlantic Monthly*, November 1988. 43-66.

Hamer, Marguerite. "Luring Canadian Soldiers into Union Lines during the War Between the States." *Canadian Historical Review*. 27:150-162. June 1946.

Hanchett, William. "Lincoln's Murder: The Simple Conspiracy Theory." *Civil War Times Illustrated*. November/December, 1991. P. 28.

Johnson, Ludwell. "Beverley Tucker's Canadian Mission, 1864-1865." *Journal of Southern History*. Vol. 29. 1963, 88–99.

Kazar, John D. "The Canadian View of the St. Albans Raid." *Vermont History*, Vol. 33, #1, January 1965.

Landon, Fred. "Canadian Opinion of Southern Secession 1860–61." *Canadian Historical Review* 1:255-266. 1920.

Landon, Fred. "American Civil War and Canadian Confederation." *Royal Society of Canada Transactions* 3rd series 21 sec 2) 55-62, 1927.

MacDonald, Cheryl. "Canada's Secret Police." *The Beaver*. June–July, 1991.

Mayers, Adam. "Spies Across the Border." *Civil War Times Illustrated*. June 2001.

Mayers, Adam. "Running the Gauntlet." *Civil War Times Illustrated*. June 2001.

Mayers, Adam. "Stolen Soldiers." *Civil War Times Illustrated*. May/June 1995.

Mayers, Adam. "They Came to Watch: Foreign Officers Follow the Armies." *Civil War Times Illustrated*. December 1994.

Mayers, Adam. "The Prisoner and the Prime Minister." *Civil War Times Illustrated*. August 1993.

Mayers, Adam. "Montreal's Posh Rebel Rendezvous." *Civil War Times Illustrated*. February 1993.

McLean, Guy. "The Georgian Affair." *Canadian Historical Review*. 42:133-44, June 1961.

McCulloch, Ian. "Billy and Johnny Canuck." *Civil War*. September–October, 1993.

Meade, Robert D. "The Relations between Judah P. Benjamin and Jefferson Davis." *Journal of Southern History*. Volume V, (1939), 468-478.

Rainwater, P.L. (ed.) "Letters to and from Jacob Thompson." *Journal of Southern History*. Vol. 6 1940.

Raney, William F. "Recruiting and Crimping in Canada for the Northern Forces, 1861–65." *Mississippi Valley Historical Review*. Vol. X, June 1923.

Roby, Yves. "The United States and Confederation." *Canadian Historical Association Annual Reports* (No.4, 1967).

Shepard, F.T. "The Johnson Island Plot." *Buffalo Historical Society Publications*, Vol. 9, 1906, 1-52.

Stacey, C.P. "Lord Monck and the Canadian Nation." *Dalhousie Review*. Vol. 14, July 1934, 179-91.

Stouffer, Allen. "Canadian-American Relations in the Shadow of the Civil War." *Dalhousie Review*. Vol. 57, Summer 1977. 3 32-46.

Trotter, R.G. "Lord Monck and the Great Coalition of 1864." *Canadian Historical Review*. Vol. 3, No. 2, June, 1922, 181-186.

White, Randall. "The Mirror of an Age: Toronto and George Brown's Globe." *The Beaver*. October/November 1988. 4.

Winks, Robin. "The Creation of a Myth: 'Canadian' Enlistments in the Northern Armies during the American Civil War." *Canadian Historical Review*. 39:24-40, March 1958.

Zornow, W.F. "Confederate Raiders on Lake Erie." *Inland Seas*, Vol. I, 4, 1945, 1-47.

"Confederate Raiders on Lake Erie: Their Propaganda Value in 1864." *Inland Seas*, V, Spring, Summer 1949, pp.42-47, 101-105.

"John Wilson Murray and the Johnson's Island Plot." *Inland Seas*, VI, (4) 249-57.

Newspapers

Buffalo Courier
Hamilton Spectator
Kingston Whig Standard
Memphis Daily Appeal
Montreal Gazette
Montreal Witness
New York Herald
New York Times
New York Tribune
Niagara Mail
St. Catharines Constitution
Toronto Globe
Toronto Leader
Windsor Star

NOTES

Chapter 1

1   George Denison, *Soldiering in Canada*, London: Morang & Co., 1901. 81.
2   *Hamilton Spectator*, June 1, 1867.
3   *Niagara Mail*, June 3, 1867.

Chapter 2

4   Clement Clay kept a diary while in Canada. What remains is in the Clay Family Papers, Records of Ante-Bellum Southern Plantations, Series F, Part 1 at Duke University. Key portions of the diary are missing, presumed destroyed by Clay to protect himself after his return from Canada.
5   The USS *Britannia* was the first Union ship to give chase. They fired round after round, but none of the shells hit the *Raleigh*. For its part, the best the *Raleigh* could do was shoot out the binnacle light on the *Britannia*'s deck. The commotion, however, brought the USS *Howquah* steaming to the *Britannia*'s rescue. In all, the *Howquah* fired nineteen rounds at the *Raleigh*, hitting the ironclad twice. Both shells bounced off. The *Raleigh* returned fire five times, scoring one direct hit on the *Howquah*'s smokestack, leaving behind an eight-inch hole as her calling card.
6   Cleary's version of events was quoted in an account of the *Thistle*'s run from Wilmington in *Southern Bivouac*, Vol. II, No. 7, December 1886, 444. The post–Civil War magazine told the stories of Confederate veterans.
7   Clay diary, 9.
8   Kinchen, Oscar. *Confederate Operations in Canada and the North: A little known phase of the American Civil War*. North Quincy, Massachusetts: Christopher Publishing House, 1970. 34 ff.

9   Kinchen, *Confederate Operations*, 25.

10 Roy F. Nichols, *Disruption of American Democracy,* New York: Collier, 1962. 91; *Southern Bivouac*, Vol. II #7 December 1886, 502; J.B. Castleman, *Active Service*, Louisville: Courier Journal, 1917.133.

11 The money was made available by Congress, which had passed a Secret Service Act in February. The Act set aside $1 million for clandestine operations, of which a large portion was destined for the Canadian operation. The government released cotton to middlemen at border points with the Union, and the middlemen issued bills of exchange payable either in pounds sterling or gold. Thompson would deposit his drafts at the Bank of Ontario in Montreal, the same bank used by his acquaintance John Wilkes Booth.

12 Clay to Texas Senator Louis Wigfall, April 29, 1864, in Ruth Nuremberger, *The Clays of Alabama*, Lexington: University of Kentucky Press, 1958. 232.

13 P.L. Rainwater, "Letters to and from Jacob Thompson," *Journal of Southern History* Vol. 6, 1940; Dorothy Oldham, "The Life of Jacob Thompson." MA Thesis, University of Mississippi, 1930.

14 Official Records of the War of Rebellion (OR), Series 2, Vol. 3, 174, April 27, 1864. Davis to Thompson, Davis to Clay.

15 A month later, on June 4, as the *Thistle* returned to Wilmington. She was captured not far from Cape Fear after a seventy-mile chase. Her cargo and manifests had been thrown overboard. Wooden cases that were thought to have contained rifles were retrieved by her captor. She was purchased by the U.S. government, renamed the USN *Dunbarton*, and served out the rest of the war as a cargo vessel. In 1867, the *Dunbarton* was sold to the Quebec Steamship Company as a passenger ship. On April 28, 1870, she was wrecked in a storm in the St. Lawrence River.

Chapter 3

16 *Toronto Leader*, August 12, 1864; *Halifax Morning Chronicle*, August 20, 1861.

17 In 1864, Canada was what is now Ontario and Quebec, one of five British North American colonies. It is used here interchangeably with British North America.

18 Harry Overholtzer, "Nova Scotia and the United States Civil War." MA Thesis, Dalhousie University.

19 Holcombe to Benjamin, June 16, 1864. *Southern Historical Society Papers*, Vol. 7 Jan.–Dec. 1879, p 293.

20 Holcombe to Monck, May 9, 1864. MS45 (103) 4-85 Or CO. 42/641.

21 Nuremburger, 235; Connolly to Clay, May 20, 1864, Clay Papers, Duke University.

22   Clay to Benjamin, October 29, 1864, in Oscar Kinchen, *Daredevils of the Confederate Army*, 21.

Chapter 4

23   The author published detailed accounts of many ways Thompson communicated with his superiors in the *Civil War Times Illustrated* issue of June 2001. The articles are entitled "Spies Across the Border" and "Running the Gauntlet."
24   George H. Whyte, "Confederate Operations in Canada during the Civil War." MA Thesis, McGill University, 1968. p. 54.
25   James Horan, *Confederate Agents: A Discovery in History*. Fairfax Press, 1954. 18.
26   George Milton, *Abraham Lincoln and the Fifth Column*, 286.
27   Official Records of the War of Rebellion (OR) Series I, Vol. 43, Pt. 2 Thompson to Benjamin, December 3, 1864.
28   Horan, 45.

Chapter 5

29   Macdonald was married to Eugene's sister Christine. The fascinating story of how the couple met and married, as well as Macdonald's plea to William Seward to save Eugene's life after his capture at the Battle of Malvern Hill in 1862, is told by the author in "The Prisoner and the Prime Minister," *Civil War Times Illustrated*, August 1993.
30   Brian Jenkins, *Britain and War for the Union* Vol. 1, 160; Donald G. Creighton, *John A. Macdonald: The Young Politician*, Toronto: Macmillan, 1952, 323.
31   S.F. Wise and A.L. Brown, *Canada Views the United States: 19th century Political Attitudes*, 76.
32   *Toronto Globe*, October 1, 3, and 10, 1849; Jenkins, Vol.1. 71.
33   Jenkins, Vol. 1. 74
34   Joseph Lehmann, *All Sir Garnet: A life of Field Marshall Lord Wolseley*, 114.
35   Anthony Trollope, *North America*, 84.
36   Sir Charles Hastings-Doyle to Sir Fenwick Williams, March 29, 1865. Williams papers NB Archives.
37   Jenkins, Vol. 1. 109.

Chapter 6

38   A lively account of this story can be found in "The Yellow Fever Plot," *Civil War Times Illustrated*, May 1974. While the evidence seems clear, Blackburn was never charged and denied any

complicity in the affair to the end of his life.

39   Dispatches of U.S. Consul at Toronto, NA (hereafter CD Toronto) David Thurston to William Seward, April 7, 1865.

40   "Northwestern Conspiracy," *Southern Bivouac*, 571; Horan, 107.

41   Horan, 94.

42   Clay to Thompson in Kinchen, *Confederate Operations*, 62.

43   Kinchen, *Confederate Operations*, 70.

44   "Northwestern Conspiracy."

45   OR, Thompson to Benjamin, December 3

46   OR Navies, Series II, Vol. III, Holcombe to Benjamin, November 16, 1864

47   OR, I, Vol. 39 Part I, P. 400, Report of CSA Captain Charles T. Biser, Post Commandant at Oxford, Mississippi, August 31, 1864; Sharron Eve Sarthou, researcher at John William Davis Library, University of Mississippi, relating a story still repeated today in Oxford about the events of August 22, 1864.

Chapter 7

48   After the war, the Niagara region was home to an assortment of Southern exiles. Between 1865 and 1869 they included General Jubal Early and General John Bell Hood, commander of the Army of the Tennessee, whose disregard for his men would destroy an army, lose Atlanta to Union general William Tecumseh Sherman, and open the heartland to the concept of total war. Confederate States Ambassador to England James Mason, the focus of the Trent Affair in 1861, rented a home there, as did the Confederacy's last Secretary of War, General John C. Breckinridge. Breckinridge's cousin John Castleman would be one of Jacob Thompson's key guerrilla operatives. Immediately after his release from prison in 1867, ex-Confederate President Jefferson Davis headed straight to Niagara to confer with the exiles living there. For a detailed account see William C. Davis, *Breckinridge: Soldier, Statesman, Symbol*; Denison, *Soldiering in Canada*.

49   Clay Papers, Duke University, Clay to Virginia Clay, July 28, 1864.

50   Clay Papers, Record Letterbook, Duke University, Clay to Benjamin, June 17, 1864.

51   Castleman, 135.

52   The letter, dated March 7, 1865, wasn't received by Davis but was captured after the fall of Richmond and published in the *New York Herald* on July 8, 1865.

53   Kirkland, *The Peacemakers of 1864*; *Confederate Operations in Canada and the North*, 77; Clay to Benjamin, August 11, 1864. Clay Papers, Duke University.

54 Jewett's note and telegram appear in Don Seitz, *Horace Greeley*, 348 ff.

55 Kinchen, *Confederate Operations*, 77.

56 Thompson to Mason and Slidell, August 23, 1864, in Hines, Northwestern Conspiracy, Southern Bivouac, Vol. 5, p 508-510

57 Kinchen, *Confederate Operations*, 87 ff.

Chapter 8

58 At the time this referred to what is now Manitoba, Saskatchewan, Alberta, and points north, including the Yukon and what is known today as the Northwest Territories and Nunavut.

59 Brown's *Toronto Globe* recorded every word of this extraordinary session of the legislature in its edition of June 23, 1864.

60 *La Minerve*, June 23, 1864.

61 Brown Papers, Ontario Archives, Brown to Anne Brown, June 23, 1864.

62 *The Canadian Encyclopedia* Vol. 1, 525.

63 *Le Pays*, June 28, 1864; *Courier du Canada*, July 17, 1864; Donald G. Creighton, "The United States and Canadian Confederation," *Canadian Historical Review*. 39:209-222, September 1958. 77, 79.

Chapter 9

64 Holcombe to Clay, July 10, 1864, in Kinchen, *Confederate Operations*, 104; Thompson to Benjamin, December 3, 1864.

65 Annie Brown's real identity is somewhat of a mystery. She was known to be a courier Thompson used to send messages to the South, and she used a number of aliases, including Annie Cole, Anna Brown, Annie Davis, Belle Brandon, and Irish Lize.

66 Edward Downer, "Johnson's Island," *Civil War History*, Vol. 3, 1962.

67 Castleman, 161.

68 During the first week of November 1863, Northern military officials learned that Confederate agents in Montreal were trying to buy two ships there and that a large sum of Confederate money had been sent to Canada West by Confederate Secretary of State Judah Benjamin. On November 9, the information was sent to U.S. Consul Joshua Giddings in Montreal and was also reported to Governor General Monck. Monck and Sandfield Macdonald duly investigated but found no evidence of an invasion force based in Canada.

69 Frederick J. Shepard, "The Johnson's Island Plot." *Buffalo Historical Society Publications*. Vol. 9, 1906, p 26.

70 Shepard, "Johnson's Island Plot," 10.

71 Kinchen, *Confederate Operations*, 111.

72   Charles Frohman, "Piracy on Lake Erie," *Inland Seas*, XIV, 172–80; Shepherd, "Johnson's Island Plot," 33; Robin W. Winks, *Canada and the United States: The Civil War Years*. Baltimore: Johns Hopkins University Press, 1960, 287; John Headley, *Confederate Operations in Canada and New York*, Neale, 1906. 249; Kinchen, *Confederate Operations*, 111.
73   The *Globe*, September 22, 1864; The *Leader*, September 23, 1864.
74   Lady Monck, *My Canadian Leaves*, 53 19.
75   Monck to Williams, Sept. 21, 1864, Williams papers, New Brunswick Archives; Ibid Sept. 26, 1864

Chapter 10

76   Winks, 238.
77   J.M.S. Careless, *Brown of the Globe*, Vol. I. Toronto: Macmillan, 1963, 86.
78   John Cooper, "The Political ideas of George Etienne Cartier," *Canadian Historical Review*, September 23, 1942.
79   *Saint John Morning Telegraph*, September 8, 1864.
80   P.B. Waite, *The Life and Times of Confederation*, Toronto: University of Toronto Press, 1961, 80; Creighton, *John A. Macdonald*, 369.
81   Clay to Holcombe, September 14, 1864, Clay papers, Duke University.
82   Kinchen, *Confederate Operations*, 71.
83   Clay to Virginia Clay, July 28, 1864
84   Horan's *Confederate Agents* has a good description of the *Condor*'s sinking on page 111 ff.
85   OR, Series II, Vol.3, 1239.
86   OR, Series II, Vol.3, 1239.
87   Headley, 258.
88   Castleman, 155.

Chapter 11

89   The issue of how the Confederates were dressed was an important part of their trial. Young maintained they wore uniforms and were commissioned soldiers of the Confederate States conducting a military engagement. The prosecution argued they were dressed as civilians and were common thieves. Young did wear a uniform, tailor-made in Montreal. Most likely, the only other matching things the raiders carried were the twenty-two satchels slung over their shoulders, ready to carry away the loot.
90   There is some dispute about the number of raiders, with estimates from as low as seventeen to as high as twenty-six. The author has

taken the word of Bennett Young, who commanded the mission, as given in his evidence at his trial later in Montreal.

91 At the trial of the raiders, townspeople, tellers at the banks, and passersby provided detailed accounts of the raid. The descriptions here come mainly from Horan's *Confederate Agents*, Oscar Kinchen's *Confederate Operations*, and newspaper accounts of the trial.

92 Winks, *Canada and the United States*, 300; Kinchen, *Confederate Operations*, 136.

93 *Montreal Gazette*, October 24, 1864; *Montreal Telegraph*, reprinted in the *Montreal Gazette* October 24, 1864,

94 Monck to Cardwell, October 27, 1864.

95 Monck to Sir Fenwick Williams, October 22, 1864 NB Archives.

96 Kinchen, *Confederate Operations*, 136.

97 Clay to Benjamin, Nov.1, 1864. Captured correspondence found in the Governor General's Numbered files, RG7,G21, Vol. 16, file 57, #1b;Young to Clay, November 21, 1864, Clay Papers

98 *New York Herald*, October 24, November 1, 1864.

Chapter 12

99 Creighton, *John A. Macdonald*, Vol. 1 p. 378; Macdonald papers, Letters on the Quebec Conference, Vol. 46, p 167-68

100 Careless, 160.

101 Waite, *The Life and Times of Confederation*, 88.

102 A.H. Colquhoun, *The Fathers of Confederation: A Chronicle of the birth of the Dominion*. Glasgow: Brook & Co., 1916, 60.

103 Waite, P.B. (Ed.) *The Confederation Debates in the Province of Canada, 1865*. McClelland & Stewart: 1963, 138; Ibid, 140.

104 Creighton, *John A. Macdonald*, 376.

105 Careless, 166.

106 Brown papers, Brown to Anne Brown, October 27, 1864

Chapter 13

107 *Montreal Gazette*, November 1, 1864

108 Monck to Cardwell, November 7, 1864

109 Kinchen, *Daredevils*, 66.

110 *Montreal Gazette*, October 27, 1864.

111 This letter is included in Clay to Benjamin, Nov. 1, 1864, found in the Clay papers and also in the Governor General's numbered files, RG7. G21, Vol. 16, PAC

112 Headley, 372; Clay to Benjamin, Nov. 1, 1864. Also found in Governor General's Numbered Files, RG 7

113 For a full account of these secret forms of communications see

"Running The Gauntlet," *Civil War Times Illustrated*, June 2001.

114   Clay Diary, 14, Clay Papers, Duke University. H.L.C. was Henry Lucius Clay, Clement's brother.

115   Six weeks after the end of the war, Castleman was banished without a conviction from the United States. He was escorted to Detroit, took a ferry to Windsor, and from there he travelled to Toronto, where he was reunited with Hines and Eastin. All three enrolled in Trinity College, later to become part of the University of Toronto, and studied French and law. One of their tutors was Castleman's uncle John C. Breckinridge.

116   Castleman, 175.

117   Kimball to Potter, November 5, 1864, OR, Navies, Series I, Vol. 3, p. 371-72

118   OR Series I, Vol. 3, 495–96

119   The *Globe*, April 17, 1865.

120   Thompson to Benjamin, December 3, 1864

Chapter 14

121   Thompson to Benjamin, December 3, 1864; Castleman, 168, 267; Kinchen, *Confederate Operations*, 151.

122   Headley, 266.

123   Headley, 271; Kinchen, *Confederate Operations*, 165; Castleman, 272

124   *New York Times*, November 5, 1864.

125   The other displays in this show included "three mammoth girls weighing 1 ton, three giants whose height totaled 24 feet and two dwarfs weighing 17 pounds a piece."

126   Headley, 275.

127   Pat Burns, "New York's Great Fire That Wasn't," *New York Times Magazine*, November 22, 1964, 109-10; Headley, 276.

128   *New York Tribune*, November 26, 1864.

129   *New York Times*, November 26, 1864.

130   Headley, 278.

131   Thompson to Benjamin, December 3, 1864.

132   Headley, 282.

Chapter 15

133   Creighton, *The Road to Confederation*, 184.

134   Variously reported, including the *Gazette*, October 31, 1864, and the *Toronto Globe*, October 31, 1864.

135   Waite, *The Life and Times of Confederation*, 100.

136   Lady Monck, *My Canadian Leaves*, 66.

137 Careless, 172; Creighton, *The Road to Confederation*, 185; *Toronto Globe*, November 3, 1864.

Chapter 16

138 Clay to Tucker, October 14, 1864, Clay Papers, NA.
139 Junius arrived in the U.S. in 1821, but was already married. It took twenty years for his Belgian-born English wife to confront his bigamy. She filed for divorce in 1851, and within a month Junius legally remarried Mary Anne Holmes.
140 Carl Sandburg, *Abraham Lincoln: The Prairie Years and The War Years*, one-volume edition. New York: Harcourt, Brace & Co., 1939, 718.
141 William Tidwell, *Come Retribution: The Confederate Secret Service and the Assassination of Abraham Lincoln*. University Press of Mississippi, 1988, 257
142 Louis Weichmann, *A True History of the Assassination of Abraham Lincoln and the Conspiracy of 1865*. (Floyd Risvold Ed.) Vintage Books, 1975, Chapter VI.
143 Tidwell, 262.
144 Nancy Baird, "The Yellow Fever Plot," *Civil War Times Illustrated*, November 1974.
145 More than a year later the bank tried to return the balance of Booth's account to his family. They refused to accept it.
146 Clayton Gray, *Conspiracy in Canada*, Montreal: L'Atelier Press, 1959, 129.
147 Gray, 51.
148 Weichmann, 432.

Chapter 17

149 *Toronto Globe*, November 4, 1864.
150 Brown to Anne Brown, November 7, 1864.
151 *Toronto Globe*, November 4, 1864.
152 Careless, 178ff.
153 Kinchen, *Daredevils*, 68.
154 *Toronto Globe*, December 14, 1864.
155 Kinchen, *Daredevils*, 71.
156 Dennis K. Wilson, *Justice Under Pressure: The Saint Albans Raid and Its Aftermath*, University Press of America, 1992, 62.
157 Creighton, "Road to Confederation," 212; *Montreal Gazette*, December 15, 1864; *Toronto Globe*, December 15, 1864.
158 Creighton, "Road to Confederation," 212; *Montreal Gazette*, December 15, 1864; *Toronto Globe*, December 15, 1864.

159 The *Times*, December 29, 1864.
160 Wilson, *Justice Under Pressure*, 64; Kinchen, *Daredevils*, 74 ff.

Chapter 18

161 In all they encompassed an area of what is now downtown Toronto between Queen and College streets and Dufferin and Ossington streets, then farmland on the west end of the city.
162 The elder Denison was also an officer of the Toronto Turf Club and was instrumental in establishing the classic of Canadian thoroughbred racing, the Queen's Plate. The social milieu included gala balls in the European style, soirees, and other venues where the nouveau riche and landed gentry could flaunt their wealth and status. During the visit of the Prince of Wales to Toronto in 1860, George's sister Lilla was one of the few chosen to dance a waltz with the future King Edward VII, a testament to the family's status. A year later, during a visit to England, she was presented at court.
163 John became the first Canadian Admiral in the British Navy. Septimus was among the first graduates from Canada's Royal Military College and joined the British Army. His career included a tour as aide-de-camp of the Canadian Governor General in the early 1880s and as a staff officer in the Boer War, where he was twice mentioned in dispatches.
164 David Gagan, *The Denison Family of Toronto*, 31.
165 Gagan, 44.
166 Diary of George Taylor Denison III, Metropolitan Toronto Reference Library.
167 Winks, *Canada and the United States*, 308.
168 Kinchen, *Confederate Operations*, 185.
169 Headley, 393.
170 Kinchen, *Confederate Operations*, 187 ff.

Chapter 19

171 Wilson, *Justice Under Pressure*, 64.
172 *Toronto Globe*, January 6, 1865; *Detroit Free Press*, December 23, 1864, January 4, 10, and 11, 1865.
173 CD, Thurston to Seward December 24, 1864.
174 Dispatches from US Consuls in Toronto, T-491, Roll 1, Vol. 1 Jan. 16, 1865.
175 Kinchen, *Confederate Operations*, 384.
176 Potter to Seward, February 16 and March 15, 1865.
177 Confederation debates, 59.

178 *Hamilton Spectator*, February 13, 1865.
179 Confederation debates, VII.

Chapter 20

180 Nuremberger, 262.
181 Thompson Family Papers, Southern Historical Collection, Duke University, North Carolina Thompson to Hines, March 14, 1865.
182 Headley, 324.
183 After the war, Burley joined the *Houston Telegram* as a reporter and later returned to England where he went to work for the *London Daily Telegraph*. His specialty was covering foreign wars. His last campaign was the Russo-Japanese War in 1905.
184 *Southern Bivouac*, Vol. II, Number 7, December 1886.
185 CD, Potter to Seward, March 29, 1865.
186 CD, Potter to Seward, March 30, 1865.
187 CD, Thurston to Hunter, April 24, 1865.
188 CD Potter to Seward, April 24, 1865.

Epilogue

189 *New York Times*, May 22, June 1, 2, and 5, 1867.
190 Denison, 81.
191 Varina H. Davis. *Jefferson Davis, Ex-President of the Confederate States of America. A Memoir by his wife,* 304.
192 *Montreal Gazette*, July 19, 1867.
193 P.L. Rainwater, "Letters to and From Jacob Thompson," *Journal of Southern History*, Vol. 6, 1940.
194 William C. Davis. "The Conduct of Mr. Thompson," *Civil War Times Illustrated,* 1970.
195 Memoirs of the Right Honourable Sir John Alexander Macdonald, 281.

INDEX

Grenfel, Col. George St. Leger, 56; arrested, 137, 204
Guelph, ON, 88

Halifax, NS, commissioners arrive in, 33, 70; Thompson in exile, 219
Hamilton Spectator, on Confederation debates, 198
Hamilton Times, 68
Hay, John, and Niagara peace talks, 68
Head, Sir Edmund, 170
Headley, Lt. John, 138; on use of Greek Fire, 142; on New York firebombing, 144 ff., 187, 192, 223
Hines, Capt. Tom, 42, 58, 204, 223
Holcombe, James, described 35; on Copperheads, 60; leaves Canada 70, 99, 221
Hudson's Bay Company, 119, 170
Hyams, Godfrey, 55, 133, 157

Island Queen, captured, 86; scuttled, 87

Jervois, Lt. Col. William, and Canadian defence, 167, 170
Jewett, William Colorado, 66
Johnson, Andrew, U.S. vice-president, 66; charges Thompson, 209
Johnson's Island prison, 81 ff.

Kelly's Island, 87
Kerr, William, defends St. Albans raiders, 171
Kimball, James, U.S. Consul in Toronto, 133

Knights of the Golden Circle, *See Copperheads*

La Minerve, on Canadian Coalition, 77
Lake Erie raid, 80 ff.
Lamb, Col. William, 21
Le Pays, 94; on Canadian Coalition, 77
Lee, Gen. Edwin Gray, 205
Lee, Gen. Robert E., 18, 23, 214, 224
Lincoln, Abraham, elected, 52; and peace talks, 66; spares Sam Davis, 202; spares John Castleman, 132; assassinated, 206
Lyons, Lord Richard, 112

Macdonald, John A., view of Republican government, 72, 92; on Lake Erie raid, 89; feud with Brown, 93; and St. Albans Raid, 113, 173; at Quebec Conference, 117, 151; and Confederation debates, 199; dies, 220
Macdonald, Larry, 133
Macdonald, Sandfield, 46, 66
Marmaduke, Col. Vincent, 140
Martin, Patrick Charles, 159
Martin, Robert, 137
Mason, James, 19, 212
McGee, D'Arcy, 150, Confederation debates, 197
Michigan, USS, 79 ff., 134
Middle Bass Island, 85
Monck, Lady Frances, on St. Albans raid, 115; on Ottawa, 175
Monck, Viscount Stanley, 45, described, 47; on Militia Bill, 54; on Lake Erie raid, 89; on